"This book is the best antidote for feeling stuck and helpless. It will teach you how to hope—which makes all things possible."

—Matthew McKay, Ph.D., author of *Self-Esteem*

"*Making Hope Happen* offers down-to-earth guidance on how to get out of the doldrums of hopelessness and begin moving forward. McDermott and Snyder teach readers to identify, tackle, and overcome obstacles to personal and professional success, using hope as a measurable skill that can be developed and refined. I recommend this book to anyone who perceives a gap between where they are and where they want to be."

—Robert A. Neimeyer, Ph.D., Professor of Psychology, University of Memphis; author of *Lessons of Loss: A Guide to Coping*

"An excellent guide to greater happiness and success in work, relationships, and life in general. Readers are guided through a series of hope-building activities that help them identify goals and ways to achieve those goals in such domains as school, family, leisure, relationships, spirituality, and fitness. The book is peppered with the inspirational and informative case-studies of people making important changes in their lives—changes that get them out of dead-end jobs and relationships and back into college, new careers, new businesses, and enjoying greater success overall."

—Donelson R. Forsyth, Ph.D., Professor of Psychology, Virginia Commonwealth University; author of *Group Dynamics*

Making Hope Happen

A Workbook for Turning Possibilities into Reality

Diane McDermott, Ph.D.

C.R. Snyder, Ph.D.

New Harbinger Publications, Inc.

Publisher's Note

This publication is designed to provide accurate and authoritative information in regard to the subject matter covered. It is sold with the understanding that the publisher is not engaged in rendering psychological, financial, legal, or other professional services. If expert assistance or counseling is needed, the services of a competent professional should be sought.

Distributed in the U.S.A. by Publishers Group West; in Canada by Raincoast Books; in Great Britain by Airlift Book Company, Ltd.; in South Africa by Real Books, Ltd.; in Australia by Boobook; and in New Zealand by Tandem Press.

Copyright © 1999 by Diane McDermott, Ph.D., and C.R. Snyder, Ph.D.
New Harbinger Publications, Inc.
5674 Shattuck Avenue
Oakland, CA 94609

Cover design by SHELBY DESIGNS AND ILLUSTRATES
Edited by Carole Honeychurch
Text design by Tracy Marie Powell

ISBN 1-57224-167-5 Paperback

Printed in the United States of America.

New Harbinger Publications' Website address: www.newharbinger.com

01   00   99

10   9   8   7   6   5   4   3   2   1

First printing

Contents

SECTION III   Hope for Special Groups

SECTION IV   Hope Is a Relationship

SECTION I

Exploring Hope

Introduction

Welcome to the wonderful journey to higher hope. In the coming pages you will discover ways to enhance your hope that will provide you with a richer and fuller life. You will learn ways to work for the dreams that you may have thought were unattainable, and you will learn to think in terms of accomplishment and success.

This journey is not always easy, but you are guided through manageable and intriguing steps all along the way. The techniques and information you will learn in this workbook build on what you already know and what you can already do. Each new step is described with easy-to-follow directions—signposts along the road. You will start with small changes, or goals, and add new goals when you are comfortable with the changes you have made. Throughout this workbook you are reminded that lasting changes are always made slowly, and patience with yourself is a key to success.

In this first section you will learn an active definition of hope, one that you can apply in your daily life. You will learn about your own level of hope by taking and scoring the Hope Scale. You will discover through your personal stories and those of your family ways to understand your hope and how it developed.

Socrates said, "Know thyself." In order to take this journey into the realm of higher personal hope, the first step must be understanding where you are now. Developing this base of knowledge is the work of the first section.

1

Is Your Life in the Doldrums? Try a Dose of Hope

I recently enjoyed a leisurely dinner with my longtime friend, Janet. As we settled in to appetizers she reopened the "back to school" question. "I really wish I could find it in me to go back to school and finish college. I think about it a lot, but I don't know if I'm really smart enough to do it. I like my job alright, but I've seen ads on TV about how people can improve their careers by going to school at night, and that sort of intrigues me. The thought of all that studying and taking tests really scares me, though."

My impulse, as always, was to present the many arguments I've used in the past. After all, Janet was a good student when we were in school together. Of course, she had to work harder in some subjects—but who doesn't? The fact that I had finished college was a frequent and not always comfortable topic of conversation for us. As long as I had known Janet, she never had been one to rise to challenges. Instead, she preferred to do those things where some success was assured. At the end of our sophomore year in college, she decided to get a job as a secretary with her father's law firm, abandoning her goal of becoming a high school teacher. Although she had job security and a livable wage, her existence was rather mundane—nothing like the initial teaching career that she had envisioned.

After our dinner conversation I began to think seriously about her dilemma, and I couldn't help comparing her situation to that of people who see the opportunities in life's challenges and run to meet them. The question, as I saw it, was why do people with seemingly equal abilities behave so differently in pursuing the things they want out of life?

High- and Low-Hope People

Considering the way my friend seems to avoid pursuing her goals, I see that her doubts become roadblocks and genuine difficulties become insurmountable obstacles. When she looks down the road toward reaching her goal, her path is full of potholes, twists, and turns that cause her to shy away from the journey. "I don't think I'm up to all that," she tells herself. "It would be better to stay where I am, even though I'm not very happy." In short, she is a low-hope person.

High-hope people, on the other hand, have the courage to pursue their goals without the cautionary self-doubt of Janet. As high-hope people look down the road to their potential accomplishments, they know there will be difficult times ahead, maybe even times when they will want to give up. But ultimately, their desires for their goals and their beliefs in their abilities to solve most problems will allow them to see a future filled with new and interesting outcomes. Rather than experiencing their dreams as causing anxiety and requiring excuses, high-hope people view their goals as exciting and energizing.

Achieving High Hope

How can you become a high-hope person? The answer is that it can be learned. Some people have learned hope as young children, while others have developed it later in their lives. The important point is that hopeful thinking can be acquired. No matter how old you are, what your family background may be, or how much money or education you have, you can raise your level of hope and have a more fulfilling future.

Hopeful thinking can be acquired, no matter how old you are.

There are a few caveats to this promise, however. Old ways of dealing with life are safe and comfortable, if not always satisfying. To change so as to face challenges can make people anxious—so they stick by the old standbys. The program we offer in this workbook, however, will show you how to break your old habits so as to become more hopeful. We have used the methods you'll learn in this book to help people change their lives—to take on exciting new challenges. If you are down in the dumps, wading through the doldrums of life, and not daring to dream, then you need a strong dose of hope. Of course, you cannot get this hope at your local pharmacy. No, instead you will produce it in the most powerful laboratory in existence—the human mind. Your mind.

Are You a High-Hope or a Low-Hope Person?

As you read the opening restaurant dialogue, did you identify with the person in the story who is questioning her ability to attain goals? If there is some part of you in Janet's saga, then learning to think more hopefully could really give you a boost. In our experience as educators and psychotherapists, it's exhilarating to encounter high-hope people. How they think about life is infectious, and high-hopers leave trails of energy and positive feelings wherever they go.

Is it only special people who can learn to be high in hope? We think not. Hope is available to most anyone who is willing to work for it. Certainly, some people seem to be more positive about life, while others are more negative and dubious about their prospects. Take Janet, for example: she was raised by parents who, out of concern for her safety, taught her to be cautious about trying new things. She was never encouraged to take risks, even moderate ones. The message she learned from her parents, whether or not it was their intent, was that it was better to not try than to fail. So the little girl grows up into the adult Janet for whom the risks of failure loom large.

What You Will Learn from This Book

Notice that you operate daily using the messages you have learned, some messages helping and others hindering you. These internal thoughts—an ongoing self-talk—are so familiar that you seldom stop to examine them, let alone discern whether they are positive or negative. You accept these thoughts about yourself as "just who you are," as though you always have been or always will be the same person. By using this workbook, you will learn to emphasize new thoughts about yourself, and that new self-messages can help you actually achieve your goals and dreams. Most importantly, you will find out how to replace your old negative, self-defeating, and low-hope self-talk with a realistic and more helpful dialogue. In brief, you will learn strategies for increasing the hope in your life.

Because this book is about changing the way you think and act so that it's truly possible to work toward your guiding dreams and goals, the methods and assignments we have provided are all geared toward your personal growth. We will show you how to determine your own level of hope by measuring the two hope-related dimensions of willpower and waypower. We will be helping you to determine where your present attitudes and beliefs have come from and where they lead you. You will learn to set new goals, even to try ones you may have thought too difficult in the past. We will structure an opportunity for you to examine your personal history and then to shake the kaleidoscope of details into a more positive pattern. And finally, you will be learning new and

It is truly possible to work for your guiding dreams.

more productive ways to think and act, and how to maintain those new behaviors for the rest of your life.

The Promise of Hopeful Thinking

This book is built upon several premises, the most important of which is that the quality of hope is fundamental to a successful, productive, satisfying, and energetic life. Hope, in its simplest form, is the inner knowledge that one has the ability to set and pursue goals, as well as to solve problems all along the way. If you can begin to think in this manner, there are many benefits you will experience. This is the promise of hopeful thinking—it helps to deliver all of the wonderful targets of our human imagination. Why just idly dream, conjuring outcomes that delight you, then let such goals fall by the wayside? By learning to think hopefully, it is as if you are purchasing a reusable ticket to help you reach those wondrous destinations that fill your mind.

For the reader who seeks to become higher in hope, it will be helpful to use this book as it is intended. It is a fairly slow, step-by-step process. In this workbook, we begin with an explanation of hope, we describe how to measure individual hope, and we provide a variety of exercises aimed at increasing your hopeful thoughts and behaviors. Our premise is that to learn to be hopeful, you must embark on a journey. In turn, hopeful thinking helps you travel the roads of life with more success. The story of Ted offers a brief example of one such journey of hope—an escape from the mundane to the joys of actually achieving meaningful life goals.

✳ Ted—Going for His Goal at Last

Ted spent his fortieth birthday just like he had his previous twenty-two birthdays. He arrived at the garden department of the large department store where he worked, watered the plants, swept the floors, and for the rest of the day waited on customers. Many customers asked for Ted because they knew he would have answers to their gardening questions.

Ted loved plants and had ever since he was a small boy. The yard in front of his parents' San Francisco home was tiny, but Ted planted as many kinds of flowers and shrubs as he could in the sandy soil. When only ten years old, he experimented with the propagation of certain flowers in an effort to develop new colors. Growing plants was the center of his life.

Ted's parents thought that gardening was a wonderful hobby, but a hobby only—nothing more. Their own lives had been difficult, and they wanted Ted's to be easier and more successful. Ted's parents had been raised to believe that life was hard, and the only way to succeed was through determination and work. Life for Ted's parents was neither pleasant nor fulfilling. Their day-to-day activities were routine, and they worked very long hours with very little time for leisure activities. What free time they had was spent doing household chores or watching television. Essentially, their lives were like those of so many other Americans, so busy getting by from day-to-day that it rarely occurred to them to dream of other possibilities. If either one of them considered doing something different—learning a new skill or developing a lucrative hobby—the idea was dismissed quickly as being unrealistic, beyond attainment.

Although Ted's parents spoke to him about the importance of an education in avoiding dead-end jobs such as theirs, their behaviors sent another more powerful message—work as soon as possible. Ted was an average high school student, and when graduation came, he went to work for a large department store in the garden section. As the years rolled by, he took occasional junior college courses but never felt stimulated enough to get his associate of arts degree. Whenever Ted fantasized about other things he might do with his life, his responsibilities to his wife Rita and their two children put a stop to such thinking. His only choice, it seemed, was to stay in his secure job.

On his fortieth birthday, Rita gave Ted a catalytic book—it was filled with stories of people in midlife changes. Ted was fascinated by these tales about real people and how they had been able to set and reach goals. Rita believed that Ted once had dreams and goals, but that he had fallen into the same pattern as had his parents. She was determined to help him take a chance to achieve a few of his goals, whatever they might be.

Rita also realized that life for their family would be much happier if Ted were working at something he really loved. Rita had gone to school to become a dental technician, something she really enjoyed. She was a positive and cheerful person, and she influenced her children, now nine and eleven, to go after their goals. If she could help her children, then why not Ted? A first step was to help Ted see that there were other options besides the safe rut in which he spent his days. This birthday book provided just such a window for Ted— a chance to see a different and better tomorrow.

As Ted read the book, each evening he and Rita talked about the things he was learning. Rita encouraged him to think about his real love—working with growing things. How could he begin a life where he could be creative with these interests? For years, as a voluntary part of his sales job, Ted had given advice to customers about planting their gardens and beautifying their yards. He would take a page from his sketch book and give a customer a sample design, complete with the specific flowers, trees, and shrubs. He made their yards and gardens come to life on that piece of paper. Over the years, his customers asked for him repeatedly, refusing to work with anyone else.

Ted knew he had a creative talent that other people valued, so he formulated a daring idea. With the interest he had since childhood and with the information and skills he had acquired as an adult, Ted believed he was qualified to become a landscape gardener. With that insight, and with encouragement from Rita, he decided to start his own landscaping business. Leaving the security of his job, however, meant that there was the possibility of failure. If he didn't succeed financially, his family would suffer, and his parents would criticize him for his "wild ideas." Ted's wife and children, however, were totally behind him—they believed he never would be truly happy until he took such a chance.

There were many details involved in beginning his own business, but Ted and Rita became excited about the future. For the first time, Ted was looking forward to tomorrow and what it and the subsequent days would bring. Rita's income was as large as Ted's, and she volunteered to support the family while Ted got started. At last Ted had a life goal about which he felt positive, enthusiastic, and engrossed, and his energy level rose. Rita was very supportive and helped him to think of ways to solve the various problems that he encountered. Pursuing a dream was new for Ted, and he occasionally slipped into the negative thinking in which he had been immersed as a child. When Ted told his parents about his plans to start his own landscaping business, they were, predictably, negative and discouraging. Ted was disappointed by his parents' skepticism, but Rita was there to sustain his new vision.

After the discussion with his parents, Ted could see more clearly how he had come to think so negatively. He could see that his parents, well intentioned as they were, had never allowed themselves to expect much from life. To them, dreaming meant that you took a big chance on being disappointed. That big chance, however, seemed worth it to Ted in his post fortieth birthday renaissance.   ✳

As is true for many high-hope people, Ted had a supportive partner with whom he could discuss his plans. Rita was encouraging and she was a good problem solver. She set an example for Ted that he had not had in his parents, and, with her help, he learned to take risks to go after what he really wanted.

Fortunately for Ted, he was able to plant his new pattern of thinking and, much like his flowers and bushes, he was able to make it grow. Through his hard work and determination, he started a successful landscape gardening business. When some of his previous customers discovered that he was available not only to plan the designs, but also to do the planting and maintenance, they were delighted to hire him. Word of mouth increased his business rapidly, and soon he was able to hire one, then two, additional people to work for him. Ted continued with his plant propagation experiments as well and eventually was able to offer customers new and unusual varieties of flowers. He never thought he would be as happy as he was in the warm sunlight, working with the soil. He made remarkable changes because he had learned to have hope in his life. Much like the sun that nourished his plants, hope emboldened Ted's thinking.

Ted's story illustrates how our childhood environments and our caregivers' thoughts influence our adult thinking. Ted's parents were not purposefully negative, but they squashed any semblance of hopeful thought in their children. They did not set an example for Ted to follow in which dreams could be actively pursued. Just as so many people do, Ted's parents lived out their lives on the verge of happiness. Their thoughts were filled with not's, cannot's, shouldn't's, and a variety of other negating, questioning, and undermining caveats. Life was not an adventure, a journey about places and things for which one could reach. Rather, life always was to be qualified and limited by what could go wrong, what would impede growth. Eventually, for Ted, plants and growth became a metaphor for reaching out, improving, trying, trying and perhaps failing—but most importantly, trying again.

The "Miracle Question"

The first question we ask of you as you begin this book, is whether you are happy and truly satisfied with your life. Here we would ask you to consider the "miracle question." Although there are variations, the gist of this question is, "If a miracle occurred and you could have your life exactly the way you want it, what would it be like?" This is not meant to be a "genie-in-a-bottle" question, nor are answers such as winning the lottery acceptable. This is a serious question that deserves some thought before you write your answer. We have designed the following questionnaire to help you consider the various life arenas in which you may wish to see changes. Not everyone sets goals in all areas, nor do they necessarily consider all areas to be important. We believe, however, that the arenas covered in this brief questionnaire are all important components to a well-balanced life. If there are some areas that are nonexistent for you, we ask that you continue with the questionnaire, noting those that are currently missing from your life.

If you could have your life the way you want, what would it be like?

Life Satisfaction Questionnaire

Consider each in terms of how you have felt over the past year. Use the rating scale below to fill in the blanks in each statement.

1	2	3	4	5
very dissatisfied	somewhat dissatisfied	neither	somewhat satisfied	very satisfied

1. I am _____ with my intimate relationships (significant other).

2. In my relationships with my family (parents, children) I feel _____ .

3. I am _____ with my friendships.

4. I am _____ with the work I do (in or outside the home).

5. As I consider my work/career achievement, I feel _____ with my accomplishment so far.

6. I am _____ with the level of education I have attained.

7. I am _____ with my financial situation.

8. In terms of my ability to meet future expenses, I am _____ .

9. I am _____ with my spiritual life.

10. I am _____ with my level of physical fitness.

11. I am _____ with those aspects of my appearance that I could change.

12. I am _____ with the status of my health.

13. I am _____ with my emotional stability.

14. I am _____ with my recreational life.

As you can see from the items on the scale, the important life arenas we are concerned with are personal relationships, career and work, spirituality, education, finances, mental and physical health, and recreation. In order to obtain an overall picture of your satisfaction, add the scores you gave yourself in each area, and then average all the ratings. If you gave yourself mostly 4's or 5's, you are fairly satisfied with your life at the present time. However, if your ratings were mostly 1's and 2's, you are clearly discontented in much of your life. If you relied heavily on the "neither" rating, you are living life in the doldrums.

You can use this questionnaire to determine which areas of your life would benefit most from a boost in hope. For example, suppose your lowest ratings center around issues of personal appearance, physical health, fitness, and recreation. You might decide, after examining these areas as they relate to each other, that beginning an exercise program will increase your satisfaction with yourself overall. Be sure to keep your answers to this questionnaire handy, because it will be useful when it is time to select personal goals as targets for your increasing hope.

Interestingly, satisfaction with one's life does not necessarily mean achievement of grand and glorious goals. It does mean, however, that you have met the goals you have set for yourself, whether they are to be the president of a company, or to raise happy, healthy children. The machinist can be as satisfied with his or her life as is the doctor or lawyer. We believe that hope, which is the ability to dream, to find routes to reach your dreams, and the mental energy to work for them, can help you to lead a more satisfying life.

Hope is a way of approaching life that says "Yes" and "I can." The hopeful person is unafraid of the challenges that lie ahead. And there are challenges ahead in this book as you travel the road to higher hope. We will be taking you into a self-examination process that may not always be comfortable. We will be asking you to think about and to write about events in your life you may not have remembered for some time. Your journey to higher hope begins with an honest appraisal of who you are, how you think about your life, what you want for yourself, and how you can get what you want. In chapter 4 we will be asking you to write a narrative account of your life as a way of understanding more about yourself. It is through such an examination of your personal story that you will begin to understand why you feel and think the way you do now. Let's continue with the story about Janet, whom we met at the beginning of this chapter. Through this narrative we can begin to see why she is so reluctant to complete her college education.

✳ Janet's Story Continued

Janet was an only child—born after her older parents almost had given up on ever having a child. Both her parents were established in their careers, Dad as an attorney and Mom as a teacher, and they continued working during Janet's childhood. Her caregiver, an *au pair* who had been brought from El Salvador, was devoted totally to Janet and her parents. Because of her parents age and their inability to have more children, Janet was treated like a fragile doll— no rough games or adventuresome activities. But, she was encouraged to develop her intellectual skills through ample reading and foreign languages.

Despite Janet's excellent private school education, she never developed much personal confidence in achieving her goals. The overprotection of her parents and *au pair* had instilled a self-doubt that was fueled by negative messages when she considered undertaking new and difficult tasks. Such self-talk included, "You might fail," and "You could fall short." Even in Janet's current adult circumstances, her thoughts about failure are preventing her from inquiring into the night school program that would lead to completing her college degree.

✳

Janet's best friend has tried to persuade her that she should "just give it a try." This friend has obtained her bachelor's degree and knows that, while it is difficult and requires a great deal of hard work, it's not impossible for a reasonably intelligent and determined person. But when Janet thinks about going back to school, she is haunted by her failure self-talk, which rolls across her thoughts time after time. The challenge then is to help Janet change these learned self-talk messages. In order to do that she will have to examine the content of those messages and how they were learned. But, before we continue with Janet and her journey into higher hope, it first is necessary to learn more about hope. Next, is a description of hope, as well as a brief review of the research that we have conducted to establish hope as a measurable characteristic.

What Is This Thing Called Hope?

You have seen how hope affects peoples lives in a positive way by invigorating them to go after their goals. You also had a glimpse of how people become low in hope as a result of the self-defeating messages they heard and internalized when young. In a later chapter, we will help you examine your personal history, focusing on the low- or high-hope messages reflected in family stories. Before proceeding with this process, however, it's important that you have a thorough understanding of what we mean by "hope."

The word *hope* has several common meanings involving expectations or wishes. As we use the term, it means something rather different than these terms with more passive connotations. Our definition is *active*, involving goals, willpower, and waypower, which are the three components of hope.

A *goal*, the first component, is something you desire to do or to have. It can be small, such as buying a pair of earrings, watching *Monday Night Football*, or finishing a term paper. Or, your goal might be larger, such as losing weight, learning to play tennis, or completing a semester in college. Goals can be such a variety of things that we even hesitate to enumerate them.

Hope is active,

involving goals,

willpower, and

waypower.

As we work with our clients and students, we ask them to set realistic objectives—goals that can be accomplished in a reasonable amount of time. For example, a first-year college student says she wants to be a famous author when she is older. In fact, she may become one, but she has many years of study and work before that could happen. Her first step, and the goal that we would suggest for her, is to take a writing class and produce one creative work. Our point here is that while goals can be very large, they also can be divided into smaller, more manageable parts. We will discuss goals in much greater detail later in the book, showing how to assess their realism and how to break them down into smaller tasks.

Waypower is the second component, and is the perceived capability to find routes to your target goals. To demonstrate waypower, let's see what happens to George, who has decided to bake a cake for the family. George is a good cook, but he has not made many baked goods. After finding what looks like a tasty recipe, he assembles his ingredients and preheats the oven. When he is ready to add the milk, he finds he is one cup short. George, up to his elbows in flour, reviews his options for getting more milk. He could wash his hands and go to the grocery store, or perhaps he could send his son. He, or his son, also could go next door and borrow the milk, which is what he decides to do. George is demonstrating waypower when he discerns the several ways he could get the milk he needs to finish the cake—his goal.

Willpower, the third component of hope, is the driving force in hopeful thinking. It's the energy that propels you toward a goal, and it is shown in internal self-talk such as, "I can do this," " I'm ready," " I've got what it takes." To illustrate this, let's look at some well-known high-hope people. Although we do not know her inner thoughts, the day that civil-rights activist Rosa Parks sat in the front of the bus she must have been driven by the energy of her desire for freedom and told herself that she could make a stand. Or consider athletes such as Mark McGwire and Sammy Sosa, who put so much mental and physical energy into their home run records in the 1998 baseball season.

Willpower does not have to be in such expansive proportions as that demonstrated by great athletes or social activists. Willpower is simply the sum of energy you can bring to bear on whatever goal is your focus. You set and achieve small goals constantly; life is made up of these small goals that you meet even when you are not paying much attention to them. For example, each day you get up, get dressed, eat breakfast, and prepare for your day. Each of these activities is, in fact, a goal. They each take a certain amount of willpower, but since you do them daily, it's unlikely to seem as if they require much of this willpower. The point is that *everyone* has willpower. It is not a characteristic that must be learned or developed from nothing, but rather it can be increased and directed toward specific goals that you may have thought unattainable.

Revisiting the case of Ted, you may not be surprised that when he first decided to start his own business, he confronted a number of problems. He had to secure some venture capital, he had to be certain his family would be financially supported, and he needed to learn how to run a small business. Rather than becoming discouraged by these roadblocks, he solved each problem as it came along, brainstorming ideas with Rita and seeking information from many available sources. High-hope people ask for help. They use whatever resources they can find in order to be certain they are taking the right course. To illustrate hope further, let's follow Janet as she decides to go back to school and finish her college degree.

✳ Janet Goes Back to College

Four years had passed since Janet was a college student at a prestigious state university. Her major original intention was to teach history at the secondary school level. During the summer between her sophomore and junior years, however, she met a young law clerk and fell in love. She had been working that summer in her father's law office and, when the fall semester came, Janet decided to stay out for the year so as to pursue her new relationship. By Christmas, however, they no longer were seeing each other.

The law office work was pleasant, the companionship of her coworkers was enjoyable, and she was earning a decent wage. But from the beginning, Janet was disappointed in herself for not pursuing her original goal. She believed she was intelligent and had thought she would be a good teacher. In fact, this had been her dream since she was in high school. Fear of competition with other students, as well as a reluctance to disrupt her comfortable life, stopped her from going back to college. In addition, her parents never encouraged her to take chances, and they naturally liked the idea that she was working for her father. Life was almost like her childhood—except for the nagging thoughts of wanting to go back to school.

Janet expected more of herself, however. Increasingly, she was growing dissatisfied, feeling stuck in the same place while all her friends seemed to be moving ahead. She remembered enjoying history, and the sense of pride in her success when she put forth the effort. One evening in the supermarket, Janet happened to meet a former high school teacher whom she had admired greatly. The teacher, Ms. Bram, was dismayed that Janet had dropped out of college and had given up her dream. She believed that Janet would make an excellent teacher. Ms. Bram encouraged Janet to look into evening courses at a local college and even gave her the name of an admissions counselor there who was a friend of hers.

Janet's confidence was buoyed by this conversation, and the very next day she called the college for an appointment with the admissions counselor. She began to feel more enthusiastic about finishing her degree, and after the appointment with the counselor, she was elated. All of her first two years of credit would be accepted at this school and she could go directly into the education program. The admissions counselor mapped out the teacher-education curriculum, and it was clear that she could complete it in two years.

By this time, Janet was truly excited about the prospect of going back to school. She began to think such thoughts as, "I'm ready for this!" "What have I got to lose?" and, "I know I can do it!" There were moments of doubt, of course, but Janet realized that she always could go back to work as a secretary.

After deciding to return to college, Janet's next decision was whether to go full-time or part-time. If she decided not to work she would have to ask her parents for money, which felt embarrassing for a twenty-six-year-old. One option was to move in with her parents, but there were problems involved in that—after several years of being on her own, a return to dependency would be awkward for everyone. After considering her options, however, Janet decided to ask if she could move back in with her parents and reduce her work to part-time. With some income of her own, she would not be totally dependent on her parents. Most importantly, this plan would allow her to go to school full-time. Full of energy for getting her degree, she wanted to get it as soon as possible.

Janet's parents readily agreed to her living at home and going to school. After all, she was their only child and they were in no hurry to lose her to the world. As planned, Janet enrolled for fifteen credit hours and went back to school. She felt ready to cope with any roadblocks she encountered this time around. She knew she could solve problems and that she could ask for help when needed. She was on her way.

✳

The Elements of Hope in Action

To examine how hope works in helping us strive for our goals, let's examine how Janet used each component of hope. To begin with, she had the dream of becoming a high school history teacher, which was a goal she had cherished since her teenage years. When she first started college, Janet allowed her uncertainties, as well as the promise of a relationship, to deter her from staying in school.

After the relationship was over, Janet was faced with the tediousness of her secretarial work, and she revived her teaching goal. She had enjoyed the subject of history in school and remembered how easy the reading and writing assignments had been for her. Janet's confidence grew with those memories, and the chance meeting with Ms. Bram ignited her building energy. She began to believe that she actually could finish college and realize her dream. She also realized that it was time to begin—with the assurance that she could fall back on secretarial work if things did not work out.

Once Janet had the decision to go after her goal, she had other problems to solve and decisions to make. She didn't want to be dependent upon her parents for everything. With Janet's developing confidence in herself, she was forging a new identity, one involving independence, competence, and courage to pursue her dreams. There were several routes to her final goal of attending college. Janet could live at home and let her parents pay for everything; she could work full-time, keep her apartment, and attend school part-time; or she could work part-time and have some money of her own, and still live at home to save expenses. She even could pay for her own food and a token amount for rent, if that suited her growing sense of independence. After examining the options and their consequences, Janet made her decision. Although that option was acceptable to her parents, Janet had some backup plans in case her parents said no—finding a roommate, or finding another job if the law firm did not allow her to work part-time.

To increase Janet's sense of willpower, she used her past successes as well as the encouragement of her former teacher, Ms. Bram. As Janet began to tell herself that she *could* do it, and that she was *ready* to do it, her willpower heightened dramatically. Discovering a few options, her waypower increased when she began to make alternative, or backup, plans.

The Elements of Hope in Your Life

You have just read about Janet's decision to finish her college degree, the problems she encountered, and the enhancement of hope that occurred when she pursued her goal. At this point we want you to identify a goal you have had recently, and describe the steps you went through as you worked for it. *The goal need not have been achieved.* This is important, because hope is not

Hope is not

dependent upon

constant success.

dependent upon constant success, but rather the experience of *some* success. Hope is a process, and it is the exercise of the process that fuels successive hopeful attempts to achieve dreams. Even though you feel empowered to reach a goal and have many plans to get there, you may not always succeed. It's a measure of hope that you can try again, change the goal, or simply reevaluate your efforts, learning from possible mistakes.

We now want you to take a closer look at your hope in action. Identify one goal you have worked for recently, and enter the description in the first blank. Next, describe the roadblocks you encountered as you worked for your target. Then describe the methods you used to cope with these impediments. On the next line, describe the thoughts and feelings you had as you worked for the goal. And finally, what was the outcome of all you did?

Goal Assessment Worksheet

The roadblocks I encountered were _____

The methods I used to cope with these roadblocks were _____

The thoughts I had as I worked for the goal were _____

The outcome was _____

Here is one example of a goal, waypower, willpower, and the outcome.

- The goal I worked for was to lose ten pounds.

- The roadblocks I encountered included eating in restaurants, keeping snacks in the house for my children, and office parties.

- The methods I used to cope with these roadblocks were eating salads in restaurants, putting snacks in a separate cupboard, and not eating at the office parties.

- The thoughts and feelings I had were, "I'm ready to do this now," and, "I did it before and I feel confident."

- The outcome was successful. I lost twelve pounds.

We use the above exercise with clients and students to demonstrate that they have the rudiments of hope in their lives. As we mentioned at the beginning of this chapter, no one could survive without some degree of hope. This book is about showing you how to augment and nurture your hope so that you can feel empowered to pursue your dreams.

In the next chapter we show you how to assess your hope. Discovering how you score on willpower, waypower, and the combination of the two, is a necessary step in the process of helping you actualize your hope potential.

2

What Is Your Level of Hope?

By this point, you are beginning to understand hope and how it may work in your life. Fortunately, hope does not have to remain ambiguous and vague. Indeed, it can be measured, and by following the steps in this chapter, you can find out your level of hope—that is, you will have a score indicating how high or low you are in this important characteristic. To accomplish this, you can take the Hope Scale, which yields a score on willpower and waypower, as well as the combination—or total hope score.

The Hope Scale has been administered to more than twenty thousand people in research and clinical settings, where it has been useful in helping people to determine their hope levels under many differing conditions. Research has been conducted to insure that the Hope Scale measures hope, rather than a different but related characteristic such as optimism. Our studies also demonstrate that the scale is measuring a trait; that is, your scores probably will be very similar each time you take the scale unless, of course, you engage in activities purposely to change your score. An essential starting point as you undertake the program for developing hope in this book is to measure your hope right now. Hope Scale scores will serve as a baseline against which you can measure your progress. Your scores will reveal which aspect of your hope—willpower or waypower—may need more work. After you have taken the hope scale, we will show you how to score it.

Hope is not ambiguous, it can be measured.

Hope Scale

Directions: Read each item carefully. Using the scale below, please select the number that best describes you and put that number in the blank provided.

1	2	3	4
Definitely false	Mostly false	Mostly true	Definitely true

_____ 1. I energetically pursue my goals.

_____ 2. I can think of many ways to get out of a jam.

_____ 3. My past experiences have prepared me well for the future.

_____ 4. There are lots of ways around any problem.

_____ 5. I've been pretty successful in life.

_____ 6. I can think of many ways to get the things in life that are most important to me.

_____ 7. I meet the goals I set for myself.

_____ 8. Even when others get discouraged, I know I can find a way to solve the problem.

Scoring Your Hope Scale

To derive your overall score, add up all the numbers you marked in the blanks to the left of the statements. The scores can range from a low of 8, indicating you marked all the items as "definitely false," or a high of 32 reflecting the fact that you marked all the items as being "definitely true" for you.

Because we have administered this scale to thousands of people, we can give some norms about your score. A score of around 24 indicates an average amount of hope, which actually may be a fairly strong hope score. In order to have obtained a score of 24, you could have marked a 3, or "mostly true," to all items. Such a pattern of responses would indicate a moderately hopeful individual. Indeed, we have found that many people have this reasonably high level of hope.

A score higher than 24 indicates that you usually think hopefully, while a score lower than 24 indicates that you may not consistently be hopeful. To be a high-hope person, it is necessary to obtain a high score on both willpower and waypower; conversely, when you score low on both of those dimensions, you are exhibiting low hope.

To determine your willpower score, add the ratings you gave yourself for the odd-numbered items. To determine your waypower score, add the four even-numbered items. If you scored 12 or more on the willpower items, but lower than 9 on the waypower items, you may have difficulties taking action toward goals. That is to say, you may be stuck when problems arise, unable to think of solutions. If, on the other hand, you scored more than 12 on the waypower items, and less than 9 in the willpower items, you probably are stuck for another reason. Namely, you may have many ideas and ways to achieve them, but are lacking in the mental energy to implement your plans.

Profiles of Hope

Examine the scores below to determine which profile fits you. Although your own story will be unique, in the coming pages you will read about individuals who typify these profiles. Do the elements in any of these stories seem familiar to you?

- **Full High** = Willpower greater than 12

- **Mixed-Low Way** = Willpower greater than 12 + Waypower less than 9

- **Mixed-Low Will** = Willpower less than 9 + Waypower greater than 1

- **Full Low** = Willpower less than 9 + Waypower less than 9

Hope in Action

What do these combinations of scores look like in real people? Embarking on your journey through this book, it's important to understand the roles that willpower and waypower play in hope. The stories that follow describe the four combinations of low or high willpower and waypower. You will meet Darcy, Larry, Shawna, and Matt. The lives of each of these people reflect a different profile of hope.

✳ Darcy—Ready to Quit: High Will, Low Ways

As Darcy's advisor, I was surprised when she marched into my office and announced that she was quitting the doctoral program. I knew she had dreamed of being a clinical psychologist since she was an undergraduate.

"I worked so hard to get good grades," she said through tears. "I even took a special course to do well on the entrance exams. I've done everything right to get into this program, and now I'm failing two of my courses. I just don't know what to do—except quit."

"Tell me about which courses are hard for you," I suggested.

"Biology and pharmacology are the hardest ones." She blew her nose and dabbed at her tears. "Honestly, the professor and the other students seem to be speaking a language I've never heard. This program is so much harder than anything I have done before, and I'm beginning to think I made a mistake coming here."

"You've had other difficult courses in the past," I said. "Tell me how you managed to get through those."

"They were nothing like these." She wadded her tissue and continued. "Sometimes I think I don't have the background for this work, but when I had problems before I usually discussed them with the teacher."

"What's stopping you from doing that now?" I asked.

"I guess I don't want to seem stupid. It just didn't seem appropriate to do that in graduate school. But I don't want to quit. I'm determined to get this degree, so I'll just have to put my pride aside and see what help I can get."

Darcy had been a highly motivated undergraduate student, but the small college she attended had not offered her enough challenges. She was not used to finding work difficult, and in the face of impending failure, she experienced anxiety and self-doubt. Her highly emotional state prevented her from seeing solutions, and her impulse was to give up. Talking it over with her advisor, and identifying the specific problems, helped Darcy to see that the total picture was not as bad as she had thought at first. Once she was able to overcome her emotional reaction, she could find ways to prepare for these difficult courses.

Larry—Words, Words, Words: Low Will, High Ways

As a college student, Larry became engrossed in philosophy, reading all the major writers and memorizing their wisdom. His professors believed he had great potential because of his brilliant class debates. But when it came to putting his ideas into writing, Larry lacked the energy necessary to do the work. Recognizing that his academic record was riddled with incomplete and dropped courses, he came to the counseling center for help.

My first session with Larry was a struggle to help him focus on what had brought him for counseling. Instead, he wandered into intellectual discussions relating philosophy to psychology and avoiding the real issue that concerned him—his academic failure. What he was finally able to reveal was that he really preferred to talk about his ideas rather than write about them. He found the discipline of writing to be tedious and uninteresting, while discussions with other people were stimulating and exciting.

"All the way through high school my teachers thought I was great. I have a lot of good ideas, but I just don't seem to have the motivation to write about them."

"When you try putting your ideas into writing, what thoughts do you have?" I asked.

"It just seems like too much work. I get tired and tell myself I can do it later. But when later comes there's always something I'd rather do that's more fun and not so hard."

Larry had many ideas that might have brought him academic success had he implemented them. For much of his life, however, he had traded on his charisma to impress others. When it was necessary to write about his ideas, without the immediate praise of others, he lacked the willpower to work alone. He had been rewarded by others for his clever ideas, but had not developed the willpower necessary to bring them to fruition.

✳ Shawna—Missing Out on Life: Low Will, Low Ways

Shawna spent her high school years like she had all her other years in school—on the fringes of what was happening. She was neither popular nor unpopular, but had a small circle of girlfriends who were very much like her. Shawna's grades were average, mainly C's and B's, and she rarely attracted the attention of her teachers. She occasionally thought about joining a club or trying out for the spirit squad, but she never felt enough "pep" to do those things.

One course Shawna did enjoy was Technical Literacy where she learned word processing and various business skills. As a result of this course, Shawna decided to become a secretary after she graduated. She thought that working for a doctor or lawyer might be interesting, but she did nothing to get that type of job. Instead, Shawna applied for work through a secretarial service, believing that one of the temporary jobs would lead to permanent employment.

Almost immediately Shawna was sent to work for an insurance agent who had a small office. His secretary was on maternity leave and he needed an energetic and resourceful individual to take her place. When Shawna realized she would be alone in the office she was apprehensive about her new duties. Her employer was patient, however, and showed her the various forms and reports he needed typed. As the first day drew to a close, Shawna's exhaustion was openly visible. Her work was slower and she heaved deep and frequent sighs. Concerned, her employer asked her if she would be able to do the amount of work there was in his office. Shawna had serious doubts.

The next day Shawna called her agency, telling them she was ill and could not go back to the insurance company. Over the next months, she worked at a series of jobs, never enjoying any of them enough to seek permanent employment. With the end of each temporary job, Shawna felt a loss of self-confidence and a desire to change her life. She saw her friends from high school get interesting jobs, marry, and have children. Her life was racing by, and Shawna's low hope was preventing her from catching a ride. ✳

Many low-hope people drift through life without experiencing the highs that come from daring to dream. Shawna, as with Ted whom we met in chapter 1, preferred to play it safe rather than to risk failure. She never dared to shine, and on the few occasions when she might have, her low energy foreclosed on her plans.

❋ Matt—From Making Coffee to Making Recordings: High Will, High Ways

Ever since the family could remember, Matt had loved music. When he was a baby he had his music box, as a toddler he beat on pans as drums, in grade school he played the trumpet, and as a teenager his boom box was blaring constantly. When, at fourteen years old, Matt was hired to work the light and sound panels for a children's theater company, his future goals were set. Matt knew he had to work in the music industry, no matter how he got there.

Because he knew what he intended to do with his life, Matt cared little for his high school classes. He began skipping school in his junior year, spending his time instead at a local recording studio. The older artists and engineers taught Matt a great deal about making records, and by Matt's senior year he knew he wanted to drop out of school. His parents understood his love of music and, while they would have preferred that he finish high school, they allowed him to attend a training program for recording engineering instead.

Once in the training program, Matt worked hard and graduated at the top of his class. He knew he was on the right track. His new credentials were valuable, but the challenge was finding work. The music industry is difficult to break into, but Matt was up to the task. With a small allowance from his parents to help him as he got started, he found work as a "gofer" in a well-known recording studio. He was asked to go for coffee, to answer the phones, and even to scrub the bathrooms, in exchange for rubbing elbows with top-name musicians.

As the months and years went by, Matt was allowed to engineer occasional songs, getting an opportunity to show what he could do. Because Matt was very good, a few musicians began to ask for him. In time, his reputation grew until his work was in demand by well-known artists. Matt had the ability to understand the sound the musicians wanted to achieve. With the levers and buttons on his console, he could translate their vision into beautiful music. As the years went by, Matt made less coffee and more music, and today he is a foremost recording engineer with several gold and platinum records to his name.   ❋

Dropping out of high school could have been a disaster, and for many it is, but Matt's high waypower and willpower fueled his dream and kept him working for success. He was unusual in deciding on his career so early in life, but once his goal was set, he kept the dream before him, always thinking of ways to make it come true.

An Overview of Hope Scores

The stories you have read depict the four conditions of high hope, low hope, high willpower with low waypower, and high waypower with low willpower. High-hope people dare to visualize themselves achieving success. They greet life as an adventure, chockful of opportunities, regarding setbacks as temporary and as chances to learn. Their energy is infectious, fueling and igniting ideas in the people around them. By contrast, low-hope people may fade into the background, or they may attempt to throw water on your fire with their negative attitudes.

Low waypower hinders the expression of full-scale hopefulness by preventing the person from thinking of ways to reach goals. This individual may have dreams and energy to pursue them but feels blocked when problems occur. Low willpower can be of long duration, as was the case for Shawna, or it may be the result of recent circumstances. Whatever the reason, low willpower depletes the person of the mental energy required to get things done.

Your next step is to take a closer look at the willpower and waypower in your own life. We have chosen the story form to describe the conditions of hope because life stories carry a great deal of information. In the next chapter you will begin writing your own story, and through this process, understand better how you have come to think the way you do.

3

Once Upon a Time—Your Story of Hope

An essential part of increasing your hope is developing an understanding of your current hope patterns. Are you high or low in waypower or willpower? Where does your overall hope level fall? In previous chapters, we have provided you with some assessments to help determine your hope. The life satisfaction questionnaire in chapter 1 allowed you to see which important life areas could use an increase in fulfillment. In chapter 2, you filled out the Hope Scale, which gave a numerical gauge of your overall hope, as well as its willpower and waypower components. You also began examining how you pursue your goals, discovering the different ways willpower and waypower determine whether you can reach them.

So far, we have shown you glimpses into the lives of a variety of people who are either high or low in hope. This method, the narrative, is an excellent method to understand the things you think and do. We have used it to describe the lives of specific individuals who represent various "kinds" of hope. As you read these stories in the previous chapters, you probably developed a clear picture of each character and how he or she was able to access willpower and waypower. Now, writing your own hope story will clarify your goal selection, the determination you have to reach your goal (willpower), and the extent to which you can perceive yourself as being capable of solving the problems that you might encounter (waypower). In this section, we ask you to write about yourself, using the guidelines we will provide, though you should go ahead and read the entire chapter before you do any of the assignments.

Tips for Writing Your Story

We know that not everyone is comfortable expressing their thoughts in writing. So, we have a few words of advice before you begin. Don't be concerned about sentence structure, spelling, or grammar. Here is what is important for you to do: *Write about your thoughts and feelings as you perceive them, without censorship or criticism of your work.* Remember, no one is going to see your story except you, unless of course you choose to share it with others.

You may wonder why it's important to write your story, instead of telling it, or perhaps just thinking about it. For one thing, a written story is more permanent than a told story, and it allows you to go back and review what you have said about yourself. In addition, writing your story allows you some private time during which you can seriously explore your personal hope. Many people find that regularly writing in a journal, which is really quite similar to writing your own story, is a source of personal growth and a means to maintain balance in their lives. Writing about yourself need not be difficult, and it may well prove enlightening. Are you ready? Let's start slowly (which is one tip that high-hope people practice). Keep in mind these guidelines and you can produce a story about yourself. For the first story about yourself, we ask that you write about a single experience, but *write about it in great detail.* As you do this, you will find that your thoughts and feelings about the experience become clear. It is almost as if you're focusing a camera lens on a small part of your life. Follow the steps described below.

Telling your own story is the way to understand hope in your life.

Step One: Introducing Yourself

To begin your story, first describe yourself. You will want to mention your age, sex, and ethnic group. Your relationships are important in your life—describe the major ones. Are you married? Describe your children, if you have any. Your socioeconomic status also may be relevant—for example, upper class, middle class, or working class. You may be at the poverty level, which may well have some effect on your level of hope. The amount of education you have had should be noted, as well as your assessment of your various abilities. Some of your abilities might include your hobbies and special interests, those activities that capture your attention. You also may wish to mention personal qualities such as sensitivity to others, and nurturance. In short, any characteristic about yourself that *you believe to be important* should be included in your personal description. Take some time with this exercise and be very complete. Write it as if you were introducing yourself to someone who did not know you.

Step Two: Identify Your Goal— Starting Small

Next, think about a recent situation in which you have wanted to do something. Or, perhaps you wanted to get something. This need not be a large or especially difficult thing, but it must be something you can identify as a goal. It is important to select single goals, and these should be fairly small. You might choose, for instance, learning a new dance, or finding the right gift for a friend's birthday. You also can describe a goal that is a step toward a larger end. For example, if your target were to run three miles a day, running a quarter of a mile each day for a week would be a realistic step toward your goal and a good subject to write about.

As you describe what it was you wanted to do or to have, take your time and paint a complete picture of this event. In this part of your story, be sure to include how long you have wanted this goal, and whether you have tried to achieve it before. Write about how your life would change as a result of achieving the goal, or what meaning the achievement of the goal would have for you.

Step Three: Describe Your Ways

Before describing the different ways you thought about reaching your goal, describe the thoughts and feelings you have about yourself as being able to generate pathways. Do you feel confident? Do ideas come readily to your mind? Perhaps you do not generate avenues to reach your goal easily and therefore feel less confident about success. The perception you have about your ability to find ways to reach your goal, especially when you encounter problems, is very important to understand. Take your time. Thoroughly explore these thoughts and feelings you have about yourself. You may begin to feel anxious or even depressed as you work on this step. These feelings are normal to have as you face yourself. Accept the feelings as a natural part of growing and write about them.

Now, describe the different ways you thought about trying to achieve your goal. Was there one major route you imagined? Or did you have several? Of the pathways you thought about, which ones did you actually try? You may have thought of things to do, discarding them as too difficult or simply not feasible. Write about those also. Be thorough in your description. Understanding your waypower is vital to your ability to enhance your total hope.

Step Four: Thoughts and Feelings— The Basis of Personal Messages

Now that you have identified one of your goals, and explored how to reach it, write about how energized you felt to work for it. As you thought about what you would need to do to reach this goal, what thoughts and feelings did you have? Did you see yourself as able to move along the paths you had thought of to reach the goal? Were your thoughts positive or negative?

Mixed? Were your feelings enthusiastic or anxious? Perhaps you did not experience any vivid emotion or thought—write about that also. Once again, give this some time, and be descriptive.

Step Five: Meeting Obstacles

This next part is very important—write about what happened when you tried to go after your goal. Did you run into roadblocks? Life can throw them in your path. Describe any impediments carefully. What did you do when encountering roadblocks? Did you try other ways to get to your goal? Did you change your goal? You may have given up at that point and decided to try again later. If you did not meet with any difficulty, achieving your goal when you first tried, write about how that felt. A key here is to examine thoroughly your response to the frustrations you may have encountered as you pursued your plan.

Step Six: Tell About the Results of Your Efforts

Finally, write about whether or not you reached your goal. How did you feel? What was it like to get there, or not get there? Was it like you thought it would be? Was it worth it? How do you think this experience will affect the next time you try for a new goal? Perhaps you did not reach your goal, but decided to try for another one. Describe that process. What changed your direction? How did it feel to give up one objective and substitute another? Write everything you can remember about what you thought and how you felt. Outcomes build upon each other, and recognizing how you think and feel at the end of a goal pursuit is another important part of learning to enhance your hope.

This is but one of literally hundreds of hope stories that you probably have in your head. Was the pursuit of your goal harder or easier than you thought? In our experience, it gets easier with more practice. And, this exercise is one that we would encourage you to try many more times. Here is an example of a hope story that focuses on how the individual worked for one goal. You can compare your story with this one. Of course, everyone is different, but perhaps you may identify with parts of Ruth's tale.

✳ **Ruth**

Step One

Probably the most important thing I can say about myself is that I'm a mom. I love being a mom, it's what I have always wanted to do, and I do it really well. Jeff and I have three children so far, but we may have more. Alison is six, Adam is four, and Jeremy is two, and they are the loves of our lives. It is also important that I am thirty-two years old, white, and this is my second marriage. I was married briefly at eighteen, but it was annulled within the year. I am a registered nurse and worked in pediatrics until I had Alison. I feel very lucky that Jeff makes enough money so that I can be a full-time mom.

I am active in my church and, now that Alison is in school, I am also in the Parent-Teachers Association. We live in a large, charming home in the suburbs. Each child has a bedroom, and we have a big back yard with a lot of play equipment. We also have two cats, a dog, and a hamster—the all-American family. I should be very happy. But I'm not. In order to understand that, I need to describe what I look like.

I have always been what people call "petite." I am five feet tall, and for most of my adult life I weighed about ninety-five pounds. As a nurse I was constantly on the go, often working double shifts. Sometimes I forgot to eat meals, or only had time for small snacks. Gaining weight was never a problem for me. When I became pregnant the first time and was no longer working, I took life easy and learned to enjoy large meals. Although I didn't gain too much weight with Alison, I didn't lose it all before I became pregnant again with Adam. Now, after three children, I'm a real "chubette." Jeff calls me his "little butterball," which I am sure he means affectionately, but which rankles me each time I hear it.

So here I am. I'm a thirty-two-year-old woman who loves her life and her family, but not herself. I am at least twenty pounds overweight, and on someone so short, that's a lot. I try not to look in the mirror, but when I have to, it doesn't look like me. People tell me I have pretty face, but I hear the unspoken "you ought to lose weight." Jeff doesn't criticize, but still I worry that he might stray to someone thinner.

✳

Step Two

Identifying a goal isn't difficult—I want desperately to lose weight! I say that, and yet I also love to cook and like to eat what I fix. Nearly every night I go to sleep with the resolution to eat less the next day. When morning comes and I am making breakfast, the resolve seems to evaporate. Those eggs and bacon look so tempting, and I can barely resist the coffee cake. I tell myself that a hearty breakfast will allow me to resist overeating the rest of the day, but by midmorning I'm ready for a snack. If I allow myself to snack (and I nearly always do), then I think the rest of the day is lost as far as dieting is concerned, and I eat whatever I crave.

It isn't just how much I eat that is a problem—it's also that I hate to exercise. I spend most of my time playing with the children, or doing things for them, and there seems to be no time to work out.

To summarize my goal: my problem is weight loss, and the solution seems to be both eating less and exercising more. I have to develop a simple plan that I can actually follow.

The goal I set for myself was to lose five pounds. I need to lose more weight, but that will be for later—after I have begun the process. I know that if I lost those five pounds, I would feel better about myself, my clothes would not be so tight, and most important, that accomplishment would make me feel empowered to continue losing weight.

Step Three

Nearly every day I have thought about ways to lose weight. Sometimes I resolve to starve myself until I am thin again, but then common sense takes over and I know that would ruin my health. I have thought about hiring a sitter and going to the gym for an aerobics class. I have bought diet drinks, read diet books, and even tried eating only one type of food for a while. Finally, I realized that trying to fix everything about my diet and exercise lifestyle all at once was over- whelming, and I decided to focus on one thing—exercise.

When Adam was born, we had purchased a three-wheel stroller, large and safe enough to carry both young children. My plan was to begin walking or jogging for forty-five minutes every other day while pushing the two youngest children. The good things about this plan were that I could spend time with Adam and Jeremy out in the fresh air, yet boost my metabolism and burn some calories at the same time.

Step Four

Dusting off the little-used stroller, planning my route, and finding warm clothes for the boys was exciting. Jeff, an inveterate exerciser, was very encouraging, too. He suggested that, on the weekend, we could take a family jog with Alison riding her bike to keep up. The only doubt I had was whether I could keep up with everyone else.

Step Five

My first jog started wonderfully! I even ran several blocks before I got too winded. In my enthusiasm I walked, jogged, and ran for well over an hour, and reached home exhausted. That night I slept soundly, but when I awoke I was so stiff I could barely move. I couldn't believe I had done that to myself; surely I knew better. However, my plan was to work out every other day, which gave me a day to rest. I decided to stretch several times during the day off, and to be certain to stretch before and after working out.

The following day I was far more careful about how long and how vigorously I worked out. I was still somewhat stiff, but after about twenty minutes, most of the aches and pains disappeared. I walked or jogged more and ran less, but felt considerably better when I was finished. The aching muscles of the past two days underscored how important it is to start small and work up.　　✳

Step Six

All of this happened two weeks ago. I have now lost nearly five pounds, and I am still exercising. Just as I had wanted, I do feel better about myself. Accomplishing this goal has encouraged me to cut down on the sweets I had been eating between meals, as well. Now I believe I can go on to lose the rest of the weight, and best of all, I'm beginning to feel more power and control over other things I do, such as how much I eat and how often. A fun by-product of my success is that we have been able to take long Sunday walks in the park, a wonderful family outing.　　✳

More Tips on Writing Your Story

In this brief story about herself, Ruth chose to tackle a problem that had been bothering her for some time. She selected a small goal, but a meaningful one. She was certain that weight loss was desirable and attainable, but it was not until she had a clear plan for how to proceed that she felt the fire to make the changes. Once the five pound weight loss target was reached, Ruth felt even more determined to reach her eventual twenty-pound goal. Notice, too, that Ruth incorporated her family into her program, giving herself added incentives.

As you write your story, be sure to describe each step along the way as thoroughly as you can. Take your time. Don't try to do it in one sitting. Thinking about the goals you have set, the plans you have had, and the outcomes, is a valuable exercise. Writing the story, however, is essential to your developing understanding of hope in your life. Remember, waypower and willpower are steps you will learn, skills you can enhance, but not until you understand where you are now. Next, we will show you how to use what you are writing to increase your hope in the immediate, and in the future.

Using Your Story to Identify Hope

Earlier you were asked to write a brief vignette about a time you identified and then pursued a specific goal. We suggested five steps to help you as you wrote about yourself. Here, we ask you to examine what you wrote for each of those steps in order to learn how to identify the markers of hope.

Exploring Markers

Markers are the words you use to signify how you think and feel about yourself. For example, if you describe your job as something you really enjoy, this statement would indicate a higher level of hope than if you stated that you found your job boring. In writing about yourself, terms such as "worrier" or "cynical" fall into the low-hope category. By contrast, descriptions such as "happy" or "peaceful" would be higher in hope. In our research with stories written by children and adults, we use markers to tell us about the writer's level of hope. In addition to scores on the Hope Scale, hope markers provide valuable information about you.

How you describe yourself and your life is important. Do you see your personal qualities in positive or negative terms? Do you perceive a number of ways to reach your goal? Do you feel energized? Perhaps you have a difficult time getting motivated or in seeing avenues to obtain what you want out of life. As you answer these questions, remember that there are no right or wrong answers. Your descriptions are unique to you, and because they are your thoughts and feelings, there is no point in criticizing them. Remember also that honesty is important here. No one will read what you have written about unless you choose to share it. When you write about yourself, it is sometimes difficult to eliminate the critic—seeing yourself through the critical eyes of others.

The first step in your story was to write about yourself. There are many ways to describe yourself and your life, and we provide some questions to use as guidelines. The words and phrases you use are important markers to your level of hope, and we ask you to examine them carefully. Identifying these markers is important, *because they are the messages you give yourself*. And guess who listens to these messages? You do. So, each time you describe yourself in either positive or negative terms, you reinforce either high or low hope. In this chapter, the task is to identify these messages. Underlining and then listing the words and phrases on a separate page highlights the messages you are giving yourself. This exercise brings these words into focus—otherwise they are hidden in the rest of your story. Here is an example of marker identification from Ruth whose story you read earlier. The descriptive phrases she used are underlined.

> Probably the most important thing I can say about myself is that I am a mom. <u>I love being a mom,</u> it is what I have always wanted to do, and <u>I do it really well.</u>

Ruth loves what she does and believes she does it well. These statements are markers for high hope. Ruth continues to use high-hope statements when she writes that she feels very lucky and that she lives in a charming home.

Not all stories reflect such high hopes, of course. Here is a brief description written by a middle-aged woman who seems ready to make changes in her life. The descriptive words and phrases have been underlined here, as well.

> The thing that stands out in my mind is that <u>I am bored</u> with my life at this point. I have been working at the same job, insurance underwriting, for the past fifteen years. My two children are grown and I am no longer married. I am at an age when men don't ask me out, and <u>I'm tired</u> of spending the evenings alone with my cat. <u>My life isn't really bad, it just isn't fun anymore.</u>

In this description, the writer reflects a general dissatisfaction with her life. Using words such as "tired" and "bored" directly reflect these thoughts and feelings. She also tells us that her life is no fun anymore. The next description gives another example of low-hope markers. Once again, these are underlined.

> Anyone who sees me can see that <u>I'm different, but not in a good way.</u> I hate my nose. It's so big, and it's all crooked. Here I am, twenty years old, in what should be the prime of my dating life, <u>but no one is going to look twice</u> at a guy who looks like I do. I know <u>there is no point</u> in asking anyone out, <u>only to get a refusal.</u>

This young man has allowed one facial feature to sour his outlook on dating. His low hope is reflected through the negative words he used. It is important to stress here that, even though these statements reflect low hope, they are not wrong or bad. These statements reflect the way he feels about himself at this point in time. His feelings are legitimate because they are his, even though an onlooker might consider his nose to be just fine or pay no attention to it at all. Low-hope thoughts must be recognized before changes can be made, which is the purpose of this exercise.

Learning to identify the messages you give yourself is not easy. To accomplish this, you will need to be sure your descriptions are very complete, using the words that best reflect the way you think and feel about yourself. After that, you will underline each of those descriptive words or phrases and then enter them in the columns labeled low hope, neutral, or high hope. A descriptor list has been provided at the end of the chapter. Before starting on your own story, however, let's revisit Janet. Many of Janet's earlier goals have been met, and she is ready to step into a new phase of her life.

✳ Janet—Mother-in-Law Woes

Step One: Who Am I? Introducing Myself

When I determined and achieved the goal I'm going to write about, I was closing in on thirty years old, which seemed like a huge milestone. As I looked back on my life I saw that <u>I had actually accomplished quite a lot.</u> I am married to a <u>wonderful</u> man, an attorney, and we have a daughter whom we both adore. After getting my teaching certification and teaching history for two years, with the birth of my daughter I stayed home for one year. Now, I substitute teach and <u>I enjoy it a great deal. My life was and is good.</u> We bought a new home last year, and <u>I enjoy decorating it. We have enough money</u> to travel if we wish, and we have a <u>congenial</u> group of friends. Mainly we are homebodies, just <u>enjoying our daughter and our lives together</u>.

All of this sounds idyllic, but <u>it wasn't quite as perfect</u> as I have portrayed it. The major problem I had is with my mother-in-law, Judith. She is a very controlling woman who, I am sure, does not approve of much that I do. She can be openly flattering, but then she'll slip critical comments into the conversation on a regular basis. John, my husband, married late in life, and it seems clear to me that Judith had believed she would have him all to herself. I don't think any woman he married would have suited her. My problem was finding a way either to tell her to stop being so critical or to learn to let it roll off my back. John preferred that I learn to tolerate it, but <u>I really didn't think that was possible.</u>   ✳

Step Two: What Was My Goal?

My goal was to find a way to have a better relationship with my mother-in-law. At that point, each time she called or dropped by unannounced, <u>my stomach knotted,</u> and I <u>felt really stressed.</u> Early in our marriage, I told John about the critical things she said, but it was obvious that he didn't want to hear about them. He would reply, "Well, that's just my mother."

A number of my friends have mother-in-law problems. In fact, they are a frequent topic of conversation. I didn't want to have to live with those negative feelings, however, and <u>I was determined to find a way to deal with the situation.</u>   ✳

Step Three: How Could I Solve My Problem? Exploring My Ways

I woke up every morning wondering if I would hear from Judith that day. As a consequence, <u>I felt on edge,</u> and <u>my good mood evaporated.</u> <u>I thought about the various ways I might have coped</u> with her criticisms, but often those thoughts turned into daydreams of witty sarcasm and brilliant put-downs—a skill I had never learned. I knew I needed a more rational approach, but <u>I didn't know how</u> to develop one. Frankly, <u>my emotions were getting in the way of my reason.</u> I needed some guidance to solve this problem.

To get a better perspective on the situation, I decided to call a family therapist one of my friends had seen during a difficult time in her life. I was able to get an appointment the next week and found her to be extremely helpful. She suggested that I keep a journal of the problem situations, including my thoughts, and what I actually did when Judith criticized. For the next two weeks I kept the journal.

Recording the events and my thoughts was very enlightening. The first thing I noticed was that the critical events were not as frequent as they had seemed. The next surprising thing was that I actually said nothing openly about the criticisms, even though I had a number of negative thoughts. As the therapist pointed out, my silence may have sent the message that criticism was acceptable. Furthermore, my apprehension and frustration made the occurrences seem more frequent than they were. In actuality, there were times when Judith visited and made no critical comments.

My next task was to find appropriate ways to express the feelings I had when Judith criticized. While my thoughts had been aggressive, I knew my behavior must be assertive. When Judith said that she didn't care for my new haircut, rather than telling her to keep her opinions to herself, I could say, "I like it this way, and that's what matters." With the help of my therapist, I practiced a number of assertive responses to the situations I had recorded in my journal. After several weeks <u>I felt strong and confident</u> enough to confront Judith. ✳

Step Four: Dealing with My Thoughts and Feelings About Judith

Yes, I felt confident, but when I saw Judith pull into my driveway <u>my courage began to fail</u>. "Wait a minute," I told myself. "<u>You are strong enough</u> to do this. What are you afraid of?" Of course I was afraid she would get angry, but I had dealt with angry high school students who were far more rude and hostile than she could ever have been. Knowing that <u>I had coped with difficult situations</u> in the past <u>bolstered my determination</u> to be confrontational with her, should the opportunity arise. As luck would have it, however, she was all sweetness on that visit. ✳

Step Five: Implementing the Plan and Exploring My Will

Because <u>I was ready</u>, and <u>I felt strong</u> in my belief that <u>I could deal with negative situations,</u> I was far more able to relax than I had ever been. I actually <u>began to enjoy</u> her visit, and found that she had some interesting things to say. My opportunity for confrontation came several days later, however, when Judith made a critical comment about the new curtains I had put in my daughter's bedroom. I was able to tell her that we liked them, and that I was sorry she found them displeasing. I also mentioned that it was a good thing it wasn't her room. Judith grunted and gave me a long lecture on respect for my elders. <u>I felt devastated</u> and wondered if all my plans had been for nothing.

Although I was disappointed in Judith's reaction as well as my own, I realized that this was the first time I had ever confronted her about the negative comments she made. Now I knew something that I hadn't known before—the type of response she was likely to make. I also realized that my comment about the room not being hers might have had too much of an edge. I vowed to practice more responses and to guard against any that might sound sarcastic.

Several days later my opportunity came again. Judith had invited me to lunch, but when I arrived at the restaurant, she stated that she was embarrassed to be seen with me because I was wearing jeans. For a moment I was stumped. I could simply leave, or I could defend what I was wearing. Instead, in my sweetest voice, I said, "I understand that women of your generation don't wear jeans, but my generation does. We find them quite comfortable." Once again Judith grunted, but this time she had no rejoinder. It was a small victory, but I felt wonderful!

✳

As you read Janet's story and note the phrases we have underlined, you will see that most of them are positive or neutral. Janet is a high-hope individual, and that is reflected in her vignette. But remember, your story should reflect the way *you* think and feel. Only by recognizing the messages you give yourself can you increase your own level of hope.

It is not always easy to recognize whether hope markers are positive, negative, or neutral. The statements you select should describe your thoughts and feelings, not those of another person. You will find the most markers when describing yourself, and when considering your waypower and willpower. On the next page is a list of a few of Janet's markers entered onto her personal descriptor list, as you will enter yours.

Hope Markers in Your Own Story

The first step to writing your story was to write about yourself. You will have described important features such as age, sex, ethnic group, marital status, income, and children, if any. You also might have described where you live, your spiritual beliefs, and your social life. Your description should be as complete as you can possibly make it. Remember, no one needs to read this but you.

At this point, we want you to read the description of yourself to see if there are things you would like to add. When you have completed it to your satisfaction, review it. Now underline all the words or phrases that describe how you think and feel. Next, transfer your words or phrases to the appropriate column of the descriptor list at the end of the chapter.

Janet's Personal Descriptor List

Low-Hope Markers

- I really don't know if it is possible
- my stomach knots
- I feel stressed
- negative feeling
- I felt on edge
- my good mood evaporated
- I don't know how
- felt devastated

Neutral Markers

- isn't quite as perfect
- ways I might cope
- courage began to fail
- I was disappointed
- I was stumped

High-Hope Markers

- I have accomplished quite a lot.
- wonderful man I adore
- My life ... is good
- Enjoy it a great deal
- have enough money
- enjoying our daughter
- I was determined to find a way to deal with the situation
- I felt strong and confident
- You are strong enough
- I had coped with difficult situations
- bolstered my determination
- I was ready
- felt strong
- enjoy
- I felt wonderful

Step Two in the assignment was to identify your goal. Many times goals are tangible, that is, objects you would like to acquire. Frequently, however, goals are what you would like to accomplish, such as weight loss or better relationships. Note the terms you use to describe your goal and your reasons for selecting it. For example, you may have chosen to lose weight because you were tired of feeling bad about yourself. The words "feeling bad about myself" would go in the low-hope column. If, on the other hand, you wanted to lose weight in order to "feel better about myself," that statement would go into the high-hope column. Although the difference appears subtle, the first description indicated that the writer habitually feels bad about his or her weight. The second description indicates a generally positive feeling that the writer wishes to augment.

In Step Three you examined the ways you thought about reaching your goal. Did you think of one way, or several? You may have sought information from someone else when you felt stymied, as Janet did. High-hope people recognize when they need to consult with others and do so freely. Examining your waypower thinking is a vital part of discovering your level of hope. We separate *perceiving* your ways from actually *trying* them, because it is often at the beginning point of perception that ways are blocked. It's important that you take a careful look at your thoughts and feelings as you considered each way to achieve your goal. What messages did you give yourself? Did you discard many of your ideas as being too difficult? Perhaps you saw few options to getting what you wanted. If that was so, how did you describe your thoughts and feelings? Underline the descriptive phrases you used, and then enter them on the descriptor list.

In Step Four you examined your thoughts and feelings about reaching your goal. This section may contain many markers, so underline all the words and phrases that describe how you thought and felt. Were you uncertain or doubtful, as Janet was initially? Perhaps you felt confident throughout your story, or you may never have reached the certainty that you could accomplish your goal. Once again, underline the descriptions and then enter them on the descriptor list.

In Step Five you described what happened when you put your plan into action. You may have met obstacles or frustrations along the way. Did you abandon your plan? Perhaps you used the first experience to learn how you could do things differently, as Janet did.

In this section you also wrote about the results of your efforts. Did you accomplish what you wanted? Perhaps you changed your goal, or simply considered it a good learning experience. Underline the words and phrases you used to describe your thoughts and feelings about the outcome and then enter these on the descriptor list. Your willpower is described by the markers you used in this section.

After you have underlined the hope markers in each section, write them in the appropriate column. Notice the number you have in each of the three columns, and identify in which of the sections you have the greatest number of hope markers. With practice, you will learn to assess the hope in your stories without going through this process each time. In the beginning, however, it's important to see the words you use about yourself. Later, this information will form the basis for restructuring your self-talk into powerful, high-hope messages.

Personal Descriptor List

Low-Hope Markers   **Neutral Markers**   **High-Hope Markers**

4

History Lessons from Your Childhood

In chapter 3 you wrote a short vignette about yourself in which you described choosing and then pursuing a goal. You examined your willpower and way-power as you wrote about yourself. We showed you how to analyze the vignette by identifying the words and phrases you used to describe your thoughts and feelings. These activities, along with your Hope Scale scores, give you insights into your current level of hope. Now you can identify which part of hope, will or ways, needs to be enhanced. No matter what your level of hope is, you will find the information in the pages to come enlightening and useful.

The Importance of History

Hope is learned. It is learned through the modeling provided by the significant people around you, as well as through the natural consequences of your actions. Each time you set a goal, think of ways to attain it, and then carry out your plans to a satisfactory conclusion, you experience the consequence of success. When your plans do not succeed, you experience a different lesson. Learning through consequences is very important, and we will focus on that in subsequent chapters. The focus of this chapter, however, is the hope message you saw modeled in your family.

You will remember Ted, from chapter 1, and the influence his parents had on his life. We have found that many low-hope people come from families with a history of low hope. In fact, there are often generations of low-hope individuals whose influence can be seen in even the youngest members of a family. We know, for example, that poverty often extends over a number of generations. It is extremely difficult for young people who are surrounded by adults with low hope to develop the waypower and willpower necessary to carry them beyond their poverty-ridden circumstances.

One does not have to be in such dire straits as those who live in poverty, however, to have been influenced by low-hope messages. In Ted's case, the family was solidly middle class, but his parents communicated the need to play it safe, work hard, and take few risks. While Ted's adult life was financially stable, he felt stifled. As Ted began to change his life, to actualize his dream, he was able to see more clearly how his parents had influenced him.

Hope is learned, in part, through the examples set by the important people in your childhood.

In order to assess the impact of family messages, it's necessary to understand your own history. In this chapter, you are going to examine your personal history—the immediate influences on you while you were growing up. Then, we are going to ask you to explore the history of your roots—those legends about distant ancestors that lend interest and pride to many families. For the moment, however, the focus will be on the young you.

Later in the chapter we will ask you to write a story. You will begin with the earliest memory you have, and then work forward in time, selecting the events that are most important to you. Other people have chosen memories of entering school, or of a parent losing a job, or of an early success. We suggest that you purchase a notebook specifically for this assignment because your life story should take many pages. As with the previous stories, honesty is very important. Remember, no one will read your story unless you permit it.

As with the other assignments, an example may be helpful. We have taken excerpts from the life of Donna, a fifty-year-old attorney.

✳ Donna

I used to think it was a dream. Then one day I told my mother about it and found that it was a memory. I was standing in the back seat of a car, looking out the rear window, and crying. The figure of a large woman in a white dress was receding into the distance. As the car moved farther away I began to play with some gold foil chocolate coins she had given me. The remarkable thing about the memory was that I was only eight months old. The woman who had been my nurse was leaving our employment, and I was devastated.

After that, I don't remember a great deal until the Christmas of my second year. On that occasion I remember clearly the brightly decorated tree, and my new rocking chair. I remember my mother and father standing in the doorway with me, and how utterly thrilled

I was by the display.

That same year, I am told, my father was elected to the California legislature, and after that, he and my mother were gone a great deal. I remember being awakened late one night by my mother, who had just returned from Sacramento. She had brought me a Winnie-the-Pooh teddy bear to go with my favorite books.

My parents do not feature as frequently in my memories as Juanita, our maid and my companion. Juanita taught me to use silverware, to drink from a cup, and of course, to use the bathroom. She was my friend and my protector, the person I ran to first if I was hurt or frightened. Juanita had a great outlook on life. I remember that other maids from the neighborhood would sit in our kitchen and tell stories. I just sat in my high chair and laughed right along with them, although I didn't understand much of what they said. What I did understand was that life's problems needn't be taken too seriously. A joke, laughter, and patience seemed to carry these ladies along.

When I was five years old, a tragedy struck. My father died of a heart attack, leaving my mother with large medical bills, a number of other debts, and no income. Although my father had been a successful attorney, a judge, and then elected to the legislature, he had neglected to get life insurance, save money, or provide for my mother and me. Needless to say, our lives changed drastically.

I was saddened by my father's death, but I was also too young to comprehend fully what the impact on our lives would be. When our lifestyle changed, I began to understand. Juanita had to leave, and we moved to a much smaller house in a less elegant area of the city. We sold one of the cars and the huge dog my father had recently purchased. The saddest memory, however, is of saying good-bye to Juanita. I knew she couldn't stay with us, but I loved her dearly. It was obvious, even to a five-year-old, that we were having a hard time financially and that my mother was worried. My grandparents came to stay for a while, and I often heard them talking about how my mother was going to be able to manage.

Throughout that difficult period, my mother set a tone of calm confidence. She had not had a career, but she had a good education. She also had the belief that she could find a way out of our problems—she was a fighter. Friends advised her to file bankruptcy, but she refused, preferring to pay off my father's debts a little at a time. I was worried about our future too, but my mother's confidence and her willingness to talk with me about my feelings made me realize that there were things I could do to help.

In the late 1940s it was difficult for a woman to find good employment, and my mother spent many hours away from home interviewing for positions. I was in kindergarten by then, and it was not always possible for her to be home with me after school. Child care was also a problem, partly because few options were available, and partly because I didn't want to stay with anyone else. I suppose I was stubborn, but I was also independent. I determined that I could save my mother money by taking care of myself. Reluctantly, she allowed me to stay alone after school. Some people may consider this to be neglect and, perhaps legally, it was. However, I felt capable and responsible, and caring for myself has fostered a self-confidence that has lasted all my life.

Through one of my father's former clients, my mother heard about a position as a story analyst at one of the movie studios. Although she had no experience with this sort of work, she did have a master's degree in English. She applied for the job, and was hired. I was delighted. Although it meant another move, the school I would attend was right across the street from the studio. I went to my mother's office every day after school. I enjoyed walking right through the studio gates, past all the teenaged autograph hunters waiting to see movie stars. Sometimes, for fun I would stand around watching them compare autographs, then, when I got bored, I would leave them gaping as I went inside.

My mother was such an energetic person, always ready to take on new projects. The studio offered her extra money if she could translate and synopsize the Spanish language scripts, of which there were many. Having only a smattering of Spanish but assuming she could learn, she said yes. That began our Mexican period.

For the next six months, my mother and I went to the Mexican movies at least twice a week, read children's stories in Spanish, and even ate quantities of rice and beans. The Mexican movies were a new and wonderful experience for an Anglo child. Huge families would come to the double feature, and the theater was filled with the noises of children squabbling and babies crying. During the intermission, a gentleman in a sombrero called out bingo numbers in Spanish. After the movies, mother and I took a bus ride home, our car having long since died. This was all a great adventure for me, but for my mother it was another step toward achieving her goal of financial security.

Life was good, despite our struggles. By the time I was in junior high school my mother had paid off the debts, and bought a small home. But my mother wasn't about to settle into complacency. She recognized the escalating value of real estate in Southern California, and her new goal was to profit from it. The home we bought was a "fixer upper," and that is just what we did. We learned how to paint, hang wallpaper, sand floors, put up wall board, and anything else we could do to improve the resale value.

By this time I was old enough to be an active participant in my mother's plans and also to develop a few plans of my own. Law is a difficult profession for a woman, but my mother told me that my father would have been proud to have me follow in his footsteps. I was a good student, and, with the advice of my father's old friends, I began planning my own career goals. I set my sights on going to college at Occidental, my mother's alma mater, and then law school at USC.

After making a substantial profit on the house when she sold it, there was no stopping my mother. She bought a much larger home and, later, two small apartment houses. Because the market was inflating all the time, they increased their value many times over the next fifteen years. She had surely achieved her financial goals, and all on her own.

As I review my life as a child, I can feel the influence of strong women. Juanita showed me a relaxed and patient perspective, finding humor in the problems of life. My mother showed me that determination, willingness to take risks, and hard work, could bring success. Those messages have been central tenets for me, and I thank these strong women daily for their influence.   ✳

Donna has written about only a few of the many memories she might have selected; however, each of these events signaled an important message. Some of Donna's experiences were sorrowful, and she does not hesitate to describe those feelings. Neither, however, does she allow those events to color her entire life. The loss of a nurse, her father, and a companion could have left Donna with feelings of irreparable sadness. Donna's mother, however, was a powerful influence in mitigating those unfortunate events.

Donna was witness to her mother's determination not to give in to misfortune. Even in a time when women were encouraged to be dependent on others, this woman was able to establish her own goals, determine the pathways to reach those goals, and then energetically go after what she wanted. Although there were other models in Donna's life, her mother remained the most powerful one. She was the driving influence behind Donna's later achievements in college, law school, and the legal profession.

Goals, waypower, and willpower are all elements in Donna's story, both for herself and for her mother. In the case of her mother, we saw her cope with the grief and loss of a husband and the difficulties of being a single parent. Having experienced the threat of poverty, she set a goal of financial security. She explored the pathways available to her, at times seeking the advice of friends. As a high-hope person, Donna's mother energetically followed opportunities when they appeared. There were times when she was downhearted and discouraged, and she was able to share those feelings with Donna. She also shared her belief that she could pull through, and made Donna an active participant in pursuing her dreams.

The elements of hope in Donna's life ran parallel to those of her mother. Recognizing that there were many problems and not wanting to be a bystander, she set her own goals in an effort to help her mother. There are not many goals of a serious nature available to a five-year-old, but she chose to become as independent as possible in an effort to relieve some of her mother's stress. The route Donna chose was to take care of herself after school. This was not an easy goal to accomplish. The neighbor women clucked their tongues at a child staying alone, and she had to be careful to keep the door locked at all times. Donna learned to avoid the gossips, just as she learned to cook and clean the house, so that her mother would have more time to spend with her. Both mother and child were acting on the principles of high hope.

Beginning Your Personal History

You have now reached a point where you can begin your own story. As Donna did, start with your earliest memories. It doesn't matter if you don't know how old you were in your recalled memories. As long as the memories are yours, not details told to you by relatives or photographs you saw, these recollections are grist for your story mill. The reason the memories should be your own is that they contain the messages you internalized as you were growing up. Another person's story is not your own. Photographs can be used to stimulate memories, but often we confuse the picture with the genuine recollection. If a photograph elicits a thought or a feeling about the event pictured, you are probably remembering.

The first time you write your personal history, it does not need to be a complete autobiography. As you saw with Donna's story, it is not long, but it does portray a picture of the messages she received. As you write your first history, try to sample memories of significant events at different stages of your life. Select a quiet and private place to do your writing. You should be able to contemplate your life without interruptions and without questions from others. Allow yourself enough time to explore your thoughts and feelings about the events you experienced, and describe them thoroughly. Don't worry about your writing style, spelling, or punctuation. The work you are doing is for you alone.

Looking for Hope Messages

Once you have the first draft of your personal history written, you are ready to assess its contents. Using the method of identifying markers that you used previously, underline any thoughts or feelings that you had about the events.

Now, reread you history and make a note of what lessons you learned from each memory. Consider, for example, the Mexican period of Donna and her mother's life. One lesson Donna learned from that experience was that taking risks could pay off. Donna's mother took a chance that she could learn Spanish—a language she barely knew—well enough to translate the scripts.

In Donna's story, the messages are detailed in each memory, for purposes of clarity. In your own work, they may not be so obvious. Here is where you will need to take the time to think about what your memories mean. You may have a general idea about the level of hope your parents conveyed to you, but searching for specific messages will be helpful later as you learn to restructure their content.

The history you have written is only a first draft. Use it as your beginning point, and find time each day to add to and enhance what you have written, including new memories, newly remembered feelings about memories, or anything that can add detail to the history. Each time you allow yourself to ponder your early life, you will find more clues to understanding the adult you. While understanding is not vital to behavior change, it goes a long way toward making the process meaningful.

Next, you are going to explore your family history. While parents and significant others play an important role in determining your hope, each family history has a unique character vital to understanding how your current thoughts and feelings have been influenced through the generations.

What Family Stories Say About Hope

In a global sense, the United States is a young country. So, many of us have ancestors who came from somewhere else, and we seem fascinated by our heritage. African Americans frequently know how many generations have passed since their ancestors came as well as where they came from in Africa. Anglos often can run through a litany of what percentage they are of which nationality. Asian Americans and Latinos have their own ancestral groups, and Native Americans have tribal affiliations. The study of family genealogy has become a favorite hobby for many people.

Our purpose in this chapter is to examine the stories that have been told in your family over several generations and how they may have influenced you. Many families have such stories, and children often hear them from grandparents or other elders. These stories suggest themes that are reflected in the behaviors of family members over subsequent generations. For example, African American elders may tell stories of slavery that depict courage. For the young people who are listening, these stories have the power to instill self-respect and a desire to continue overcoming racism. Many families had forebears who traveled across the plains in covered wagons, or who fought in various wars. Tales of hardship and struggle and stories of heroism all convey important messages about hope to the generation who hears them.

Family stories convey important messages about hope.

Family stories need not be long or involved—sometimes they are brief incidents that capture interest. Importantly, however, they are told generation after generation. For example, knowing that your ancestors came to the United States to escape persecution, even if you do not know the details, is an important piece of information about hope in your family. Other times, if you are lucky, there are detailed stories about the early lives and struggles of your foremothers and forefathers. Grandparents and great-grandparents are a good source for these tales.

Stories may be told to young children as a way of conveying the values in a family. For instance, parents may tell children about their experiences when growing up in an effort to convince them to behave in a certain way. If you remember such lessons, or hearing the words "When I was a child . . . ," you probably heard such lectures. Children seldom believe that their parents know best or that anything that happened in the past could be relevant to today. Our point, however, is that there were important messages in those stories whether or not you heeded the advice. You may have heard about courage and determination, or you may have gotten the message that life is an uphill battle and one should expect failure. Whatever the messages, they have an impact on your level of hope today—even though the impact may be largely beyond your awareness. We are going to ask you to remember some of these family stories for your second assignment in this chapter.

The Value of History

Our research shows that hope is conveyed in a variety of ways. Earlier, we described modeling, that is, learning through watching significant others. We also mentioned the learning that occurs through the consequences of one's own actions. Another important process for conveying hope is through stories that illustrate the types of behaviors that are characteristic of members of your family. We use the term "family" in its broadest sense. We are speaking of generations of people who represent your hereditary line.

Because immigrants developed so much of America, most of us represent a series of interesting family lines. Marriage, for much of the world, is conducted within small circles of acceptable mates, and it frequently is driven by social rather than personal reasons. In the United States, on the other hand, marriage for love is the accepted standard. Because of this, many family lines are woven together, resulting in a uniquely fascinating person—*you*.

Hope is communicated from person to person, generation to generation. Your family history gives insights into the hopefulness of past generations. Those stories create real people out of names on a genealogy chart. They become people with whom you can identify and from whom you can learn wisdom. They also serve as distant and subtly powerful teachers of hope—both low and high.

It's important to recognize that not all stories are uplifting. Many families have a tragic history that has left thoughts and feelings of defeat in a long line of ancestors. Some stories are told with anger, resentment, or other negative emotions. Parents may relate terrible incidents so as to "prepare" their children for trouble or grief. Although the motivation of the older person in telling such tales of woe is to somehow toughen their youngsters for what is ahead, such "preparation" actually serves to lock these malleable young minds into repeating the disappointments and hardships. That is to say, such stories have low-hope scripts that children unfortunately embrace. And, in taking a hold of the child's dreams, low-hope stories make for yet another tale of unhappiness for that child.

In examining your family history, you may find traces of hope, but you also may discover that some of the low hope you experience today has its roots in the past. The second assignment of this chapter is writing one or more of these family stories then reviewing them for the messages that they carry.

Donna, whom we met in the previous chapter, had a close relationship with her grandfather. He and she would take long walks, always ending at the Atchison train station where his cronies sat and told stories. Fred told exciting stories about his life as a soldier; later Donna came to understand these fine tales were not entirely true. As an ancient veteran of the Spanish-American War, Fred had been awarded many medals over the years simply for staying alive so long. He wore his medals proudly on their walks, and young Donna was convinced that he must have been a hero. Fred's real story, however, was even more interesting and a more important influence on Donna's adult life.

※ Fred

Fred was born in late 1882 in New York City, the son of a wealthy shipbuilder. He decided he wanted a life of excitement. Spending his time in an office, pouring over blueprints and arguing with craftsmen like his father did was not what he envisioned for himself. At that time, the United States was threatening to go war with Spain over her colonialism, and Fred had dreams of riding up Cuba's San Juan Hill next to Teddy Roosevelt. Forsaking his father's money and refusing a college education, Fred chose to enlist in the cavalry. Fred excelled in his basic training at Fort Sam Houston, Texas. Because he was far better educated than most of the enlisted men, and he comported himself as a gentleman, Fred rose quickly to an officer's rank. Good men were in short supply, and he was highly valued. A robust and energetic young man, Fred had an unusual talent for horsemanship. His superiors had high hopes for his future in the Army—and so did Fred.

Unfortunately, Fred's good health did not last. Houston's hot and humid summers, with mosquitoes carrying malaria, provoked an epidemic. Fred succumbed and was unable to ship out with the rest of his unit. Fred's dream of fighting in the Spanish-American War was over. He might have gone back to New York, but he still loved the outdoors and, most of all, adventure. When the Army offered to send him to be a guard at Fort Leavenworth, Kansas, that seemed good enough until something better came along.

Something better did come along—in the shape of a young school-teacher named Jenny, who was visiting friends in the town of Leaven-worth. Their courtship was not long by the standards of those days because she lived far away, and it was difficult for them to spend time together. The solution was for them to get married, right away.

Although he had little to offer Jenny in the way of material goods, they both were caught up in the romantic appeal of life on the frontier and decided to homestead in the new Oklahoma Cherokee Strip that was just opening for claims. As a member of the cavalry, Fred was allowed to be among the first to make the dash to stake out land for farming in the new territory. When the ribbon was cut, Fred galloped his horse as fast and as far as he could, until he got to an area by a stream that looked suitable. Although the land was dusty and bleak, there were hundreds of men on horseback rushing to stake their claims, and Fred decided to go ahead and stake his.

As soon as he had his claim registered, he sent for Jenny. They then began building their farm. At first, they lived in a sod hut, but after a time Fred built a two-room cabin. They lived in that cabin for four years, subsisting on Fred's Spanish-American War pension and what little they could grow.

Farming was difficult for a young man raised in New York, and Fred was far more comfortable on top of a horse than walking behind a plow. Farming did not seem to come naturally to Fred, and he had neither the money nor the land to become a cattle rancher. During their fourth year in the Oklahoma Territory, with a child on the way, Fred and Jenny decided to relinquish their claim and move back to Kansas.

They settled in the country outside a tiny town near Atchison. Jenny got a job as a schoolteacher for a short time, and Fred worked as a jack-of-all-trades. He enjoyed fixing broken things, and helping his neighbors with general farm work. This work, together with Fred's pension, barely met all their needs, which by that time included raising three daughters. Despite being very poor, Jenny kept their small home clean, and the girls were always well groomed. They had a cow, some chickens, and a vegetable garden, so at their very worst they always had enough to eat.

Living on the edge of poverty, Jenny unexpectedly inherited a large furnished home from her great-aunt. At that point, the family moved to Atchison, where life improved for Jenny and the growing girls. Fred continued his work as a general repairman, bringing in a minimal but adequate amount of money for the family. Although Jenny was tolerant of Fred's general lack of ambition, his daughters were not. They worked hard to overcome the image their father portrayed to the town by driving around in his horse and wagon in his old clothes. Jenny, for her part, instilled in her daughters a love of learning, good manners, and the courage to persevere. All three went on to attend college and lead successful lives. In the years to come, however, they never forgot their poverty. Each daughter worked hard, saved and invested her money, and made certain she would never be poor again.   ✳

This is a story that can be found in many American families. It tells of people settling the West and the struggles and hardships that they often experienced. Why is this story important? How does it relate to hope? The answer to both questions is that the story depicts the character of a family. It shows an individual, Fred, who wanted to carve out a life different from that into which he had been born. He set goals and he made decisions. In retrospect, he might have made better decisions for his family, but he lived and worked outdoors, free of the constraints of business suits and stuffy offices. Jenny presents a somewhat more complex figure—part obedient wife and part courageous woman. Her goal was marriage and a family, which she accomplished despite austerity and disappointments. Jenny's daughters, having watched her cope in silence with the consequences of Fred's choices, were absolutely determined to make better lives for themselves. Knowing their parents' past and experiencing poverty firsthand, all three girls took advantage of opportunities to become educated and to assure their own financial security.

Stories are influential whether they illustrate high or low hope. In Fred and Jenny's case, while there are many high-hope aspects of their lives, neither of them felt empowered to make significant changes that would have bettered their situation. The influence on their immediate offspring, however, was to generate a reaction that produced high-hope thoughts and behaviors. Virginia, who is Fred and Jenny's oldest daughter and Donna's mother, has lived her high-hope life motivated by the poverty she experienced as a child.

✳ Virginia—No More Secondhand Clothes

By the time Virginia was in high school, the family had moved to a four-bedroom home in Atchison. Her mother, Jenny, had inherited the house and all its furnishings from a great-aunt, so to outward appearances the family was not poor. Virginia's father, Fred, did not hold a regular job, however, and the family had very little money to spend. Jenny made underwear for Virginia and her sisters out of the fancy printed material on flour sacks. She haunted church bazaars for clothing that could be altered to fit her daughters and repaired the holes in their shoes with cardboard. By the time Jenny was finished working her miracles, her daughters looked nice—even occasionally stylish.

Despite Jenny's efforts to save her daughters from experiencing shame, all three girls were constantly embarrassed by their father. Wearing his shabbiest clothes, he drove a battered wagon pulled by a broken-down horse. No matter how well groomed or how polite the girls were, they were always known as Fred's daughters. Virginia, however, discovered a way to become known for her own accomplishments.

Every year in Kansas a statewide short-story competition is held, with the winner getting one free year at the college of his or her choice. Virginia loved to write and had been getting high marks from her teachers for her poetry and stories. She entered a story she had written called "Prisoner's Fudge," and, astonishingly, she won! She was building a reputation of her own as a smart and creative young woman. With her scholarship she decided to go to the University of Kansas and major in journalism. During the summer before college she began a correspondence with William Allen White, the famous journalist, which lasted many years. His advice, which she sought and took, helped her make good decisions about the future direction of her career.

In the years to come Virginia transferred to a California university, eventually earning both a bachelor's and a master's degree in English. After a brief marriage during which Donna was born, she had a long and successful career as a story analyst at a large movie studio. Virginia, true to her goal, invested her money wisely, became a wealthy woman, and was never poor again.   ✳

Virginia's story shows that having a low-hope example can, at times, spark high-hope thoughts and behaviors. The point here is that, even if you find many elements of low-hope in your family tales, you can alter the course of your generation. We cannot stress enough, high-hope people learn from the experiences of others and change their actions accordingly. Virginia observed her father's behavior and, although she loved him, she didn't want to be like him. She also loved her mother dearly, but Virginia was not one to sit complacently by, letting someone else control her life. Virginia exercised high waypower and high willpower to take her out of the life she had known. When she left the poverty of her girlhood, she never looked back.

Examining Your Family Stories

Take some time now to recall stories you may have heard from parents, grandparents, or other family members. You might try to remember what your home environment was like when you were young, or what it was like to meet Grandma or Grandpa. If you have no recollections, talk to others in your family to solicit stories that they may remember. If you are lucky enough to have parents or grandparents who are still alive, ask them to relate their adventures to you. Most oldsters love to tell the younger generation about the days gone by, and these stories can be fascinating. Even if the stories they tell are not ones you heard as a child, the adventures they describe would have influenced your parents and thus you. *Their stories live in you*, often without your being aware of it. If you think about it, this involves good detective work. And *you* are the case.

After you have written the story as you remember it, examine the general theme that it depicts. Markers of hope are found in words and phrases, but they are also found in *themes*. In the story of Fred, the main theme was self-determination, which is an important component of high-hope behavior. Let's look at some other hope themes in this story.

Fred experienced major disappointments twice in his life, and each time he was able to change his goal. The first time, when malaria kept him from going into battle, he was able to channel his military service into guard duty. The second time, when he gave up his homestead, he was able to support his family while continuing to do things that he enjoyed. These events illustrate a moderately high-waypower theme in Fred's life.

As we follow Fred through his life, we see that his willpower seems to diminish. He began with high energy for military service, defying his family's wishes and forfeiting a secure career. In his dreams he saw himself valiantly riding into the fray, rifle and sword at hand. As he encountered obstacles, however, his fire seemed to die out, even though he found routes to continue a life that he enjoyed. Eventually, his low willpower stalled him, however, in a life far less fulfilling than that which he had imagined. The theme conveyed by Fred's low willpower is one of settling for less. Many people do this. Is settling for less part of the implicit script of your family?

Finding the Messages

For Fred's daughters, the messages acted as stimulants for hope. They wanted their lives to be very different from his. For Fred's granddaughter, however, a message of a different kind was heard. She was impressed by his ability to defy convention and strike out on his own. In her teenage years, Fred's life gave her the courage to challenge her family's expectations. She felt a connection with her grandfather through the stories she had heard over and over again.

As you review the stories from your family, find not only the themes, but also the messages conveyed. Some stories go back through a number of generations. Through the values and behavior of your parents, even your grandparents, can you identify how messages were constructed? And finally, consider how your own life has been influenced by these stories. Have your actions been reinforced, as they were for Fred's granddaughter? Do you feel a connection to past generations? Does that sense of connection bolster you? Or perhaps, if the stories are full of disappointment and struggle, you see your life continuing down that same road, with the same unhappy road stops and a final destination that is disappointing. These are the messages from the family history that tug at people's sleeves to remind them of their roots. Recognizing these influences provides one more piece of the puzzle of hope. And as that puzzle begins to take shape, you can understand yourself better and make whatever changes you want.

Where Are You Now?

All of the writing assignments and questionnaires in this workbook have been designed to provide a better understanding of your hope level. You now have a general idea of areas in your life that need hope enhancement. You have taken the Hope Scale and have information about which component of hope may be high and which may be low. You have examined one or more situations in which you set a goal and then applied waypower and willpower to pursue that goal. From that assignment, you learned whether or not you use this process effectively. Next, you reflected on your childhood and began to develop an understanding of the messages about hope that you heard in those formative years. And finally, you explored the flavor and character of your family as described in its stories and legends.

Throughout these chapters, you were encouraged to write down your thoughts and feelings and to examine them for markers and themes of hope. At this point, you're able to place yourself along a continuum from low hope to high hope. You can identify areas of your life in which you feel less hope and areas in which you are more hopeful. And, most importantly for the work in the next section, you have begun to identify the self-talk you use, which can bring down your hope, or serve to heighten it.

The following checklist can be used to keep track of your progress. Put a checkmark next to the statements that are true for you. You may not have achieved all of the items on the list because some take longer than others to accomplish. And, *everyone moves at a different pace*. Do not let the fact that you have not completed everything in the first section stop you from continuing with the work in the following sections. Continue writing your stories—you will find that they get easier with practice. Recognizing family influences is important, and it often takes time to synthesize what you're learning. The better you know yourself, the more you will recognize these important connections with the past.

Progress Checklist

1. I understand how high hope can change my life. _____

2. I have determined which areas of my life need hope enhancement. _____

3. I understand the role of goals. _____

4. I understand the role of waypower. _____

5. I understand the role of willpower. _____

6. I can identify my own goals, waypower, and willpower. _____

7. I have taken and scored the Hope Scale. _____

8. I can identify my hope score configuration (i.e., waypower/willpower). _____

9. I have written one or more stories about myself. _____

10. I can identify markers and themes of hope in my stories. _____

11. I have developed a personal descriptor list. _____

12. I understand how my hope markers and themes inform my experience of hope. _____

13. I have written about one or more childhood memories that hold lessons about hope. _____

14. I understand how hope is conveyed through messages heard in childhood. _____

15. I have sought information about my family's stories and have written down what I remember. _____

16. I have identified the influence this history had on the family in which I was raised. _____

17. I can identify a progression of hope messages through my family line. _____

SECTION II

Hope Building Strategies

Introduction

Now that you have a general understanding of hope, and, more importantly, *your* hope, it's time to learn some strategies to enhance that hope. This section of the workbook presents a number of useful techniques that you can employ to raise your hope level. We recommend that you practice all of them. Remember, the more you exercise these strategies, the more hope you will experience in your life.

Each of the techniques described in the following chapters is designed to build upon the previous one. We begin with goal setting, because it's fundamental to any consideration of hope. In chapter 1 you made a preliminary assessment of your life satisfaction; in chapter 6 you will take a closer and more thorough look. You will determine your satisfaction with each life area and how important that area is to you.

In chapter 7 you will continue with an investigation of your hope level in each specific life domain. Because selecting goals is such an important part of success, you need to develop a clear understanding of which life domains are in need of hope enhancement, and which area will be the best place for you to begin. At the end of chapter 7 you will be ready to select the goals you will use for the work in this book.

We continue in chapter 8 with waypower, showing you how to increase your perception of choices and options. Thinking of many ways to accomplish your goal is a skill that can be taught. With increased waypower, you will develop the flexibility of thinking that can be applied to many situations. You may be surprised how helpful this will be in your life.

In chapter 9 we show you ways to increase the energy you have at your command to follow your pathways and pursue your goals. With increased willpower you will feel confident and empowered to reach for your dreams. You will learn to envision yourself doing new things, and you will learn positive, high-hope self-talk that changes the way you think.

The strategies detailed in the chapters in section II are both physical and mental in nature. Increasingly, medical and psychological research tells us that human beings are best viewed from a holistic perspective—that is, in their totality. Consequently, what you *do* is as important as what you *think* and *feel*. To enhance your hope, we advocate the holistic approach and present tactics for heightening hope by employing all three of these important functions. The Life Domain Scale and the Domain-Specific Life-Hope Scale both are designed from a holistic standpoint.

In subsequent chapters you will learn that physical fitness and health are important foundations for hope. You will be encouraged to watch your nutrition, rest, and exercise, in order to be in optimum condition to do the things you dream of doing. We recognize that illness, disability, and chronic pain afflict many people. The strategies we suggest for enhancing physical well-being, however, apply to individuals with chronic suffering as well. In a later section a chapter is devoted to those who have chronic suffering, for theirs is a special challenge to maintain high hope.

Changing negative self-talk to messages that empower, is a must for high-hope people. Because of your earlier work, you have a head start toward understanding the words you use to describe your thoughts and feelings. In the following chapters we will show you how to change these messages in significant ways to heighten your hope. When you modify the messages you automatically give yourself, you are affecting a transformation in your thoughts and feelings, and you become the person you want to be.

In the coming chapters you will be taught to use visualizations, checklists, models, and other methods to increase your hope. The exercises we suggest are both interesting and enjoyable. Take the time to complete each one as thoroughly as possible and practice the suggestions often. Case studies and research have shown that these techniques work. Throughout these chapters you will see examples of people using the strategies and enhancing their hope, as you will do. Invest the energy to make these changes. Be patient with yourself—however, making significant changes in thoughts and behaviors takes time. We want you to learn lessons that you can use through the years. We want you to infect others with your hope. We want your hope to last a lifetime.

5

Take a Closer Look
at Your Goals

Goals are essential to life. Whether or not you consciously look at it this way, everything you do can be described as a goal. Take, for example, getting up and around each day. You expect this of yourself, so you probably don't think about all the individual actions that you accomplish in order to achieve this feat. In fact, getting up when the alarm sounds, dressing, eating breakfast, making your commute if you work away from home, and the myriad other things most people do each morning, require sustained efforts and resolve. Anyone who has raised children, especially teenagers, knows how difficult these habits are to acquire. Yet you probably do them every day, perhaps more easily some days than others, without considering what an accomplishment they are. Many aspects of your life are as routine as getting yourself ready for the day. Pay attention to the things you accomplish every day and notice how many goals you achieve.

Give Yourself a Pat on the Back

One of the characteristics of high-hope people is their recognition that the things they have done in the past will help them in the future. A first step toward this recognition involves taking a close look at what you actually have accomplished, the problems with which you have coped, and the good habits you have developed. You may think that the many small things you do each day are unimportant, or that they are not real goals. Be aware that many people struggle each day to cope with the demands of living. If you are having a difficult time coping, the hope strategies in this book are of vital importance, and you will want to keep your initial goals small. If, however, you glide through your day, meeting all your obligations with a minimum of strain, you still may feel dissatisfaction with your life. You will want to reappraise the goals you have already achieved, and set new ones that will provide more pleasure. In whichever group you find yourself, give yourself a pat on the back. You have already achieved a great deal. Recognize your successes and be proud of yourself!

Your Hierarchy of Goals

In the mid 1960s, a psychologist named Abraham Maslow proposed that human needs could be categorized into a hierarchy ranging from the most basic to the loftiest. The basic needs were safety, food, and shelter, while the highest needs were esthetic and spiritual. Maslow's hierarchy culminated in a state called self-actualization. Although not all goals are needs by Maslow's definition, all needs are goals. If your basic needs for survival are routinely met, you will probably not think of them as goals. However, if you are living in poverty, then the basics of existence become your most important objectives.

As you take a closer look at your dreams, it's important to keep the hierarchy in mind. For example, a young single mother who can barely meet the expense of feeding and clothing her children finds dreams of a glamorous career beyond her reach. While such a career might actually be possible for this young woman, there are basic steps she must take and goals she must reach before tackling that particular long-range goal. If she cannot see how to get out of poverty, the dream of a glamorous career will die on the vine. While it's very important to aim high, it is also important to know where to begin. High-hope people are not afraid to have big goals, and they can envision the basic steps they will need to take along the way to achieve these goals.

High-hope people can visualize big dreams and the small steps to take along the way.

In this chapter you will select several goals for your hope-enhancement work. As you decide on your targets, consider where you are in your hierarchy. Are there conditions in your life that might interfere with your efforts? For example, suppose you have always wanted to learn to paint, and now you believe that you have the time to try your hand at watercolors. In your hierarchy there may be other needs and responsibilities, such as child care, a job, or a relationship, that will have to be met before you will have the time to paint. Don't be discouraged—simply be aware of the position your goal holds among all the life goals you have. This will allow you to make realistic plans, have more energy to carry out those plans, and thereby increase your chances of success. Goals that hold a high-priority status are more likely to generate high waypower and willpower and less likely to be discarded along the way.

Long-Range and Short-Range Goals

Goals can be divided into short range and long range. Most major achievements in life, such as career success, educational attainment, or raising children, take a long time to accomplish. There are many small goals along the way, and these are usually short range in nature. You will also have other short-range goals that may not be immediately related to your long-range plans but that enliven and enrich your life. For example, learning a sport may not be related to your goal of career advancement, but it certainly will bring you enjoyment. Activities, such as sports or hobbies, contribute to other important spheres and help you live a balanced life. High-hope people have both long- and short-range goals. They can divide their long-range goals into small steps, which then become more easily achievable and manageable goals. Each time you accomplish one of your smaller goals, you realize that you are one step further toward your larger achievement.

High-hope people know how to prioritize their goals.

In chapter 1 you filled out a brief questionnaire as a preliminary screening of your overall life satisfaction. In this chapter, you are going to examine the important areas of your life in a far more detailed way. From your ratings on these questionnaires, you will select several goals that will constitute the material for your personal hope work.

We begin this examination with a rating scale for both *satisfaction* and *importance* of each life domain. You will assign yourself a number on the Life-Domain Questionnaire, which will allow you to see which specific areas are most and least important to you and which you are the most and least satisfied with. Each life domain has its own section in which it's described and which includes a series of questions for you to consider as you make your rating.

The Domain-Specific Life-Hope Scale that follows the Life-Domain Questionnaire gives you a rating of your hope level in each of the important domains. For each area, you will read a brief vignette of a person setting a goal in that domain. These descriptions show you hope in action and provide models and suggestions you can use in your own hope enhancement. After completing both questionnaires contained in chapters 6 and 7, you will be ready to select your goals for the work in this book. Careful selection is important if you are to learn the strategies well and maximize your chances for success.

What Are Life Domains?

Your values, attitudes, and behaviors can be classified into the groups we call *life domains*. There are nine areas, and each will be described in detail. Knowing what each domain consists of will help you judge how important it is to you and how satisfied you are with that part of your life. The domains are described alphabetically, not in order of importance. Their significance in your life is for you to decide. Remember, too, there are no right or wrong answers. Decide honestly how important and satisfactory each domain is for you.

The Academic Domain

The academic or educational domain includes your formal training—kindergarten through college or graduate school. It also extends to other courses you may have taken, whether or not they led to a degree. You should also include seminars, workshops, or any continuing education you have acquired. Don't include classes you may have taken for fun, such as painting, dance, or the like. Those will contribute to the leisure arena.

As you think about your academic domain, ask yourself if you are pleased with your current level of education. Does your education allow you to do the type of work you want to do? Do you feel knowledgeable about the subjects that interest you? Do you ever wish you had more formal education or training in order to feel more competent? Many individuals who lack formal education are very well educated. These people may be self-taught, and are always interested in reading and learning new things. How important is learning to you? Notice whether or not there is a discrepancy between your rating of the importance of academics, and your rating of how satisfied you are with that area of your life.

The Family Domain

Family, in this context, refers to your spouse or life partner, children, parents, grandparents, and your extended relations, including relatives by marriage. Family may also include individuals who live with you, but to whom you are not related, such as foster children. In some families, a courtesy relationship is extended to godparents and very close friends, often given the honorary title of "aunt" or "uncle."

Family relationships are often taken for granted, especially when they're good. When considering how important this domain is to you, ask yourself how much time and energy you presently devote to these relationships. Are you meeting all of your responsibilities? Are your relationships as fulfilling as you would like them to be? Are there relationships that need work? There may be conflicts you need to resolve or positive things you need to say to your loved ones.

Not everyone has family with whom they are close. Many people choose to be independent from others, and this domain may not be an active part of their lives. Again, there are no right or wrong answers—only honest ones.

The Leisure Domain

In this era of dual-career families, with most households having two wage earners, you may have forgotten the meaning of leisure. Leisure is defined as time without duties or responsibilities, what we used to call "spare time." If you have leisure time, how do you spend it? Your interests don't need to be inactive to be considered leisure. Sports (observing or participating), gardening, refinishing furniture, shopping, and artistic pursuits, all come under this heading. So do movies, television, reading, and other, more sedentary activities.

You may wish for more leisure time, for the chance to do a few of the things you dream about. Do you make it a high priority? Do your other responsibilities always seem to absorb your time? Do you have books that you'd like to read sitting unopened on the shelf? Do you have projects, such as the birdhouse you were building or the quilt you were sewing, just collecting dust? These are important questions to consider as you rate the importance of leisure and how satisfied you are with its role in your life.

The Personal Growth and Development Domain

Personal growth and development is a domain that includes the type of work you are doing in this book. Self-knowledge and introspection have always been valued by philosophers but in recent times a plethora of books devoted to aspects of personal growth have appeared. For some people, personal growth constitutes a large part of their mental activity. If you are in this group, you may have read a number of books to gain insights into your thoughts and feelings. You may have sought counseling or therapy to help with specific problems and get you through especially difficult situations. You may use dreams or other means to discover new aspects of yourself.

Other people may find that personal growth through these activities is a lower priority. People in this group seek concrete and immediate answers to the questions that concern them. They want information, ideas, and solutions to their problems, and they want to get on with the business of living. Consider which group you are in. How do you cope with problems? Do you see yourself as a work in process? Or do you want solutions you can implement to help you move on to the next goal?

The Health and Physical Fitness Domain

Physical fitness and health, judging by statistics on exercise and obesity, is a domain that is often ignored. The United States Initiative, *Healthy People 2000*, states that less that 30 percent of us get regular exercise, and that 55 percent of us are overweight or obese. This area of your life includes eating the right foods to be healthy, getting regular physical exercise (especially aerobic workouts), monitoring alcohol and tobacco consumption, and getting enough rest.

Are you satisfied with your health habits? Do you build into your week enough time to exercise? Do you eat fast foods rather than fixing more nutritious meals? Have you vowed to quit smoking or to lose weight? Are you satisfied with your personal habits? Consider these questions as you rate the importance of health and physical fitness in your life.

The Romantic Domain

Romance is the special feeling you have for a significant person in your life. These feelings often, but not always, involve sexual intimacy. Your romantic relationships may be with people of the opposite sex or of the same sex. You may be married, living together, or maintain separate residences. There are many configurations to romantic arrangements, including the choice to have no romantic relationships at all. Ask yourself if you feel comfortable with potential romantic partners. If you are attracted to someone, do you feel confident pursuing that person? As you rate this domain, be honest and accurate in your assessment of its importance to you and your satisfaction with your present level of romance.

The Social Domain

The social domain includes relationships with others outside of those you considered family members or romantic partners. This aspect of your life involves your membership in groups, your friendships, and your ability to approach others with whom you would like to develop an acquaintance. Are you able to make friends when you want to? Do you have as many friends as you would like? Do you feel that you belong with your friends and acquaintances, or do you feel like an outsider? You may choose to have a small social life because it suits your personality. There are no right or wrong ways to evaluate this domain, just be honest when deciding what level of importance the social arena has in your life and how satisfied you are with your present situation

The Spiritual Domain

The spiritual domain can be described in a number of ways. It can be defined as your relationship to God or a higher power. If you are an atheist or an agnostic, you may experience a spiritual relationship with nature, or you may rely on a conviction that scientific knowledge is enough for you. Whatever your belief system is, you have formed some idea of the nature of life. It is this idea that constitutes the spiritual side of you.

Do you find yourself puzzling over spiritual issues, or searching for answers to ease your mind? Do you feel a need to develop that aspect of your life? Perhaps you find spiritual concepts irrelevant to your life and therefore unimportant. Or, perhaps you have a strong belief system that allows you to tackle other goals in your life. Again, there are no right or wrong answers, only honest ones.

The Work Domain

The last life domain is that of work. You may have a career, or you may hold a job. You may work full-time or part-time, for pay or as a volunteer. You may work in or outside the home, or home and family might be your career. Whether you are a professional or an unskilled worker, you spend some time directing your physical and mental efforts toward the accomplishment or production of something. This is your work. Do you find the work you do fulfilling? Is your work challenging and interesting? Or, perhaps you wake up each day dreading what is to come. How important is your work to you, and how satisfied are you with it?

Below we have provided you with two scales ranging from a low of 0, to a high of 100, with a mid-point of 50. Using the first scale, assign yourself a number to rate how *important* you believe each life arena to be. On the second scale, assign yourself a number to rate how *satisfied* you are with your life in each arena

Life-Domain Questionnaire

0	50	100
not at all important	moderately important	extremely important

Academic _____   Family _____   Leisure _____

Personal Growth _____   Physical Fitness/Health _____   Romantic _____

Social _____   Spiritual _____   Work _____

0	50	100
not at all important	moderately important	extremely important

Academic _____   Family _____   Leisure _____

Personal Growth _____   Physical Fitness/Health _____   Romantic _____

Social _____   Spiritual _____   Work _____

What Do Your Ratings Mean?

Now you can compare the rating you have given to the importance of each domain with the rating you have given to the satisfaction with each domain. If the two ratings are similar, then they are consistent with the way you wish to balance your life. If, on the other hand, they are not similar, then your life may be out of balance in that area. You may have found that several areas of high importance are giving you low satisfaction. For example, work may be very important to you because you are responsible for supporting a family, and you have high expectations for your career. If you are not making the money you need or deserve, or if you are not getting the promotions you want, you probably rated your satisfaction in this sphere lower.

In a different vein, you may have rated the romantic domain as highly important, and you find yourself distressed if you do not have a significant other. Even though you may not have trouble getting dates, you may not be satisfied with the fact that it is difficult for you to be alone. You may wish to be more independent and less reliant on others. If this is the case, you would probably rate your satisfaction lower in that area.

In another example of disparate ratings, Janet placed a high importance in the academic domain, but having quit college, she was dissatisfied with that part of her life. She made finishing college a long-range goal, and with the completion of many small goals, or steps, she was able to bring into balance the importance and satisfaction she experienced in that domain.

The disparities in your rating will give you a clue about where to look as you think about choosing your goals. Keep your hierarchy and your priorities in mind as well. A domain may be extremely important to you, but it may be crowded out of your life by other, less important but demanding duties. For example, if you rated physical fitness and health as extremely important, but find your time to exercise eaten away by other things, a rearrangement of your priorities may be in order.

You have made a good beginning by rating yourself on these two scales. You may find it helpful to write a short narrative about those domains in which you found discrepancies between what you rated as important and your satisfaction rating. Writing your thoughts and feelings will help you clarify which areas you would like to change and the direction your change can take.

Before we move on to chapter 10 and the Domain-Specific Life-Hope Scale, here is Donna's narrative describing the importance she places on romance, and her lack of satisfaction with that part of her life.

✳ Donna—Divorced and Alone

I have been married twice. The first time I was twenty-three, in my first year in law school, and inexperienced where men were concerned. We were only together for four years, and for most of that time we argued. People might expect that of two attorneys, but it was an unpleasant situation. When he was offered an opportunity to join a firm in San Francisco, I decided to remain in Los Angeles, and we filed for an amicable divorce.

I remained single for four more years, dating occasionally, but socializing mainly with a large group of old friends from college. I was fairly satisfied with my life, but with each passing year my biological clock reminded me that if I wanted to have children, I had better get to it. When I was 32, I met Robert and fell in love. He wasn't a lawyer; I didn't want to make that mistake again. Robert was a family-practice doctor, and he was totally dedicated to his work.

We had a wonderful honeymoon in the Cayman Islands, during which time I became pregnant with our first child. After Robert Jr. was born, we had twin girls, Dawn and Marie. I continued my work part-time, and we had an excellent nanny who filled in for me when I had to be away. Robert, it seemed, was always away, so I tried to be both mother and father for the children.

By the time the children were in their early teens, Robert had taken an apartment closer to his clinic, ostensibly so that he wouldn't have to make long commutes at late hours. Perhaps I should have been suspicious, but my life was so busy with work and family that I accepted everything Robert told me as truth. He had, in fact, been involved in a long relationship with his nurse and finally asked me for a divorce.

At first I was devastated and felt as though my life had collapsed. There were weeks spent in tears and the comfort of my bed, sleeping the grief away. Eventually, however, with the help of a psychologist and many friends, I began to pull my life together. I realized that, with the exception of the very early years, Robert and I had not had a close relationship. We had spent much more time apart than together, and there was little congeniality between us.

The children were not nearly as hurt as I was. They had spent very little time with their father and had learned to expect little from him in the way of an emotional relationship. Of course he had always provided money and material goods and would continue to do that. We remained in our home, the girls kept their horses, and in fact, our lifestyle did not change.

That brings me to where I am today, fifty-one years old and without a satisfying intimate relationship. It's important to me to be able to share my life with another adult. I crave warm and intimate moments, and I even dream of another trip to the Cayman Islands with a wonderful man. Although I know I'm still attractive, I also know that my age, my educational level, and my profession place me at a disadvantage for meeting eligible men. I am at a point in my life where most of my family responsibilities are at a minimum. I am secure in my career as a partner in my firm. I have felt for some time that my romantic life was out of balance, and now I can focus my attention on changing it.

❋

6

Your Domain-Specific Hope

In the last chapter you learned about life domains. You rated how important each domain was to you, and how satisfied you were with that area of your life. Next you compared your *importance* rating with your *satisfaction* rating, looking for discrepancies between the two. We asked you to write a brief narrative about the domains of your life, especially where there was a difference between the two ratings. Donna's is an example.

The next step in the process of goal selection is for you to evaluate your level of hope in each domain. To help you do this, we have provided the Domain-Specific Life-Hope Scale. This scale is similar to the Hope Scale you used in chapter 3; however, the statements you will rate this time deal specifically with each domain. The Domain-Specific Life-Hope Scale has been used with thousands of individuals and has been found to be a valid method of assessing hope in particular life areas. The original scale dealt with six domains: social relationships, academics, romantic relationships, family life, work, and leisure. In keeping with the holistic approach of this workbook, we have added the domains of personal growth, health and fitness, and spirituality.

Your hope scores on each of these domains are important pieces of information you will need as you decide on the goals to use for your work in this book. Each domain scale is followed by two brief vignettes describing individuals who show high or low hope in those areas. Each item on the scale will be identified as either willpower or waypower, so that you can add the separate scales for each domain, as well as the total hope score.

In chapter 8 you will use these ratings to help you decide on your goals. Please rate yourself on the scale that accompanies each domain, and when you have completed it, read the vignettes that describe high- and low-hope behavior and thought in each area.

The Academic Domain

1	2	3	4	5	6	7	8
Definitely False	Mostly False	Somewhat False	Slightly False	Slightly True	Somewhat True	Mostly True	Definitely True

_____ 1. I could think of lots of ways to make good grades in school. (way)

_____ 2. I energetically pursue(d) my school work. (will)

_____ 3. There are lots of ways to meet the challenges of any class. (way)

_____ 4. Even if a course is difficult, I can always find a way to succeed. (way)

_____ 5. I've been pretty successful in school. (will)

_____ 6. I can think of lots of ways to do well in classes that are important to me. (way)

_____ 7. My past academic experiences have prepared me well for future successes. (will)

_____ 8. I got the grades I wanted in my classes. (will)

✳ Henry—Called to the Bar?

"You should be a lawyer." Perhaps my argumentative nature is the reason that I heard this injunction so many times growing up. The truth of the matter is that I really would like to be a lawyer, but I never seemed to make good enough grades to consider it. I was lucky to get into college at all, and then I scraped by with a C average. I've been a car salesman for ten years now, and while I make fairly good money, the work is not what I really want to do.

I admire a person with a good education. I think getting an education is the best thing a person can do for himself, and I often think that I would be a better student if I went back to school now. I have looked into doing some remedial courses to bring up my grades. I think I might try a few of those and see how I do. I know law school is very demanding, and I just don't know if I have the right stuff.   ✳

Henry clearly has low hope in the academic domain. Although education is important to him, he is very dissatisfied with his own level of achievement. He has had a dream of becoming a lawyer for a good part of his life, yet he perceived few ways that his dream could be accomplished. In addition, he expresses serious doubts about his ability to succeed in law school, even though he believes he could do better with undergraduate courses now. Henry might decide that becoming a lawyer will be his goal.

Henry recognizes, however, that there will be a number of steps that he must take before he can attempt law school. By succeeding in the smaller goals, such as making good grades in the coursework he is considering, his willpower and his waypower will begin to increase. Before we leave the academic domain, let's revisit Janet's hope. Remember that Janet went back to school after dropping out prior to her junior year.

✳ Janet—A Love of Learning

I did it, and I'm so proud of myself! There might have been a few doubts along the way, but I always believed I could finish college. I wanted to be a teacher, and here I am. My first two years of college were successful enough that I believed I could do at least as well in the junior and senior years. My parents were understanding and wonderful to allow me to move home for a while. When I started back to school I was a bit apprehensive at first, being an older student. But soon I realized that I had an advantage. I could focus my attention on schoolwork, and I could usually think of ways to get good grades.

My education has really paid off. I'm a good teacher, and I can stimulate my high-school students to continue their education, too. Still, I think the time I spent working in my father's office was good for me. It gave me a chance to mature, so that when I went back to school I was really energized for the work. ✳

Janet's satisfaction with the academic domain matches the importance she places on it. Both are high, as is the hope she instills in her students. Her narrative is full of high-hope markers. She speaks of the energy and focus she had for her schoolwork, and she clearly believes she is competent in that sphere of her life. She states that her academic work prepared her well for her teaching responsibilities, and moreover, she can now help her students develop hope in the academic domain of their lives. Janet wanted to continue her education, and she decided to make that her long-range goal. Her story, as told in chapter 2, described the smaller goals she accomplished that led to her final achievement. If you decide to select an academic goal, consider the steps you will take. How long will your journey be? How important did you rate the academic domain, and how satisfied were you with your existing education?

The Family Domain

1	2	3	4	5	6	7	8
Definitely False	Mostly False	Somewhat False	Slightly False	Slightly True	Somewhat True	Mostly True	Definitely True

_____ 1. I can think of lots of things I enjoy doing with my family. (way)

_____ 2. I energetically work on maintaining family relationships. (will)

_____ 3. I can think of many ways to include my family in things that are important to me. (way)

_____ 4. I have a pretty successful family life. (will)

_____ 5. Even when we disagree, I know my family can find a way to solve our problems. (way)

_____ 6. I have the kind of relationships that I want with family members. (will)

_____ 7. There are lots of ways to communicate my feelings to family members. (way)

_____ 8. My experiences with family have prepared me for a family of my own. (will)

✳ Nan—I Don't Belong

Until a few years ago I had no idea who my birth-parents were. My adoptive parents, a wonderful couple in their forties who had been married for over twenty years, had not had any children of their own. There is no doubt in my mind that they wanted me. They doted on me, spoiled me in fact, to the dismay and criticism of my adoptive aunts, uncles, and cousins. I had everything a little girl could want, except the feeling that I really belonged to that family.

Clues about why I felt different from the others in my adoptive family are found in the reason my adoptive mother had no children of her own—she was terrified of childbirth. In fact, she was frightened of so many things that most of her life was spent in the narrow confines of home, and the small town in which she lived. My adoptive father was always protective of her, accepting the things that frightened her as real. To some extent, the anxiety that pervaded my household also infused my cousins' homes, and they, too, were cautious in the extreme.

I, on the other hand, was never afraid of anything. I learned to swim and dive, to ride horses, and I loved the roller coaster when my church group took a trip to a theme park. My adoptive parents were constantly worried that something dreadful was going to happen to me, but their fretting made me even more daring. As a teenager I felt more at odds with everyone than I had as a child. I wanted to experience life, not be protected from it.

From the beginning I had known I was adopted, and when I was in my late teens I began to wonder if my birth-mother would be more like me. When I told my adoptive parents that I wanted to find the woman who had given me life, they were hurt, and, of course, frightened. I continued arguing my point, however, and finally they agreed to help me. It was surprisingly easy to find my birth-mother because the agency had kept records that they were permitted to share. A meeting was arranged, but as the time grew near, I wasn't so sure it was a good idea.

Not being afraid of things, however, was an important part of my self-image, so I forged ahead with the meeting plans. I traveled to a small town in West Virginia where my birth-mother lived with her husband and the four children she had kept. The meeting was both strange and sad. Although we look somewhat alike, and we had the same tendency to gain weight, our personalities were nothing alike. Perhaps, if she had been able to go to good schools, as I had, or if she had been able to have the other advantages I had, we might have been more alike. But the woman who was my birth-mother was uneducated, overweight, and apathetic about life.

If we were not alike, and I felt so different from my adoptive family, who was I? Where did I belong? After the meeting I felt as if I was at a crossroad. All my life I had assumed that there was someone with whom I really belonged, now that assumption was shattered. Or was it? Was it possible that I could create a family of my own in which I'd feel at home? Perhaps that was the answer to where I belonged.   ✳

Nan placed a high importance on family, but not the family that raised her. Her early life appears to have been a reaction to the overprotection of her adoptive parents, and that, combined with the knowledge of her adoption, produced feelings of isolation and of being different. Although her willpower and her waypower scores are low when she thinks of her adoptive family, she expresses the beginnings of hope when she thinks of creating one of her own. Let's take a look at Angie, whose high will and ways carried her through to the successful birth of twins.

✳ Angie—Determined to Have Children

I was raised in a big Italian family, one of five children, and always planned on having children of my own. Unlike my two older sisters, however, I decided to go to college and have a career before I married. By the time I married Troy, we were both in our mid-thirties, and ready to start a family. Coming from such a long line of fertile women, I thought getting pregnant would be easy for me. How wrong I was! We spent two disappointing years before we finally sought medical help.

We had heard stories about fertility treatments with women having multiple births, and I was somewhat wary of getting involved with these medical miracles. On the other hand, Troy and I really wanted to have at least one child of our own, and after that we might adopt more. We had a good income, a large home in a good neighborhood, and an extended family waiting with open arms to welcome our child.

The first step was medical tests, many of them. The doctors said they had to find the source of our infertility problem, so Troy and I both underwent a series of uncomfortable procedures. In the end, the problem was the endometriosis that had plagued me for years. As it was explained to us, the egg I released each month didn't get to my womb as it should, therefore, it never got fertilized. The solution was to gather a number of eggs, fertilize them in vitro, and then place them back into my womb.

Sounds simple, but it wasn't as easy as that. For two months before the procedure of removing the eggs, I had to take fertility shots. I hate needles, so Troy gave me the injections. I took especially good care of myself, too, exercising and eating very nutritious food. We were determined to do everything we could to increase our chances of having healthy children. Finally the day came when seventeen eggs were removed from me, and four were fertilized in the laboratory using Troy's sperm. When they were ready, all four were place back into me. We waited eagerly to see what would happen, wondering if we would have as many as four babies.

We would have cherished all four children, although it would have been a struggle to meet all their demands. As it turned out, we had beautiful twin girls. The girls are fraternal twins, of course, and it just happens that one looks like Troy's side of the family with light blond hair, while the other has the more Italian looks of my family. We are delighted with our girls, and for the present we have our hands full. In time, though, we may adopt a child or two. We always wanted a large family.   ✳

Angie epitomizes the high-hope person who places a high importance on family life. Her experiences growing up not only prepared her for a family of her own, but fostered her waypower when it appeared she might not have children. Angie's high willpower is shown in her willingness to undergo painful injections and treatments, as well as chancing quadruplets. She and Troy pursued their goal of having a family, helping each other overcome each obstacle they encountered, and encouraging each other along the way. As they held their rewards in their arms, they knew their struggles had been well worth the effort.

The Health and Fitness Domain

1	2	3	4	5	6	7	8
Definitely False	Mostly False	Somewhat False	Slightly False	Slightly True	Somewhat True	Mostly True	Definitely True

_____ 1. I can think of many ways to maintain my health and fitness. (way)

_____ 2. I actively work at being healthy and fit. (will)

_____ 3. Even when I am tired, I can usually make myself work out. (will)

_____ 4. I can find ways to continue my health and fitness routines in a variety of situations (e.g., traveling). (way)

_____ 5. I believe I can sustain my health and fitness as I grow older. (will)

_____ 6. Habits of health and fitness I acquired in the past will help me in the future. (way)

✳ Sherri—Supermodel

They always said I looked anorexic, but the camera adds at least ten pounds to the way a person looks. Designers make clothes for girls who look like I do. Well, anyway, the clothes they show at the couture collections are for extremely thin people. Although I started modeling when I was fourteen, everyone said I looked at least twenty. Now I am twenty, and I'm beginning to feel old. But let me start at the beginning.

I was born in New York City where my mother had been a well-known runway model before she married my dad. He is a freelance writer, and between them they have a lot of connections in the theater and in the publishing industry. I was always tall for my age, and people expected me to follow in my mother's footsteps. By the time I was fourteen, I was quite well developed, but I also had baby fat on my hips and thighs. I knew that if I wanted to model, the fat had to go. That was when I started dieting, smoking, and using uppers anytime I could get them. Of course, my parents didn't know about any of this—they were off in their own worlds.

I didn't like sports and I couldn't be bothered exercising, but nevertheless the pounds seemed to melt off. The fact that I was eating very little, energized by the amphetamines, was a pleasant experience. When I landed my first modeling job my statistics were perfect. I was five feet, ten inches, and weighed one hundred and fifteen pounds. Everyone was delighted when I was signed by one of the best agencies in New York, and my career took off.

During these past six years I have been on the cover of every major fashion magazine, traveled around the world for shows and shoots, and made enough money to last me the rest of my life. Was it worth it? The answer is, I don't know. I managed to finish high school by having a tutor, but I really didn't have an adolescence. I have starved myself, taken drugs, and smoked cigarettes to stay thin for so long that I have a tremor and a serious cough. I'd like to get off the merry-go-round, but I'm not sure how. I need to start taking care of myself because, in this business, no one else looks out for you.

I feel as if I've lived a lifetime already. It's strange to be twenty and facing retirement.

✳

Sherri's health and fitness were so unimportant to her when she was younger that she was willing to throw them away. Staying thin so that she could be a model was the only goal she had, and her waypower only extended to a few, maladaptive behaviors. Like so many adolescents, Sheri no doubt felt immortal. When she reached the ripe old age of twenty, however, her poor health and fitness habits were beginning to catch up with her. At the end of her story, she stands at the brink of change. Developing her willpower and waypower in the health and fitness domain will increase her chances for a longer and healthier life. Here is the story of Buddy, a man with outstanding hope, who had a great misfortune to overcome.

✳ Buddy—Off the Field and into the Wheelchair

My dad was the football coach at our high school, and sports were the most important activities in our house. My mom was a nurse, so you can imagine that health and fitness was an important part of our family life. Every day after school, my brothers and I played football or shot baskets until it was time to come in for dinner and homework. I guess we had a picture-perfect family because my parents didn't fight, nobody drank or used drugs, and we all watched out for each other.

By the time I got into high school I was the tallest and heaviest guy in my class, and even with all that weight, I was a fast and agile runner. As a freshman I was good enough to be a starting offensive lineman for the varsity team. I played hard and aggressively for three years and planned to go to college on a football scholarship. In the middle of the season in my senior year, I was blocking and missed the tackler. I felt my head snap back, something crunched, and suddenly I blacked out. When I woke up I was lying on the field with everyone around me. I was terrified because I couldn't feel anything from my waist down, and I couldn't move my legs.

In the hospital the doctors told me that I had snapped my spine just below the shoulders—I was now a paraplegic. I would spend the rest of my life in a wheelchair. My parents and brothers put on a false cheerfulness when they visited me, and I knew their dreams for me were shattered. I felt shattered too. For many weeks, while I strengthened my upper body and learned to use a wheelchair, I felt empty and confused. I couldn't graduate with my class, I couldn't envision going on to college now; I didn't have an identity.

One of the constant visitors I had while I was recuperating was our parish priest, Father Vince. He understood how angry and frightened I was, and he even let me rail against God for letting this thing happen. Slowly, as the weeks turned to months, I began to accept the accident and learn about this new wheelchair-bound person who was Buddy. I didn't have my legs, but I had a good mind and a supportive family. I also had a fundamentally healthy and sound body, despite missing the use of my legs. I made up my mind to go to college and major in physical education. Why shouldn't I do that? I loved sports, and just because I couldn't do them anymore didn't mean I couldn't teach them. Legislation mandating equal rights for the disabled could work to my advantage.

Now I'm finishing a doctoral program in sports and ready to embark on a career as a college professor. True, there were some difficult times during college and graduate school when I felt like giving up, but I knew I could be successful if I just stuck to it. Once I made up my mind to live a full life, I discovered many options available to me. I won't say I'm glad for the accident—I'll always wonder if I would have been a star. But my life has developed in ways I would never have dreamed. ✳

Buddy's story is an inspiration to all who know him. High-hope people often have that effect on others, and Buddy's hope is infectious. His early health and fitness habits contributed to his ability to recuperate from his accident. The high willpower and waypower he learned in childhood helped him face his limitations and build a successful life.

The Leisure Domain

1	2	3	4	5	6	7	8
Definitely False	Mostly False	Somewhat False	Slightly False	Slightly True	Somewhat True	Mostly True	Definitely True

_____ 1. I can think of many satisfying things to do in my spare time. (way)

_____ 2. I energetically pursue my leisure time activities. (will)

_____ 3. If my planned leisure time activities fall through, I can find something else to do that I enjoy. (way)

_____ 4. I can think of lots of ways to make time for the activities that are important to me. (way)

_____ 5. Even if others don't think my activities are important, I still enjoy them. (will)

_____ 6. My experiences with hobbies or other leisure activities are important to my future. (way)

_____ 7. I have satisfying activities that I do in my leisure time. (will)

_____ 8. When I perform in leisure activities, I usually succeed. (will)

✳ Virginia—A Stranger to Leisure

Having been left with numerous debts and a small daughter to raise when my husband died, I felt it necessary to work long hours. I was determined to provide a good home, and never again did I want to experience the fear that we might become destitute. I had a good education and was a talented writer. I went to work for a movie company and, in short order, was one of their valued story analysts. I was willing to do whatever the job required, even learning Spanish, to make myself essential to the story department.

I made an excellent salary and invested my money wisely. Over the years I bought real estate, mutual funds, and utilities, building up a sizable nest egg. What I didn't do was relax. On many occasions my daughter, Donna, would try entice me to ride her horse, go to the movies, or do some other frivolous activity, but I never believed I had the time. When I had a day off, I was restless. It always seemed as if there was something I should be doing.

I worked as a story analyst and a writer until I was sixty-five years old. Perhaps I could have convinced the studio to let me work longer, but young people now have such different ideas about what a movie should be. No one wants to be regarded as an antique, especially not in Hollywood, so I retired to a small home in Leisure World where a number of my friends had moved. The community is beautiful, with colorful flowers against red tiles and whitewashed walls—very Spanish California. It fills the eye, but it leaves the mind hungry.

It isn't that my friends are dull, or that there aren't activities galore. I enjoy talking about the old times at the studio with a few of the people who also worked in the industry, but that doesn't happen often. I never enjoyed swimming, I don't like needlework, I left the shopping to Donna, and I can't bear daytime television. So what do I do? I do what I always did—read and write. I'm not pleased with my leisure life, but I don't know what to do about it. I might try writing a novel about a widow who has a daughter to raise.   ✳

The leisure domain had never been important for Virginia. She, like so many hard-working people, didn't consider what she would do in retirement until it was upon her. Many people of Virginia's generation thought of the term "leisure" as synonymous with "lazy." Virginia is a high-hope person in so many domains of her life, and we might expect her to turn her retirement into a successful experience. To do this, however, she is going to have to use her waypower to explore a wide variety of activities and apply her willpower to do things she has never done before.

Not every domain may be important to you, but remember that each one helps to balance your life. Eli's story shows how a dose of leisure can keep life interesting.

✳ Eli—The Renaissance Man

I'm not a scholar or an artist, the occupations you might expect of a man with interests like mine. I'm a tailor by trade, and a good one, too. Perhaps it was because so many of my clients, men of distinction, always talked to me about their work and hobbies as I fitted their clothes that I developed some unique interests of my own. One of my gentlemen, an English lord living in New York City, introduced me to British history. For a time, I spent every spare moment reading about kings and queens, wars and treaties. After that I moved into Roman history, and then on to ancient Greece and Egypt.

Reading about history began to spark an eagerness in me to see the actual countries where the history took place. My wife and I began to plan trips abroad, and we even took a course in Italian to make the most of our experience. My interest in history and travel expanded to art and literature. With each area I studied, I had more to discuss with others and made many new friends with similar interests. I am still a long way from retirement age, but when I finally stop tailoring I'm looking forward to an abundance of time to study and travel.

✳

Eli's leisure time activities will carry over into his retirement in future years. His high waypower enables him to find many new and exciting avenues to explore. His high willpower enables him to investigate his interests with sustained enthusiasm.

The Personal Growth Domain

1	2	3	4	5	6	7	8
Definitely False	Mostly False	Somewhat False	Slightly False	Slightly True	Somewhat True	Mostly True	Definitely True

_____ 1. I can think of many ways to enhance my personal growth. (way)

_____ 2. I energetically pursue my personal growth. (will)

_____ 3. The personal growth I have done in the past will help me with my future personal growth. (way)

_____ 4. I've learned a lot and been pretty successful in my personal growth endeavors. (will)

_____ 5. Even when I learn things about myself that I do not like, I continue my personal growth in that area of my life. (will)

_____ 6. When one method of personal growth is not working for me, I can think of other methods to try. (way)

✳ Dean—Playing the Cards He Was Dealt

Perhaps it's because I come from a long line of people who worked
the land that I consider myself pretty down to earth. Of course,
I work in an office and I don't rely on the vagaries of weather to
determine my fate. Even so, I accept things pretty much as they
come. For example, I know I have been a stern father, using a belt
on my children when they needed it, but that's the way I was
brought up. My wife tells me that spanking with a belt is wrong
now, even though many people used to do it. I figure that if it was
good for me, it's good for my kids. I see no reason to question the
things I was taught in the past. My parents are good people, and
they would not have taught me things that were wrong.

My wife doesn't agree with me, however. According to her,
I am a morose person who is no fun to be around. She seems to
think I should be happier than I am, but in fact, I rarely think about
whether or not I am happy. It just isn't important. I think the world
is a hard place, and that, if you face reality, you don't have a lot to
be happy about. She didn't grow up as I did. She has never faced the
prospect of a late snowfall ruining your wheat crop and plunging you
into debt. My parents always lived that way, and if they didn't find
a lot to laugh about, it's understandable.

My wife wants me to see a psychologist or take an
antidepressant. She thinks it would make me feel better and help
our marriage. She doesn't understand that this is just the way I am.
People are all different, and if she didn't like my personality, she
shouldn't have married me.   ✳

Dean sees himself as a finished product. He is working hard to support
his family and has no time or interest in exploring ways to change himself.
Because of his hard childhood, he may not know what happiness and joy feel
like, and he tends to see these states as frivolous. That his wife is discontented
with his somber approach to life tells him that she does not understand the real
world. What will happen to their marriage? What attitudes about life will their
children have? We know that hope is learned, and the prospects for this family
appear grim unless something changes.

✳ Kay—A Work in Progress

It's difficult growing up in a small town where your father is a
minister and everyone expects you to be perfect. That's the way it
was for me, and I tried my hardest to live up to expectations. Since
I was an only child, it was up to me to show the town what a perfect
family we were and what wonderful parents I had. They were good
parents, and we were happy. Although their demands were difficult
at times, I learned to examine my own thoughts and feelings in an
effort to become a better person. This is something I have carried

with me throughout my life.

I cannot say that my adult life has been as exemplary as my childhood would have predicted. I started college and was doing well when I fell in love for the first time. We decided to marry, even though we were not yet twenty and everyone advised against it. We should have listened, because after several years we realized we had grown in very different directions.

My second marriage was more suitable, although the romance wasn't as exciting. He was twenty years older than I, but he doted on me in ways no one ever had before. He had retired early from a successful business, so we had time to travel and explore the world. We decided, because of his age, not to have children. We were married for fifteen contented years, and then he died of a sudden heart attack.

At thirty-eight I was a widow with enough money to do whatever I wished. I had many friends and many interests, but when I considered my life, I found very little that was meaningful. What was I supposed to do with all the years ahead? Was there a purpose to all I had done so far? What was I really like? I began to look for answers to these questions—not because I was unhappy, but because I had always wanted to be the best person I could be. That meant self-knowledge and personal growth.

I began my personal journey at my favorite bookstore. Which of the many books available to help people with their personal growth would be the most appropriate for me? There were several books about being alone later in life, and I found one on widowhood, but these didn't quite appeal to me. I decided to ask a friend, a psychotherapist, what she would recommend. She had a number of favorites that her clients had found helpful, so, armed with her list, I tackled the store again.

Since then I have done a great deal of reading and have also attended lectures and taken a few seminars on topics that interested me. I never considered myself deficient in any particular area, and I was wide open to trying new things. If a topic turns out not to interest me, I don't hesitate to change my direction. Developing myself, learning about how and why I think and feel the way I do, has been a creative and interesting enterprise.   ✳

Kay approached her personal growth from a strong position. She was essentially a high-hope person who found her life further enriched by self-knowledge. As a child, her desire to be the best she could be had formed habits that carried her through difficult times in her adulthood. When her search for self-knowledge took her in directions that were not fruitful, as a high way-power person, she always had other options available. Kay tackled her personal growth with the enthusiasm and energy characteristic of a high willpower person.

The Domain of Romantic Relationships

1	2	3	4	5	6	7	8
Definitely False	Mostly False	Somewhat False	Slightly False	Slightly True	Somewhat True	Mostly True	Definitely True

_____ 1. I can think of many ways to get to know someone to whom I am attracted. (way)

_____ 2. When I'm interested in someone romantically, I actively pursue them. (will)

_____ 3. I've been pretty successful in my romantic relationships. (will)

_____ 4. There are lots of ways to convince someone to go out with me. (way)

_____ 5. I can think of many ways to keep someone interested in me when they are important. (way)

_____ 6. My past romantic relationships have prepared me well for future involvements. (way)

_____ 7. Even when someone doesn't seem interested, I know I can get their attention. (will)

_____ 8. I can usually get a date when I set my mind to it. (will)

❋ **Dean Revisited—Single Again**

I guess the divorce was inevitable; my wife and I were so different. It just doesn't work when two people have such different backgrounds. So here I am now, back in the singles scene and wondering how to do it. I never was any good at meeting girls—never thought they would be interested in me. I met the girl I later married in the public library. I knew she was flirting with me, but I was so dense that she had to ask me out.

It isn't that I'm so shy, and it isn't that I feel bad about myself. I just never learned how to "put the moves on," as they say. I'm a pretty straightforward guy, and I just don't like game playing and flirting. All my life, women have initiated the relationships. I know it's supposed to be the other way around, but I never felt very competent doing it. Now that I'm single, perhaps a woman will come walking into my life again. They tell me there are a lot more single women than men in my age group. The odds are in my favor.   ❋

True to type, Dean will let external events determine his romantic life. If a nice woman shows interest in him, he will respond. He won't be looking, though, because he doesn't have either the willpower or the waypower to determine his own love life.

✴ Donna—Never Say Never

At fifty-one, I know that it's unlikely that I will find another romantic relationship. My standards are high, and that narrows the field of acceptable partners. He would have to be well educated, interested in sports and the arts, near my age, have a good sense of humor, and be as financially secure as I am. In my work as an attorney, I meet interesting men all the time, but most of them are married or too young. It isn't that I'm desperate for romance in my life. In fact, I rather enjoy living alone. I doubt that I would ever want to marry again, and so I had resigned myself to being on my own.

What a pleasant surprise it was, then, to discover that a man I had always admired from afar had become available. I learned from mutual friends that his wife had left him some months previously, and that he was just now emerging from a period of grief. Although I knew him distantly, I became determined to get to know him much better.

In my younger years I never had any trouble attracting the men I wanted. Although it had been a long time since I had dated, and even longer since I had flirted, those are skills you don't forget. My first step was to arrange, through friends, to be invited to a small dinner party where he would be. I figured that, given an opportunity to get him into a conversation, I could interest him enough to arrange a date. When I arrived at my hostess's home, she pulled me aside to tell me he had asked to bring a date. I was momentarily distressed, but I was determined not to give up.

I proceeded with my plan, drawing the other woman into the conversation to be polite. It turned out that he was a horseman with several Tennessee walkers, so we had an interest in common. We talked most of the evening about our experiences training and showing horses, leaving the other woman to seek conversation elsewhere. Before we left that night, he and I arranged a riding date for the next weekend. He seems like a nice man, and he appears to meet my standards. Whatever happens as a result of our date, I had fun that night, and I guess the old skills aren't too rusty. ✴

Donna, like so many middle-aged women, is coping with the issues of being alone versus being lonely. She had come to a point of relative comfort with her solitary life, so she was in an ideal position to start a new relationship. Her high willpower and waypower from past romantic experiences held her in good stead, and she was pleased to see that she could still attract the person she wanted.

The Social Relationship Domain

1	2	3	4	5	6	7	8
Definitely False	Mostly False	Somewhat False	Slightly False	Slightly True	Somewhat True	Mostly True	Definitely True

_____ 1. I can think of many ways to make friends. (way)

_____ 2. I actively pursue friendships. (will)

_____ 3. There are lots of ways to meet new people. (way)

_____ 4. I can think of many ways to be included in the groups that are important to me. (way)

_____ 5. I've been pretty successful where friendships are concerned. (will)

_____ 6. Even when someone seems unapproachable, I know I can find ways to break the ice. (way)

_____ 7. My past social experiences have prepared me to make friends in the future. (way)

_____ 8. When I meet someone I want to be friends with, I usually succeed. (will)

❋ Anna—A Solitary Life

I love to read. To quote Emily Dickinson, "There is no frigate like a book." Books people my life with wonderful characters who have far more exciting lives than I could ever have. I've seen faraway places, envisioned curious customs, lived in other times, and had romances far beyond my dreams. Books are more desirable to me than any of the real people I have ever met.

As far back as I can remember I was shy and reluctant to meet people. I began reading when I was four, and simply never stopped. I hated adolescence and avoided doing things with people my age. I didn't mind talking to adults because they always treated me with respect, often telling me I was mature for my age. I liked my teachers and found occasions to talk to them after classes so I wouldn't have to spend much time with other students. Naturally, this earned me the title of "brown noser," or "teacher's pet."

Now, as an adult, I still have very few friends. Perhaps knowing how to socialize is a skill that has to be learned early. In any case, I don't seem to have it. I became a librarian and, while I converse with the patrons and my coworkers, I'm still surrounded by books. Sometimes I get lonely and wish I had people to do things with or someone to telephone. I worry that when I get very old I will be alone. I don't know how to make friends, and I wonder if it's too late to learn. ❋

It is clear that Anna has both low waypower and low willpower where social relationships are concerned. She never learned the basic social skills, finding her life in books far more rewarding. Most people, and Anna is no exception, need some social contact. Anna is beginning to doubt the viability of the lifestyle she has chosen and may find it necessary to learn how to make friends.

✳ Maria—A Smile and a Kind Word for Everyone

When we moved to Santa Fe and began attending St. Anthony's, I volunteered right off to help the altar society. That's what I had done in Pueblo, and I had a lot of experience keeping the silver and linens clean. At first the other ladies were a little stand offish. After all, I was a newcomer and the altar society is supposed to be for the longtime members. Father Paul seemed glad of the extra help, however, so I just smiled and did what they told me to do.

At first the other women spoke Spanish, thinking that I would not understand them. They said a few things that were not so kind, but I didn't let them know I understood for quite some time. I just continued smiling and being friendly to everyone. What turned the tide, I suppose, was when Mrs. Martinez, the oldest altar lady, found that she had cancer. When a person has cancer, other people don't know how to treat them. The disease isn't contagious, but the way cancer victims are treated, you would think it was. My mother had died of cancer the previous year, and I had been the main person to care for her. I knew what to do.

Helping Mrs. Martinez was not something I did in order to make friends, but everyone suddenly knew my name. I am friendly by nature, so I returned all the smiles, and soon I knew nearly everyone in the parish. My husband and children were also greeted warmly by people who hadn't known we existed a few months before. It was wonderful to feel so welcome, and I look forward to many years of service to the church and many friendships to be made along the way. ✳

Maria's smile and her gentle caring personality had helped her make many friends in her previous church, as they were helping her at St. Anthony's. She held friendships to be an important part of her life and had confidence that she could find a way to break through the cold reserve of the altar guild. Maria's high hope served not only herself, but her family as well.

The Spiritual Domain

1	2	3	4	5	6	7	8
Definitely False	Mostly False	Somewhat False	Slightly False	Slightly True	Somewhat True	Mostly True	Definitely True

_____ 1. I can think of many ways to express my spirituality. (way)

_____ 2. I energetically work to enhance my spirituality. (will)

_____ 3. My experiences with spirituality in the past will help me in this domain in the future. (way)

_____ 4. Even when I question my spirituality, I can use my beliefs to pull through. (will)

_____ 5. I derive the satisfaction and comfort I expect from my spirituality. (will)

_____ 6. There are many avenues to develop my spirituality. (way)

✳ **Margaret—Too Many Views**

By the late 1950s the public education in my city had deteriorated, and families who wanted their children to have a good education sent them to private schools. Even though we were not Catholic, I was sent to a parochial school near my home. I loved the school, and I loved the nuns who taught me. I even learned catechism alongside the girls who planned to make their first holy communion that year. I wanted desperately to be a Catholic too and asked my parents if I could convert. My family were staunch Protestants, however, and they disagreed with the things I was learning. They told me that the Catholics held many wrong ideas and that our religion was the right one. I was confused. Who should I believe?

The next summer I spent two months visiting my grandparents in the Midwest. My grandmother was a very religious person, but she had different beliefs from my mother and also different from Catholicism. She took me to her church, where I attended Sunday school regularly. From those teachers I learned that the other religions had the wrong idea, and that the way to salvation was by being baptized in their church. No one seemed to agree, and I was even more confused.

The problem with being confused about spiritual issues is that they are basically matters of faith, and each person you ask has their own point of view. There didn't seem to be any outside source to verify or negate what each person said. I realized, even then, that nobody knew the answers, though they tried to convince me they did.

For many years I tried to ignore spiritual issues, but events in my life have kept me yearning for something in which to believe. I have lost both my parents and a friend who died at an early age. I have seen war and disaster, hardship and struggle. I want to know why. I want some spiritual answers, but I don't have the ability to believe. If this is called a crisis of faith, then mine started when I was nine years old.   ✳

Margaret experienced too many views about religion at too early an age to understand the nature of spirituality. Each of her religious teachers presented their information as fact, and each seemed to want her as a convert to their faith. Margaret may have started her religious education with high willpower and high waypower in the spiritual domain, but such confusion was too much for a child to comprehend. She no longer wanted to explore religious paths, and she had little energy to continue the effort.

✳ Frank—Creating His Own Spirituality

It was many years ago that my family escaped from Hungary, fleeing the domination of the Communist Party. When we came to the United States, we had no money, no relatives to take us in, but we survived. Both my parents worked hard to put my brother and me through school, recognizing that the way to succeed in this new country was through education.

It was not only the communists my parents dreaded—it was also the bigotry of the rest of the family. You see, my father was Jewish and my mother was Catholic, and neither group seemed to agree on religious teachings. Both sets of grandparents applied pressure to have me raised in their religion. My parents resisted, and out of protest, turned their backs on all organized religion. I was left to discover my own spirituality.

Although I had many friends of different faiths, no one seemed to think it strange that I didn't attend a church or synagogue. And I didn't think much about it myself until I took a history of religion course in college. To my surprise, I found it fascinating. There I discovered a whole new world of ideas, different ways of solving moral dilemmas, and courageous people whose lives I could study. At that point it became important to me to define my own belief system.

I took more courses in theology and learned about the world's great religions, past and present. It seemed they all had something to offer. Certainly there were differences among them, but there were also many similarities in the core tenets of each. I didn't want to choose between them, so I combined many of the teachings to create my own. It was not a new religion, simply my own brand of spirituality. I also found that I wanted to talk about my beliefs with others, perhaps argue the validity of my ideas. Most people I met, however, were firmly ensconced in the teachings of one church, and they seemed threatened when challenged by my ideas.

Eventually, I found a group of people who shared my sometimes iconoclastic ideas. We "worshipped" whatever our idea of a higher power was without any overriding rules or regulations. My spirituality is completely personal, and it has helped me through many trying times. It isn't necessary for me to believe in a personalized God, only to know that I am part of a larger, well-ordered system. I accept that there are many things I cannot know, but I can live in the present, and be the best person I know how to be.   ✳

In some ways Frank was fortunate not to have been caught in a competitive struggle for his soul, as Margaret was. He was free to develop a spirituality that suited him at a time when he was ready to accept it. Frank's beliefs were born from studying many great theologians, and he could never limit himself to the teachings of a few. For many other people, however, one set of beliefs is enough to carry them through life. Frank's story is not written to place more value on one spirituality than another. All forms of spirituality, or even none at all, are valid for the individuals to whom they belong.

The Work Domain

1	2	3	4	5	6	7	8
Definitely False	Mostly False	Somewhat False	Slightly False	Slightly True	Somewhat True	Mostly True	Definitely True

_____ 1. I can think of many ways to find a job. (way)

_____ 2. I am energetic at work. (will)

_____ 3. There are lots of ways to succeed at work. (way)

_____ 4. Even if it's a lousy job, I can usually find something good about it. (will)

_____ 5. I have a good work record. (will)

_____ 6. My previous work experiences have helped prepare me for future successes. (way)

_____ 7. I can always find a job if I set my mind to it. (will)

_____ 8. I can think of lots of ways to impress my boss if the job is important to me. (way)

✳ **Patty—It's Only a Job**

I hear my friends talk about their careers, how they are working their way up to bigger and better things. Personally, I feel lucky just to have a job. I know the want ads are full of intriguing-sounding positions, but they're not as good as they sound. They are also not so easy to get; I know because I've interviewed for some of them and they never hired me.

Maybe I thought I'd never have to support myself, that I could get married and just keep house. It didn't work out that way though, or at least not yet. I'm nearly thirty, and I'm still single with no prospects in sight. After high school I went to junior college and took a word-processing course. I thought I might get an "MRS" instead of an AA degree, but that didn't happen either. Now it looks like work is all there is for me, and I feel stuck.

I'd look for another job, but why bother? I haven't been successful getting jobs in the past, and I don't know where to look for something that would be different from what I do now. At least I can live on the salary, and I can do the work well enough. I suppose I should just be glad I have any job at all, with so many people on welfare.

✳

Patty had never considered that the work domain would be important in her life. She made an assumption that she would be taken care of by someone else and never developed the waypower to help her find interesting jobs and secure them. She lacked the willpower to work energetically enough to achieve satisfaction and recognition in the jobs she had. Patty also made the assumption that marriage and family was not part of the work domain. As we see, in the story of Laura, homemaking can be a valid and interesting career.

✳ Laura—Motherhood, a Proud Profession

In college I studied to be a nurse and worked in that profession for ten years. I enjoyed the work, especially when I was in the pediatric unit, because I had always wanted a large family of my own. When I met Howard and realized that we had the same goals in life, my dreams seemed to be coming true.

Because of my age (I was thirty-two at the time) we decided to start our family immediately. I wanted to stay at home with the babies, at least while they were young, and Howard agreed. Homemaking was a new challenge for me, and I had fun decorating the nursery, learning to cook new foods, and reading voluminously on child rearing. I had always worked and had a successful career, so I saw no reason to expect less of myself as a homemaker. Besides, I loved it.

When the children were born, the work increased by leaps and bounds. We had three children in three years, and keeping up with them was a real challenge. Both Howard and I were interested in their upbringing, and we devoted many hours to reading and playing games with them. As they got older, my homemaking duties changed to include chauffeur, room mother, Scout leader, and Sunday school teacher, as well as the chief cook and bottle washer. My work domain is busy and fulfilling, and I wouldn't trade it for any other job in the world.

✳

Homemaking may not a suitable career for everyone, but for Laura it was perfect. She brought to it the high energy she had for her nursing career, and the expectation that she would be successful. Laura's high waypower helped her find solutions to the many challenges motherhood presented. Most importantly, however, Laura and Howard provided a high-hope model for their children, in both the work domain and in many other aspects of their lives.

Now that you have completed each domain-specific scale and read stories typifying both low- and high-hope people in each life arena, you are ready to set the goals you will use as you learn hope-enhancing strategies. In the next chapter, you will set goals that are reasonable in scope and that arise out of your own hope assessment.

7

Six Steps to Effective Goal Setting

In the previous chapters, you determined which life domains were most important to you and how satisfied you were in each area. You rated your hope in each domain and read about examples of individuals who had either low or high hope in each arena. In all of those stories, whether hope was high or low, the people described were on the brink of setting goals that would improve their lives. In this chapter, you will select goals to use as you learn hope-enhancing strategies. The groundwork you have covered so far will help you make enlightened and workable choices. You will use your ratings of satisfaction and importance in the life domains, as well as your waypower, willpower, and total hope scores from the Domain-Specific Life-Hope Scale, to aid you in your selection. Here are some characteristics of goals to keep in mind as you consider what you will target.

Characteristics of Goals

The first criterion for a goal is that it should be *important* to you. You will work more energetically and sustain your efforts better if the goal is something you really desire or need. Working for some goals may be an enjoyable process, while working for others may be no fun at all. For example, having an aching tooth extracted is not pleasant, but it's important to stop the pain. There are many daily goals you set and achieve that may not be enjoyable while getting there, but you deem them necessary or desirable enough to merit the struggle. Many people do not enjoy their jobs, but go to work each day in order to support themselves. Many individuals may not enjoy housework, but they do it in order to maintain order in their environments. Still others, because of a desire to be physically fit, can be seen jogging, whatever the weather.

Some goals are achieved through an enjoyable process, even though the effort may be substantial. For example, learning to ski requires you to suffer many aches and pains before you can glide with ease down the mountain. Short of breaking a limb, however, learning to ski can be a great deal of fun. The same can be said of many sports and leisure activities, and since these are not vital to your existence, the pleasure you take in the goal pursuit helps you maintain your efforts. When you enjoy your activities, they are easier for you to accomplish. In most people's lives, however, it is often necessary to set goals that require unpleasant and difficult activities in order for them to succeed. These goals build high hope and are well worth the effort.

Many goals you set for yourself are important but not necessary. Importance does not always equate with need. You may not consider some domains, for example leisure or romantic relationships, particularly important. If you rated importance and satisfaction at approximately the same point, above the 50 percent mark, that domain may be in balance for you. If, however, you rated both satisfaction and importance low, this may be a domain in which setting a goal is appropriate. A very low importance rating indicates that you do not believe you need that life domain, but a low satisfaction rating indicates that you may not be pleased with its lack of importance.

To illustrate this situation, consider Anna whom we introduced in chapter 6. Anna had preferred characters from books to relationships with real people all her life. The importance she gave to social relationships was low, but as she aged and began to realize that she might be facing isolation, her satisfaction with this domain began to drop. Anna's goal to develop friendships would raise both the importance and satisfaction she expressed about that life domain. As you select your goals, consider the needs they will meet in your life. You will find your waypower and willpower increase when you recognize the goal as important in meeting your needs.

Another important characteristic of goals is that *they can be broken down into small, manageable steps.* Large goals are accomplished best by focusing on each small step at a time, but even small goals will be easier to handle in this manner. Long-range goals, such as completing your college education, can be divided into steps, such as semesters. Each semester has a number of goals—completing each course, for example. These objectives can be divided, again, into the separate tasks it will take to accomplish them. Examples of these small tasks are reading chapters in required texts, writing papers, or taking tests. It's important to recognize the contribution each step makes to your eventual success. As you consider what goals you will choose for your hope-enhancing work, think about whether they are large or small and the ways you might divide them into manageable steps.

Goals can be large or small, long range or accomplished quickly. In addition to the other facets of goals, you should *consider how feasible the goal is for you* to accomplish at this point in time. Setting realistic goals is one way to boost your willpower and increase you waypower. Your dreams may be achievable, even though other people try to discourage you. If you live in a low-hope environment, it can be difficult to tell which dreams are reachable and which might be impossible.

How can you tell which goals are feasible and which are not? If you are a low-hope person, it will be difficult to know the right answer—that is, until you have higher hope. We recommend that you store away your largest dreams until hope-enhancing strategies have become part of your life. Keep your dreams in a private place and don't discuss them with others. If you are a low-hope person, there is a chance that many of the significant people in your life are also low in hope. As you learned in section I, hope tends to run in families, and one characteristic of low-hope people is that they send messages that can discourage others.

High-hope people are not discouraged by the low hope of others

Keep your large goals a private matter for now. As you build your waypower and willpower, you will become more confident of achieving these important objectives. Hope is infectious, and as you learn to exercise your waypower and flex your willpower, it will be easier to convince others that you can succeed. You will also be a model of high hope, and promote hope in those you love.

Goals, if carefully chosen, have characteristics that will help increase your chances of success. Select goals that are important and reflect your needs. If you decide on a large, long-range goal, be prepared to take many small steps before reaching your objective. Consider the feasibility of your goal. Ask yourself if this is the right time and whether you have the resources to be successful. Big dreams are wonderful, but if the timing is not right, don't be discouraged. Nurture your dreams. As you build your hope, you will find that you can reach higher and higher.

Goal-Setting Steps

Here are six steps that high-hope people frequently use when they set goals. Once you have mastered these steps, you will want to use them whenever you have a major objective in mind. Along with each step you will be reminded of the vignette from chapter 7 showing that step in action.

Step 1: Selecting Your Domain

On the Goals Worksheet at the end of this chapter, write the satisfaction and importance scores you gave to each domain. Next, select an arena that is important to you, but where you are not as satisfied as you would like. Write that domain in the appropriate space on the worksheet. Now consider the vignettes of Henry and Nan.

Henry valued education but never felt capable of achieving the goal of becoming a lawyer, and yet he never felt satisfied with his sales career. For step 1, Henry selected the academic domain. He believed that continuing his education was the answer to a successful career. The domain Henry chose would also impact other areas, such as work. When a significant change is made in one area, changes are likely to occur in other domains as well.

Nan's needs were in the family domain. She didn't share interests or personality characteristics with her adoptive family, and she occasionally felt lonely and angry in their presence. She decided that, in order to have a family to which she truly belonged, she would have to start her own. Her goal, which originated in the family domain, overlapped with the domains of romantic relationships and social relationships. If Nan was going to find a partner with whom to create a family, she would have to meet appropriate people and develop a romantic relationship

Step 2: Using Your Domain-Specific Life-Hope Scores

For this step, examine the hope scores you gave yourself in each domain. Is your hope low or high for the domains you selected as your target areas in step 1? If your hope score is low, determine which component of hope—waypower or willpower—is low. Are they about the same? Or, perhaps one component is lower than the other. These factors are important in your goal selection because they influence your thoughts and feelings about your potential for success. You want to raise your hope, so you will choose areas that are in need of improvement. At the same time, while you are first learning the hope-enhancing strategies, you may not want to select a goal about which your hope is so low that you are likely to quit. You may want to select a domain in which you have ratings in the 3 to 6 range of scores on the waypower and willpower items. Determine the highest and lowest possible scores for the domains you select. Your best chances for success will be in areas in which your scores fall around the midpoint. Because the domains have different numbers of items, the total scores will be different.

For example, on the academic domain, a somewhat low total-hope score would be 24, and a somewhat high score would be 48. For the spirituality domain, because that scale has six items rather than eight, a somewhat low hope score would be 18, while a somewhat high hope score would be 36. Your optimum chances for success, as well as your best learning experience, will occur when you select domains that fall within that range.

Margaret's hope in the spirituality domain is very low, yet she feels a need to fill a void left by her childhood experiences. Her waypower may be so low that she can no longer perceive ways to search for meaning. Her willpower may be exhausted by her previous unsuccessful experiences. If she were to decide that the spiritual domain was important enough, she might explore avenues to create her own belief system, as Frank was able to do, taking small enough steps to ensure early success that will boost her confidence. Frank approached his spiritual goal with high waypower, exploring many different theologies—or paths to enlightenment. He met with success each time he discovered a new teaching that added to his personal system. When he encountered teachings that did not enhance his philosophy, he was able to discard them and move on to others. His interest and success fueled his energy to continue the search.

Creating a spiritual belief system is a large goal, one that took Frank many years to accomplish. A smaller goal for Margaret might be to take a world religion course in which the material was presented from an anthropological, rather than a theological, point of view. Learning about religion in an academic setting would put her under no pressure to accept or reject the ideas being taught. At each step along the way, Margaret would be free to stop her inquiries or continue wrestling with this domain.

If your willpower and waypower scores are very low for a specific domain, your chances of success are heightened if the goal set in that area is very important to you. If you begin with high willpower and waypower, your chances of achieving even less important goals increases. Use your Domain-Specific Life-Hope Scale scores to help you find areas where your hope needs enhancement. You might want to avoid those domains where your hope is so low that you might easily give up. Save those goals for when you have higher hope. What is the hope score on the domain you chose in step 1? Does it fit the criteria of somewhat low to somewhat high hope?

Step 3: Deciding What You Really Want

Now that you have selected a domain that is important to you and in which you have somewhat low hope, ask yourself the following question: What would I have to do to improve the satisfaction I experience in this domain? Try not to censor your answers. Allow yourself to dream a little. Many low-hope people are taught to be cautious and not to set their sights high because they might fail. You can always scale down, so don't be afraid to dream. For now, allow your thoughts to expand and imagine yourself satisfied in the domain you have chosen. What would that be like? After you've done some dreaming, write down your ideas on the worksheet.

Virginia had never prepared for retirement, having spent her entire adult life working to ensure her financial success. When she moved to Leisure World and a life without work, she felt bored and empty. When she finally asked herself what it would take to make her retirement satisfying, her answer was to write—to do for fun what she had done for work.

Virginia's daughter, Donna, found herself single again in her early fifties. Although she was not unhappy, she recognized that a romantic relationship would balance her life. She asked herself what type of person she would like for such a relationship and was able to articulate the qualities she wanted.

Asking yourself questions such as these helps clarify your goals. It's important to see the big picture before you can divide it into smaller parts. Donna's primary goal was to have an intimate romantic relationship. It was only after she could articulate the larger goal that she could begin to see the separate steps to such a relationship. The purpose of asking yourself what you really want is to articulate your primary goals. On your worksheet, write the goal you have identified.

Step 4: Determining Feasibility

Now that you have selected a domain on the basis of importance, satisfaction, and level of hope, and you have identified your goal, it is important to examine its feasibility. One way to determine your prospects for achieving a goal is to itemize the steps necessary for completion.

Buddy's goal in high school was to go to college on a football scholarship. When he was injured and became a paraplegic, he had to change his plans and rearrange his goals. When Buddy viewed his life domains in the months immediately after the accident, he found that his satisfaction was low in most of them. Because he could no longer meet many of his needs, they all seemed very important. Prioritizing them was his first step.

The academic domain became Buddy's first priority. He recognized that a good education was going to be necessary if he were ever to support himself. He was also comfortable in the academic area, having been a better-than-average student, as well as a top athlete. Buddy identified getting a college degree as his major goal.

To determine feasibility, Buddy asked himself first how possible it was for a paraplegic to go to college. It would be necessary to learn about the provisions made for disabled students on campus and to learn to drive a hand-operated car. He thought about how other students might treat him—the last thing he wanted was pity. He also had to consider how college would be financed, since he would no have a football scholarship. After answering these questions, and after discussing his goals with his parents, he decided that going to college was a feasible goal.

High-hope people seek advice, and they learn from the experience of others.

Notice the types of questions Buddy asked. After first determining that a college education would be the best solution to problems that involved nearly every domain in his life, he had to decide if this goal was possible for him. The questions he asked also indicated some of the roadblocks he would encounter. Knowing what's down the road as you pursue your goal helps to eliminate surprises that might bring you to a standstill.

On your goals worksheet, write the questions you asked, along with the answers you found, about the goal you selected. Think carefully about both the questions and the answers. Consulting with others is a good idea, especially if your goal will involve their participation or cooperation. If your waypower is low, you may not know what questions to ask. If that's the case, it may be necessary for you to seek the advice of others, especially people who have succeeded in achieving your goal. Remember that high-hope people seek advice, and they learn from the experience of others. Planning your course, detailed in the next step, is another tactic used by high-hope people as they select goals.

Step 5: Charting Your Course

To determine feasibility, you asked questions about the steps you would have to take to reach your goal. Charting your course of action involves a more detailed examination of those steps, describing each of the smaller goals you will accomplish along the way. On your goals worksheet, write all the steps you can think of that will be necessary to reach your goal.

If you are a low-hope person, this may be an unfamiliar task for you. One way to develop the ability to chart a course is to think of a goal you accomplish frequently and easily. If you cook, preparing a meal might be a good example. Your first step is to decide what to fix, often starting with the entrée. After you have determined what the main dish will be, you decide on the side dishes. Next you check for the ingredients and see what you will need to purchase. Before you begin to cook, you must consider the cooking time of each dish so that the entire meal will be ready at the same time.

Most people who prepare meals frequently give little thought to the many steps involved. In fact, they may operate on automatic pilot. For an inexperienced cook, however, preparing a dinner can be an imposing goal. If the new cook can chart the steps in advance, the task becomes less formidable.

When your goal is something you have never done before, the course will be unfamiliar. The best way to develop a plan is to ask someone who has done it successfully. When you chart your course of action, ask others how they have reached their objective. Even if you have decided to accomplish something that is unfamiliar to family and friends, you can seek the advice of someone outside your acquaintance who has succeeded. Most people enjoy talking about themselves and will be happy to answer questions from a person who is genuinely interested in their accomplishments. For example, if your goal were to become an actor, you might seek an interview with the star of a local theater production. Or, alternatively, interviewing the drama teacher at a high school or college would provide you with many ideas to help you chart your course.

On your Goals Worksheet, write the steps you have discovered through your questions. Ask as many questions as you wish, and if you cannot think of questions, ask the successful person what he or she considers to be important about the goal. Acquire as much information as possible and enter it on the worksheet. You are now in a position to arrange your steps in order, leading to your goal.

Step 6: Arranging Sequential Steps

Now your worksheet is filled with questions and answers, ideas and goals. It's time to make sense of it all, arranging your steps into the order you'll need to follow in order to reach your goal. Your list of steps will necessarily be limited. As you begin working for your goal, you will encounter events that may add or subtract steps. Listing these preliminary steps is the beginning of waypower thinking. In the next chapter, we will show you how to develop your ability to think of different ways to reach your goals. High-hope people are flexible in their thinking—a characteristic of high waypower.

To illustrate the six steps you have learned, meet Meredith. She is a forty-five-year-old woman who raised three children then found herself divorced and without a way to support herself. She chose the domain of work from which to select her goal, although she felt bereft in many areas of her life.

✳ Meredith—Living Well Is the Best Revenge

I wasn't destitute because he gave me five hundred dollars a month in alimony. But it wasn't enough to allow me to keep the house, or even my car, let alone buy new clothes or travel. We had lived a good life, in relative comfort, until the children were on their own. Then he announced that he had met a younger woman, and he wanted a divorce. It's a familiar story to many women who devoted their lives to the care of home and family. I had never planned to earn my own living, and, although I had three years of college, I had never learned any marketable skills. Or so I thought.

Among the many skills required to be a homemaker, several stood out as marketable. I was a great cook, but in order to become a chef I would have to get formal training. I had decorated our home comfortably, but a course in design would be required before I could sell myself as an interior decorator. I liked gardening but not all the time, and child care didn't pay enough. What could I do?

The idea came to me when I was having coffee at a neighbor's home. She mentioned that she was considering hiring a maid service to clean her house when she started back to work. It occurred to me that housework was something I could do fast and well. Maybe there was a way to market that skill. Obviously I could hire out to individual people, but the amount of money I could make would still not cover my expenses. What would it take to start a cleaning service of my own? Running my own cleaning business was the best goal I had thought of, but there were still many questions to be answered.

That night I was so excited and full of questions that it was hard to sleep. How much money would I need? Where could I get the money? Where could I find competent, honest workers? How would I get clients? How much equipment would I need? Will I need a fleet of cars to get my workers from home to home? I could hardly wait until the next day to start finding the information I needed to get going on my plan.

I considered interviewing the manager of a cleaning company, but discarded that idea. There were already several cleaning services in my community, and I might be viewed negatively as a competitor. I went to my banker instead, as I knew he often made small business loans. He had answers to many of my questions, and he was willing to process my application for a small loan, using my home as collateral.

My goal was feasible, and it addressed a real need in my life. I had asked the right questions, and I had obtained a lot of information. Now it was time to chart my course and put my steps in order. The first step was to secure the loan, not a difficult feat as it turned out. Next I placed an ad in the newspaper for people between the ages of twenty-one and forty-five to work in the domestic field. A surprising number of men and women applied, and interviewing them was fascinating. They had to furnish references from prior domestic work, be bondable, and be in good health. I selected an initial group of nine people, all of them willing to start as soon as we had clients. I decided to pay my employees a higher salary than that paid by the other cleaning services, because I understood how hard it is to be poor, and I also wanted their loyalty.

While I was interviewing prospective employees, I was advertising our service, Meredith's Maids, in the newspapers. People began calling with requests for domestic help almost immediately. Soon, all my teams were working full time, and I had to hire more people. I had teams of three cleaners, with one person from each team providing transportation. The company paid mileage and supplied all the cleaning equipment.

There were many new things to learn along the way, such as how to deal with all the red tape involved in having a business with employees. There were many decisions to make, headaches to contend with, and problems to overcome. I did it, though, and now I have an adequate and independent income. I'm living well, and having my own business has given me satisfaction and confidence. ✳

Meredith's story details each of the steps presented in this chapter. She decided upon the work domain because of its importance, as well as her lack of satisfaction in that area. She was able to identify a goal and test its feasibility by asking the appropriate questions. Her next step was to chart her course of action and then arrange the steps in sequential order. The steps gave her the needed direction to begin.

At this point, you will have selected a goal and charted your course. Use the following checklist to be certain you have completed all the steps, and use your Goals Worksheet to review your goal-setting process. As you begin taking the small steps toward your goal, you may encounter unanticipated problems.

In the next chapter you will learn strategies to increase your waypower, so that roadblocks do not bring you to a stop.

Goal Selection Checklist

Put a check by each step you have completed.

Step 1: I have selected a domain that was important to me but with which I was not satisfied. _____

Step 2: I have reviewed my scores on the Domain-Specific Life-Hope Scale, with attention to the domains I selected in step 1. _____

Step 3: I have asked myself what would improve my satisfaction most in the domain I have selected. _____

Step 4: I have asked questions and obtained information that allows me to determine the feasibility of my goal. _____

Step 5: I have charted my course. _____

Step 6: I have arranged my steps in sequential order. _____

Goals Worksheet

Domain	Importance Rating	Satisfaction Rating
Academic	_____	_____
Family	_____	_____
Leisure	_____	_____
Personal Growth	_____	_____
Health/fitness	_____	_____
Romantic	_____	_____
Social Relationships	_____	_____
Spiritual	_____	_____
Work	_____	_____

My selected domain is: _____

Domain-Specific Life-Hope Scale scores for this domain is: _____

What would I have to do to increase my satisfaction in this domain? _____

_____

_____

_____

My goal is: _____

To determine feasibility I asked these questions: _____

_____

_____

_____

The answers I obtained were: _____

_____

_____

_____

Charting my course: The main steps I will take to my goal are: _____

_____

_____

_____

Here are the steps arranged in order from first to last: _____

_____

_____

_____

_____

_____

_____

_____

_____

_____

_____

_____

8

Building Your Waypower

You've come a long way so far, and you know a number of things about yourself. You have measured your hope in a general sense, and you have measured hope in specific domains of your life. You have a step-by-step guide for goal selection that takes you through the importance and satisfaction of each of the important areas of your life. You learned that it's important to ask questions and chart courses to reach your goal. You saw that those steps could help you determine the feasibility of the goal that you selected. All of that information along with your Domain-Specific Life-Hope scores allowed you to identify at least one important goal to target as you do the work of the next few chapters. You are now ready to begin learning strategies to enhance your hope—beginning with waypower.

In chapter 7, you had a preliminary glimpse of high-waypower techniques as you were learning to set goals. Chapter 8 builds upon what you've learned and augments your ability to find ways to reach your goals. You will learn a series of techniques used by high-hope people, and you will see examples of individuals using these strategies as they search for the routes they will use to reach their goals.

A Closer Look at Waypower

What is this part of hope that we call waypower? Simply put, it is *your perception that you can find ways to reach your goals*. Easy? Not necessarily. For low-hope people, this is the very point at which stumbling blocks may stop them from achieving what they want. If you are low in waypower, learning to search for ways to reach your objectives is a skill that you can develop—the skill we are enhancing in this chapter.

We speak of "perceived ways" of reaching goals because even if the pathway to a goal is obvious to others, if you do not see it, then it's not an available route for you. Enhancing your waypower means learning to *perceive* routes and learning to *envision* possible methods that you can use to reach your target. Low-waypower individuals frequently see only one or a few ways to attain what they want, and when those ways are blocked, they give up the goal. They cannot see further than a few readily available methods, often the old familiar routes they may have tried before. When these methods fail, low-waypower people conclude either that the goal was not reachable or that they are simply not capable enough to accomplish it. Usually, neither conclusion is correct. The fact is, these individuals have narrow perceptions of their ways. They have not learned to look for other possibilities when the paths that they are accustomed to treading are closed.

After deciding on your goal, perceiving your ways to reach that goal must be the next step. You might have a tremendous desire to accomplish your objective, but if you cannot see how you will do it, you're stopped before you begin. For that reason, we show you how to build your waypower before we show you how to enhance your willpower. Imagine your goal of high hope is a tall and imposing building, a skyscraper perhaps. Developing your pathway perception is the foundation upon which this building is erected. In order to have a solid building, one that will last a lifetime, you need to have the strongest base that you can construct. In your foundation there are a number of smaller building blocks, and these are the strategies and techniques you will use to build your waypower perception. With each technique you learn, your ability to find ways to reach your goal will increase. Each strategy you learn, each technique you practice, adds floors to your tower of hope.

Thus, waypower is not made up of the actual routes that you take to reach your goals; waypower is your ability to perceive the many routes that may be available to you. Low-waypower people see few paths, whereas high-waypower people can see many ways to get what they want.

Characteristics of High-Waypower People

What are the people who can see many ways to get what they want like? How are they different from those who can envision only a few routes to their goals? Our research shows us that high-waypower people use some distinct methods that cannot only be described, but more importantly, *they can be learned*.

High-waypower people look not only at the larger goal, they can also see ways to break the goal down into small parts. Large goals frequently look so imposing that it's tempting to procrastinate, or worse yet, give up before you start. Seeing the smaller parts that comprise a goal puts the whole endeavor into perspective. An example from our own experience illustrates this point.

At the conclusion of formal coursework, our master's and doctoral students must write a thesis or dissertation. This task, as seen from the bottom up, is imposing to most students. They view it as writing a book—impressive at any time, let alone in graduate school. To help our students have increased waypower about this task, we show them that this "book" is composed of five "chapters," each of which has a specific format. When seen in this light, the book is actually a series of term papers they will write, a task that is very familiar to these students. Their view from the bottom changes when the goal is broken down into smaller parts. Suddenly it all becomes possible—things begin to look up.

Getting the Help You Need

Another method used by high-waypower people to increase their perception of routes is to ask for help from others. It's especially helpful to ask people who have accomplished your goal successfully to tell you the ways they found that worked for them. In business, academia, and the professions, this is referred to as "mentoring." Since the early Greeks, when Socrates mentored Plato, this technique of passing on the necessary information for success has been used and valued. Many people, however, do not take advantage of the information available to them from the experiences of others.

Questioning others who are successful in what you want to achieve requires you to be able to articulate your goal. Our experience has shown that low-hope people often find that they have difficulty developing the types of relationships in which they are comfortable asking for information, let alone mentoring. It may be necessary for you to develop your communications skills, perhaps even taking some assertiveness training, in order to learn how to state your goals clearly and ask for the information you need.

In addition to asking others for information, you may also ask for their help. The rugged individualist ethos of our country has tarnished the notion of asking for assistance. Many people believe that if a goal is not accomplished single-handedly, somehow the achievement is diminished or doesn't really belong to them. This is not true! In fact, nearly all the major achievements throughout history have been the result of group efforts, even though one leader may have been given more credit than the other group members. To expect yourself to have all the answers, to know all the ways to reach your goal, is unrealistic. Be prepared to ask for advice, and to ask for help when you need it. This is one of the most available techniques used by high-waypower people. Furthermore, once you have successfully reached your goal, be a helpful friend to others who are struggling as you were. Share your information.

Skill Building

High-waypower people also recognize when they lack the necessary skills to achieve their goals—and are prepared to learn them. This may require taking a step back before you can forge ahead. Separating your goal into small parts and then charting your potential course of action is a good way to determine whether or not you have all the skills necessary to follow the path you have outlined.

Many goals, the ones you achieve every day for example, require skills you already have. Some goals, especially larger ones that you have never tried to reach before, may involve some very specialized expertise. Assume, for a moment, that you enjoy music and can strum a guitar. What you would really like to do, however, is to join a folk music group that plays and sings every weekend. You know some of the members, you have attended some of their get-togethers, and you believe that this goal would bring you a great deal of pleasure in your leisure time.

As you listen to the guitar, banjo, and mandolin players, you realize that you have a long way to go to reach your goal. What paths do you perceive? How can you break down your goal into small steps? Since all you can do with the guitar at this point is strum a few chords, you will need to learn many more chords and how to pick the individual strings. You will probably want to take lessons and can get the name of some teachers from the folk-group members. Once you have asked for information and help in finding a teacher, you can begin learning the skill that will get you to your goal.

Be Willing to Bend

High-waypower people are also willing to alter their goals if necessary. Flexibility is a characteristic of high-waypower thinking, and it's a skill that also can be learned. There are times when your original goal is not feasible, although you may have believed it to be at the beginning. There are many reasons a goal may not work out that are beyond high-waypower thinking to overcome. You may not have enough money, someone you counted on may no longer be available, or perhaps the skills you need would take too long to acquire. There can be many reasons why you may wish to change your goal.

Changing your goal is not to be confused with failure. Even if you decide that a goal is no longer achievable and you abandon it, you have gained valuable waypower experience in the process. The point here is that you don't have to accomplish every goal you set in order to increase your hope. The very act of targeting an objective and then searching for the ways to get you there is bound to develop your waypower thinking. Changing or abandoning your goal once you have examined the ways you might reach it can be a positive learning process for you. Benefit from it—you need not feel like a failure.

Taken all together, the characteristics of a high-waypower person show us an individual who knows how to divide large goals into small, manageable parts, and can change the goal, or even abandon it, if this seems the best course of action. If the goal is dropped, the high-waypower individual learns lessons from the experience that will be helpful in pursuing the next goal. The high-waypower person knows how to articulate the goals so that helpful information can be obtained from others. If achieving the goal requires skills the high-waypower person does not have, then he or she will expend the effort to acquire that expertise rather than giving up on the goal. Let's follow Stephanie's waypower thinking as she pursues her goal to own and operate a toy store.

✳ Stephanie—Just a Kid at Heart

All my life I have loved toys and not just to play with. Collecting is my main interest. I began with Barbie and Ken dolls, and as I got older, I amassed a huge collection of action figures. I love Matchbox cars, boats, planes, and all sorts of mechanical toys. Maintaining and enlarging this collection has been my primary interest for years. After I developed a successful home page and began trading on the web, I got the idea to open a store.

In college I majored in fine arts, so I hadn't learned anything about the business and finance I thought it would take to open a store. On the other hand, I had a close friend who, along with her mother, was operating a successful vintage clothing store. My first step was to ask my friend and her mother for all the information they could give me about getting started in your own business. They were a wealth of knowledge, and when I ran out of questions, they told me what additional questions I needed to ask. In short, they taught me a short course on small business operations.

I realized early on that I already had two important requirements. I had inherited money from my grandmother—not a great deal, but enough to get started. The other asset I had was years of accrued knowledge about toys and collectibles. My next step was to prepare a business prospective for my bank, where I could use both my money and my knowledge as selling points for more venture capital.

After I was assured that I had enough seed money, my next step was to choose a location. Once again I sought information from others about how to find a desirable location. I asked the reference librarian for some useful sources, and she directed me to several books specifically for opening small businesses. Why hadn't I thought of that before? Sometimes the most "obvious" routes are not obvious at all. From those books I learn to look for high foot-traffic areas and about how much square footage I might need. I learned some additional helpful facts from these books and my personal interviews gave me the firsthand information I needed about having a business in our town.

After I had collected all the information and had found a suitable location, the next step was to order my stock and design my store layout. While I was waiting for my merchandise to come, I had a party during which my friends helped me paint and assemble display cases. I had already begun advertising with "coming soon" posters, radio spots, and newspaper announcements. Soon my store would be open to the public, and my dream would materialize. ✳

The steps the Stephanie took to actualize her dream are quite clear. Of course, she encountered roadblocks along the way, but for the sake of a concise picture, we have omitted them for the moment. Stephanie also had two advantages, money and knowledge, that made her goal seeking easier. Realizing that she had very little business knowledge, however, she was willing to spend the time it took to learn. Now let's examine the ways you can learn the steps taken by high-waypower people as they go for their goals.

Learning to Search for Ways to Your Goal

We have described a number of methods that high-waypower people use to reach their goals. The task, at this point, is for you to learn how to use these same strategies. Building upon the waypower thinking of high-hope people, we will show how each of the strategies they use can be used by you as well. With each strategy we will present a case example for you to use as a model in your own waypower thinking.

Strategy 1: The Goal Equals the Sum of Its Parts

After you have decided on your goal, the strategy of primary importance for you to learn is how to divide that goal into smaller, manageable steps. As we have pointed out, large goals can look imposing, and even small goals can get confusing if you cannot identify the small parts of which they are composed. In order to divide your goal into manageable steps, you will need to understand, at least in a general sense, how that goal is achieved. This may at first appear to be common sense. However, a surprising number of people have dreams that they will never attempt to materialize because they cannot visualize the steps it would take to do so.

If your goal is one with which you have little familiarity and perhaps you don't know anyone who has achieved it, separating out the small steps will be difficult. That's why we stress that you must be willing and able to ask for advice and guidance from someone who knows how to reach your goal. One of the authors of this book worked for a time in a counseling situation with poverty-level clients. Some of these individuals wanted to attend college but had no friends or family members who had ever done so. Although this goal was not unrealistic, many of these clients felt stymied by the unknown. Breaking this imposing goal into its component parts of entrance testing, applications, registration, semester courses, etc., helped to diffuse the mystique.

Often times you have a general idea of what will be involved in reaching your goal, which allows you to begin thinking of the smaller steps. As you proceed and you learn more about your goal, you may find that you need to add steps. Outlining the steps, as you did on the worksheet in chapter 7, is very helpful. Once you have divided your goal into small steps, go back over those and divide them again into even smaller steps. When you have written them onto a copy of the worksheet, arrange them in the order in which you think they should be accomplished. This sequential order becomes the course you will chart to achieve your goal.

The sequential arrangement of your goals is very important. High-functioning, high-waypower thinkers usually keep lists detailing what steps they need to take, what they have already done, and what they have yet to do. Your list serves both to keep you informed and to remind you of your focus. Additionally, it serves as a reinforcer each time you can cross something off. Even if your goal involves things you have done before, we urge you to do a sequential arrangement of the steps. You will find that your focus is improved—each time you return to the task, you know exactly where you are and what you have to do.

In the first example of this technique, the goal is to start a vegetable garden. Our novice gardener has grown flowers but has no experience growing vegetables. Here is the sequential list she made. Her list is organized beginning with the first step and follows through to the final goal of picking the vegetables. Some people find it easier to work backward from the goal to the first step. Make you own list in whichever way works for you—but make the list.

✳ Creating a Vegetable Garden

1. Consult with nursery, friends, and neighbors. What grows well in our area? When to plant? How much sun and water? What type of soil? (March)

2. Choose location based on sun and water access. Decide on size. (March)

3. Cultivate soil. (early April)

4. Condition soil. (mid-April)

5. Decide on vegetables and make plan of garden. (April)

6. Purchase vegetable plants and seeds. (late April)

7. Plant above. (late April)

8. Water and weed when needed. (throughout summer)

9. Fertilize and spray for bugs. (when needed)

10. Pick vegetables! (throughout summer and fall)

The goal of having a vegetable garden is not necessarily long-range, nor is it complex. This gardener is inexperienced, and so she has been as precise as possible in her steps. She has also provided a time line to follow, which is a good idea whenever timing is an issue as it is in gardening. Our list maker has never grown vegetables before; however, even experienced gardeners make detailed schemas and outlines—for them, planning is part of the fun.

✳

The next example is more complex and will require a longer time to complete. Ken had always loved dogs, and as a boy he had a Siberian husky. He was especially attracted to that breed because of their friendliness and their wolf-like masks. When Ken became a successful attorney he decided that he wanted to develop his own husky kennel. Here is his narrative about the steps he took to accomplish his goal.

✳ Ken—A Love of the Breed

My first dog, a Siberian husky I named Nika, was a Christmas present. My parents had stuffed the tiny puppy into my stocking just before I came downstairs. From that moment on, I was in love. I house broke her, took her through obedience training, and she and I were inseparable. Nika lived 15 years, which is old for a dog, and by the time she died I was in college. I missed her, of course, but I also knew she had lived a wonderful life.

When I graduated from law school and joined a firm, the first thing I did was to buy a small plot of land in the country. Although I had not admitted to myself that I wanted a kennel, I think, looking back, that I was laying the groundwork for such a goal. The idea of a kennel began to form when I got another husky and then decided that I should breed her. At that point I knew what I really wanted to do—I set my goal. I wanted to breed Siberian huskies for their disposition and coloring, and establish a kennel with an excellent reputation among breeders.

Although I knew quite a lot about Siberian huskies, I didn't know a great deal about breeding and kennel management. My goal looked intimidating, but it was something I really wanted to do. I decided to make a list of the smaller steps that would comprise my goal, beginning with learning the things I didn't know.

1. Interview other kennel owners to find out about costs, problems, etc.

2. Call county health department about specific regulations.

3. Contact the American Kennel Club (AKC) for lists of husky breeders.

4. Design fencing and dog housing. Contract for these to be built.

5. Purchase a dog and another bitch to begin breeding.

    a) Interview Siberian husky kennels.

    b) Review breeding lines of dogs and bitches from AKC records.

6. Have a veterinarian check all dogs prior to purchase and breeding.

7. List kennel and register all pups with AKC.

8. Advertise in *AKC Journal* and *Dog Fancy*.

9. Begin obedience and show-ring training.

10. Show dogs in local shows.

11. If successful locally, show in regional and national shows.   ✳

Ken's goal was both large and long-range. The steps he listed were not the smallest ones that he actually took, but they provided him with a general outline to follow. When you have set a large goal, we recommend that you make as detailed a list as possible. This is the first step toward enhancing your waypower thinking.

Strategy 2: Asking for Help from Others

Throughout this book, and in each case example, we have stressed the importance of involving others in your plans. Over and over again, high-waypower people demonstrate the effectiveness of this strategy. In the cases just given, both the novice gardener and Ken, the husky breeder, asked for information from other people in order to plan their steps. Neither of these people knew where to begin, so asking for help was vital to their plans. But you may not be a novice or unfamiliar with the ways to reach your goal. Depending on the size and complexity of your goal, asking others for input remains an excellent idea.

Even individuals who are experts in their fields seek consultation. Major corporations have found that a team approach to problem solving is far more effective than relying on one individual. Scientists consult with others in their field when designing experiments. Political figures always have large staffs to help with speech writing and decision making. Novelists must consult with experts in order to gain the background knowledge to give their books credibility. Even painters and sculptors, in areas known for individual creativity, often have students and technicians working with them. Very few successful people reach their goals in isolation. As a species, we need and benefit from the stimulation of others.

Here is an example drawn from our experience teaching graduate students. Jeannie, a doctoral student in counseling psychology, was preparing to write her dissertation. She had some good ideas, and she had worked closely with her professors on previous research projects. Jeannie had a strong mathematical background and was quite confident of her research design. Nevertheless, she consulted with her advisor and other members of the faculty, soliciting their advice and their confirmation that her research was going to be acceptable. One reason Jeannie asked for assistance was that she wanted to be certain she had not overlooked any important details. Another reason for the consultation was that all students are expected to work with a committee of three to five faculty members as they write their dissertations. It is an acknowledged fact that even people who are advanced in their fields need help reaching their goals.

Consulting, or asking for help, is one of the salient features of high-waypower thought. We have stressed this in every story and example you have read. In the next story, we follow Erin as she prepares for her wedding.

✳ **Erin—Wedding Bells, Not Wedding Blues**

I began to plan for my wedding over a year in advance. Since I had never been married and planned to only do it once, I wanted it to be absolutely perfect. I knew nothing about weddings, having only been to one when I was ten years old. My mind was a blank slate, ready to be filled with as much information as I could get. And it turned out that I could get plenty.

As soon as I began to think about weddings, I found information galore. There were magazines, pamphlets, mail advertisements, billboards, and brides everywhere. The problem wasn't getting information, the problem was sifting through what I found. The first decision I made was to locate a good bridal consultant. Although I interviewed several, the woman I hired had an immediate grasp of the simple style I preferred.

Once my consultant was on board, I found that there were at least a hundred items I hadn't thought about or even known about. She had long checklists of details that had to be arranged, and she also had good ideas about how to save money. We consulted on almost every important decision, and as the day grew near, the arrangements were actually under control. The wedding proceeded with only a few minor glitches, thanks to the organization and preparation we had done. I can't imagine planning a large wedding without expert advice.

✳

This brief example clearly shows the benefit of asking for assistance. Erin's aim was to have a perfect wedding, and she achieved that goal. In this case, the consultation had a price, and there are many times when the results are worth the expense. When you ask for assistance with your goal, don't overlook professionals who have the necessary experience and expertise. Many times, however, you will find that help is readily available just for the asking.

Strategy 3: Stepping Back to Learn New Skills

There may be goals that you desire strongly, but for which you lack a fundamental skill. High-waypower thinkers are able to step back from the original goal for a time and focus on the skills they need to acquire. As an example of this strategy, one of the authors of this book relates his personal experience.

I do a lot of writing, including reports, student feedback, manuscripts, reviews, as well as letters of recommendation and general correspondence. Throughout graduate school and afterwards, I had written by hand on legal pads and begged, bartered, or paid people to type my scribbles. In l986 I decided to learn how to type so I could become less dependent on others. I got a self-instruction program and taught myself. This fundamental skill enabled me to reach an important goal of efficiently and accurately getting my ideas into the necessary printed form.

Learning a new skill can be difficult and discouraging. There were times when it would have been far easier to give up and go back to the old way of jotting down notes. But he persevered, and found that, as expected, his efficiency was greatly enhanced.

Low-waypower thinkers frequently believe they lack the skills to achieve their goals. If this fits you, you must decide first if your presumed lack of skill is based in reality or if it's a reflection of a generally low opinion you hold of yourself. If you genuinely need to acquire a skill in order to achieve your goal, put the first goal on hold and make learning the new skill your immediate goal. Henry, whom you met in chapter 6, is an example of an individual who felt low efficacy in the academic domain but had set his sights on becoming a lawyer.

✳ Henry—Second Time Around

I had never applied myself in high school, and then when I got into college, it all seemed like a big party. I took the path of least resistance and majored in communications, the subject where I made the best grades. All my life, though, I had thought about being a lawyer. I considered taking the law school exams, but I had heard that law schools favored people with history or political-science majors.

For ten long years I worked as a car salesman. I suppose my communications background served me well, because I earned good commissions. The problem was, I really hated selling cars day after day. I knew there must be some career for me that was challenging—and I thought law was it. I was older, and I decided that with my new maturity law school might be achievable.

I called law school admissions counselors and found out what requirements were necessary. I discovered that I could take the admissions exams with my degree in communications, but that my chances of getting a high score would be enhanced if I took a course specifically designed for achievement on that test. I enrolled in the course, which was both expensive and time consuming. I studied every night, no matter how tired I was. I learned to think analytically and substantially improved my vocabulary. I took the test a month ago and am eagerly awaiting the results.   ✳

Henry recognized that he would not reach his goal of becoming a lawyer with the skills he had when he graduated from college, let alone ten years later. He sought information, and then he stepped back from his original goal in order to prepare himself for the quest for his main goal. Henry had not felt capable of law school at the time he graduated from college. His ten years of successful work experience had matured him, however, and he was able to look at his past behavior and learn from its lessons. Correcting your course, learning from your errors, is the next strategy used by high-waypower people.

Strategy 4: Fallibility Insurance

Everyone makes mistakes; no one does it right all the time. Rather than allow errors or poor choices to deter them, however, high-waypower people learn from their mistakes. The ability to benefit from an experience that others might consider a failure, is an important characteristic of high-waypower thinkers. In one sense, when you can learn from all experiences, successes or failures, you will never lose.

You met Donna in chapter 6, and then again in chapter 7. After a divorce she found herself single again in her fifties. Her story illustrates how a high-waypower thinker can learn from a painful event that many would consider a failure.

✳ Donna—Better Decisions and a Better Relationship

I had grown accustomed, even comfortable, in my life as a single person. When I renewed my acquaintance with Tom, I was cautiously optimistic about a future relationship. We had interests in common and enjoyed many of the same things, so we began seeing each other on a regular basis. From the beginning, however, I was determined to avoid the things in this relationship that I believed had led to my divorce.

After my divorce I wanted to examine what I could have done differently to make the marriage more satisfying. I'm not saying that I was totally to blame, but in every relationship both people are responsible for the outcome. I simply wanted to examine my role in the dissolution of the marriage. I discovered several things about myself that limited my own satisfaction and probably that of my husband. For one thing, I discovered that it was important for me to control nearly every aspect of our lives together. Essentially, that meant that very little real sharing was taking place.

I am a very nurturing person, or so I believed. It was under the guise of caring that I managed every detail of our lives that could possibly come under my control. Such exertions left me exhausted and unfulfilled. I believed that I did everything for everyone else, and that they did little for me. The truth is, I never let them.

In my relationship with Tom I am determined to change that behavior. I continue to work with my therapist, who helped me see how I demonstrated my desires to control. I told Tom what I was working on and asked him to tell me when he felt I was infringing on his life. We are taking our relationship slowly, but it's going well. My goal is to have a better relationship than I have had in the past and the only way to accomplish that is to learn from my past experience.

※

Donna has taken a hard look at herself and found that her past behavior was not conducive to the goal of having a satisfying relationship. Such an intensive examination takes courage, but can be the best way to discover the things you need to learn. High-waypower people do not shrink from learning difficult lessons, and in the learning, they experience success.

Strategy 5: Rehearsal

Once you have routes to your goal identified, you can begin to try them on mentally for size. You can imagine yourself taking various courses of action that may lead you to your goal, and often you can recognize in advance the roadblocks that you might encounter. As you rehearse these routes in your mind, you can develop a general idea of whether or not they are appropriate for you. Remember, there are many, many ways of reaching goals. Some routes suit some people, while other routes suit other people. You must find the best ways for you, and rehearsal is one way to do that.

Here are some guidelines for rehearsing your routes to a goal. Find a quiet place where you can be comfortable and undisturbed. Relax and clear your mind of thoughts and feelings. Some people find it helpful to imagine that they are on a wide expanse of warm sand, perhaps at the beach. Another way to clear your mind is to imagine a blackboard filled with many thoughts. Then, take an eraser and wipe the board clean. Next, call up a goal and think of the various steps you have developed. Clearly it's necessary to have identified the steps you might take prior to beginning this exercise. During your first rehearsal, go fairly quickly over what you will be saying and doing. Be sure to picture yourself in the situation. Once you have finished this first quick rehearsal, go through the sequence of steps again very slowly. At each step, visualize yourself handling it in a competent and positive manner. Visualization and rehearsal are also good strategies for enhancing willpower thinking and will be developed further in the next chapter.

Now you have a thorough description of waypower, and you know the characteristics of high-waypower thinkers. We have given you five strategies to practice as you enhance your waypower. Here is a list to use each time you exercise your waypower. It's a handy reminder of waypower do's and don'ts that can be copied and posted around your house or office.

Waypower Strategies

Do

- Break your long-range goal into small steps.

- Begin pursuing your distant goal by concentrating on the first small goal.

- Practice making different routes to your goals, and then select the best one.

- In your mind, envision what you will need to do to attain your goal.

- Mentally visualize what you plan to do when you encounter a roadblock.

- Instead of harshly blaming yourself, realize that you simply didn't use a workable strategy when you don't reach a goal.

- If you need a new skill to reach a goal, learn it.

- Cultivate friendships where you can give and get advice.

- Be willing to ask for help when you don't know how to reach a desired goal.

Don't

- Think you can achieve your big goals all at once.

- Hurry in devising routes to your goal.

- Rush to select the easiest or first route to your goal.

- Get hung up on the idea of finding one perfect route to your goal.

- Stop thinking about alternate strategies when one doesn't work.

- Conclude you are lacking in talent or are "no good" when your first strategy fails.

- Be caught off guard when one way doesn't work.

- Get into friendships where you are praised for *not* coming up with solutions to your problems.

- View asking for help as a sign of weakness.

9

Building Your
Energy Base

In the last chapter we described waypower and showed you strategies for increasing waypower thinking in your life. When you increase your perceived ability to think of routes to reach your goal, you are enhancing one part of hope. To be a fully high-hope person, you also need to develop your will-power—which is the purpose of this chapter and the next. Here, you will learn to prepare yourself physically so that you have the maximum energy available. You will be guided through health habits that will help you to increase your well-being and decrease your stress. These strategies help you develop a reservoir of energy with which you can fire your willpower. Let's begin by understanding willpower.

Willpower—It's Not What
You Think

What's the first thought that comes to mind when you hear the word "will-power"? If you believe you need to lose weight, you probably think of abstinence and doing without the things you like. If you are a fitness buff, you may think of sweat, endurance, and aching muscles. Whatever your thoughts are about willpower, they probably involve deprivation and determination. In addition, they are probably more negative than positive. The common

High-hope meanings of the term have given it a bad rap, but we'd like to challenge the idea that willpower must be a struggle.

people realize When we use the term "willpower" in this book, we mean this: Willpower is the reservoir of commitment and energy that you can call on as you work toward your goals. While way-**that making** power charts your course, willpower is the driving force behind your efforts. Willpower is made up of such thoughts as, "I can **important changes** do this," "I'll do my best," "I'll try." High-willpower thinkers know that they can tap into their reservoir of mental energy, **takes time.** and that they can work full steam ahead toward their desired goal.

The strategies you will learn in this chapter are designed to boost your willpower using several methods that require some amount of commitment on your part. For you to embrace this concept fully and do the assignments required for the strategies to be effective, it's important for you to shed any negative views you have about willpower. Approach your assignments with an open mind, take your time completing them, and do not be discouraged if changes do not happen immediately. Please remember—you will not change overnight, any more than you became who you are now overnight. High-hope people realize that important changes take time. They have learned patience.

Hope Is Part of Your Total System

We introduced the idea of holism when we explained life domains. Although people can be divided into many different parts (e.g., mind, body, emotions, spirit), holism views people in their totality, as complete beings. When you want to increase your willpower, it's especially helpful to think in a holistic way, valuing all parts of yourself, for each has a contribution to make. For example, if you are not physically fit and you lack the energy required for everyday accomplishments, you will have a hard time getting fired up to pursue a new goal. Similarly, if you are consistently depressed you will not feel energized to seek new experiences or set new objectives. Many people who are depressed also are not in top shape physically, a situation that illustrates the relationship between the mind and the body. If you happen to be either depressed, physically sluggish, or both, your willpower is probably at a low ebb. In this chapter you will learn how to energize yourself in ways that effect your whole being, greatly enhancing your perception of the energy you have at your command.

Willpower is a positive, energizing force within you. Willpower thinking drives your goal pursuits. High willpower is not garnered through force, deprivation, or hard labor. You will heighten your willpower in increments by making small and manageable changes in the things you do and the ways you think. This chapter is filled with strategies to help you develop physical energy. If practiced, they will develop into powerful habits that will benefit you for the rest of your life.

Energize Yourself

Think of something you would really like to do, something that is new and exciting. Do you feel energized and eager as you contemplate this new activity? Or, perhaps you consider the activity for a moment, and then, overcome by feelings of fatigue, you put the idea out of your mind. Many people lead such stressful lives on a daily basis that they have little energy or enthusiasm left to do the new and unusual things that make life exciting. Often, these people are mildly depressed, bored, or burned out on the activities that comprise their lives.

You may not lead a hectic life, but you may still find yourself fatigued, bored, and generally unsatisfied with your daily routine. In our experience, low-hope people are often mildly depressed. If you believe you are seriously depressed, we recommend that you consult with your doctor. An antidepressant drug or other form of treatment may be recommended. Please follow your doctor's orders in combination with the good health strategies in this chapter.

Your hope generally, and your willpower specifically, will be enhanced if you are in good physical health. It's possible to demonstrate high waypower and willpower even if you are ill or otherwise limited in your physical capacity. A few remarkable individuals have demonstrated unusual courage and achievement in the face of great suffering and pain. For most people, however, hope is diminished in proportion to their sense of well-being. If your health and fitness are ebbing, then your hope will be correspondingly low. The strategies in this chapter provide you with ways to increase your sense of well-being. Learn these good health habits, practice them, and see how your zest for life increases.

Your hope, and specifically your willpower, will be enhanced if you are in peak health.

Before You Begin—A Few Guidelines

You may already be familiar with the health and fitness suggestions given in this chapter. They are found in many contexts—health and wellness guides, diet plans, and exercise books. However, these strategies are usually presented in the narrow context of a single goal, such as weight loss, and not from the standpoint of enhancing hope. By developing these good health habits, you are laying the beneficial groundwork for embarking on your journey to higher-willpower thinking. And specifically, you are providing yourself with the energy necessary to carry out your dreams.

Here are a few guidelines to help you on your way. If you already have established one or more of these good health habits, you are a step ahead. If you are just beginning to examine your health and fitness, you're venturing into new territory, and the road may be unfamiliar. Old habits can be difficult to change, and your new habits offer challenges you may not have expected.

The point to understand here is that making important changes in your life will take time. You have spent many years becoming the person you are today, and the habits you have developed have been well reinforced, or you would not have them. You can't just drop them and pick up new behaviors quickly. A change of any significance must be accomplished in small steps, with each step well in place before the next one is taken. If you attempt to make changes that are too big and too fast, you'll find it difficult to maintain the efforts and be tempted to quit. If, on the other hand, you take the small steps that are advised, and you do not move on until you are comfortable with that level of accomplishment, you will find that you can change your habits with greater ease than you expected.

Learn to be patient with yourself. American culture stresses fast cures and leads people to expect immediate success. These expectations are unrealistic, however, and high-hope people are willing to spend whatever time is necessary to reach their goals. In this case, the goal you set is a foundation for developing higher willpower. Each of the strategies presented in this chapter will fuel the others. As you learn and accomplish one, the others will be easier. Let's start down the road to higher willpower now with the first strategy.

Nourish Your Hope

This is not a diet and exercise book, and some of the recommendations you find here are most often found in that context. Usually, when you change your eating or exercise patterns you do so to achieve a physical goal, such as losing weight or developing better muscles. These are common goals, and research shows that once those goals are achieved people tend to lose interest in maintaining the good habits they had tried to establish. Those objectives are admirable, but they are limited in the scope of your life. As you take the small steps to develop good health habits now, remember that you are laying a foundation for high willpower, and thus high hope, which will sweep through your life with broad strokes of achievement and pleasure.

The Elements of Good Nutrition

The elements of a nourishing and healthful diet have been widely publicized by the U.S. Department of Agriculture. Essentially, they consist of a pyramid where the largest amount of your daily food intake is breads, pastas, cereal, and rice. The highest level on the pyramid and the smallest recommended intake is fats, oils, and sweets. The USDA recommends ample daily servings of fruits and vegetables—three to five vegetables and two to four fruits. Protein foods are divided into dairy products and meat, fish, poultry, dry beans, and eggs. These foods are represented on the pyramid just below sweets, fats, and oils, and the USDA recommends that their intake be limited.

The typical American diet is high in fats and sweets. These foods can create sluggishness and lead to obesity. Sugary foods may create an instant feeling of well-being due to your raised blood sugar level, but they also produce a rapid fall in energy, often leaving you depressed and deflated. In addition to the physical damage an excess of fatty and sugary foods can do (such as obesity, heart disease, and cancers), having any of these conditions also produces a lowered sense of self-esteem. The result of poor eating habits is the decreased energy level available to you for your goal pursuits. The need to develop healthy eating habits is important if your body is to become a good source of energy for your willpower.

Good nutrition builds a foundation for high energy.

The Small Steps

We asked you to change your habits in small steps. With eating habits this is especially important, because food has many meanings in addition to nourishment. Eating can reduce anxiety, and some foods help you to feel nurtured, warm, and comfortable. Many so-called "comfort foods" are also high in sugar and fat—chocolate, for example. If you eliminate foods you have used to make yourself feel better, you are likely to feel deprived and therefore prone to give up on the change process. Don't try to eliminate all your comfort foods or to change your diet drastically. Here is a simple way to nourish yourself for higher willpower.

First, keep track of the food you eat each day for a week. Making a list of these foods will help you remember. Keeping your record for a full week is important because the type of food you eat may change depending on whether you're at work, at home, or eating in a restaurant. A week should provide enough examples for you to see the pattern. Don't try to keep track of calories, fat grams, or even quantity. The point of the exercise is to familiarize yourself with your current food choices so that you can determine the next small step.

The second step is to compare your food record with the USDA food pyramid. Are you eating the proportion of each food group recommended by nutrition experts? Note which areas are out of balance and how you would have to change your food selection to correct that balance.

For the third step, select one area in which you might make a small change. For example, you may not usually eat fruit. Make a list of the fruits you like and be sure to include those in your weekly shopping. Set the goal of eating at least one portion a day for the next week. Notice that you are not asked to substitute the fruit for another food, such as cookies or a candy bar. You are asked only to add the fruit to your diet for the week.

When you have successfully added the fruit, you can choose another food to add, such as vegetables or a salad. Remember, do not force yourself to substitute these foods for your usual foods—simply add them. You will find that once you are accustomed to making healthier selections, you will experience fewer cravings for the high-sugar and high-fat foods. When you find yourself wanting the less healthy foods, don't deprive yourself, but don't neglect the foods you have incorporated as your goal.

Start the Day Right

Another important nutritional habit is eating breakfast. Research shows that people who don't fuel their body's energy needs before they start the day do not think as well, and they do not have as much energy the rest of the day as people who eat breakfast. This is as true for adults as it is for children. If you are not a breakfast eater, and you are not accustomed to food early in the morning, you may not believe you can acquire the habit. Start small with this, too. Try drinking a glass of juice or milk and having something small, such as toast or a muffin. Having your piece of fruit with a small tub of yogurt is also a small yet nutritious breakfast. Avoid cereals that are high in sugar, however. They only build you up to let you down with the eleven o'clock sugar blues.

How you nurture your body with nutritious foods is fundamental to having high energy. If you wish to learn more about this interesting and useful topic, you will find a number of books in the resource guide at the back of this workbook. The information presented here is only a fraction of this fascinating topic. The more you learn, the better informed your choices will become, and the more capable you will be of designing a high-energy lifestyle.

Health Habits That Drain Energy

Cut Back on Caffeine

In addition to the foods you eat, there are other habits that have a powerful effect on your health and wellness. For example, how much coffee, tea, or soda do you drink? Caffeine is a stimulant found in these drinks (and in chocolate, as well) that, if used judiciously, can give you a lift. However, many people sip these drinks throughout the day, coming to rely on them as a source of false energy. Caffeine is an addictive drug as well, and if you doubt that, notice the headache you will get when you withdraw from its use. An excessive use of coffee, tea, or soda also has the effect of diminishing your appetite for genuinely healthful foods. If you use sweetened drinks, then you are getting calories, but they are empty of nutritional value.

The energy you need for high willpower should come from natural sources, such as good food and exercise.

The energy you need for high willpower should come from natural sources in your body. If you like caffeinated drinks, restrict yourself to one or two and consider drinking water the rest of the time. Doctors recommend at least eight glasses of water a day, and this small adjustment would be an excellent way to accomplish two health goals at the same time. Remember to take changes in your caffeine intake slowly. If you cut back a little at a time, you won't experience the unpleasant side effects of withdrawal. If you are adding nutritious food to your diet at the same time, you should begin to feel a boost in your energy.

The Smoking Issue

It would be difficult to live in the United States and not be aware of the dangers of smoking. The media is filled with stories about lawsuits and the statistics of how many people die each year from smoking-related illnesses. Smoking cigarettes, however, is a very difficult habit to stop. If you are a smoker, and if you are aware of the impact of tobacco on your health, you are certainly addicted to that drug. As one of the authors knows from personal experience, it's distinctly possible for an intelligent person to engage in a destructive behavior even while knowing the consequences. However, it is possible to change the habit, and the rewards for doing so are great.

Why is it important to change that particular habit? After all, you probably believe that nicotine relaxes you and relieves your stress. You may not know that nicotine is a poison and a stimulant, and as such it does a considerable amount of damage throughout your body—not only to your lungs. In the long term, smoking will weaken your body, promoting illness rather than wellness and substantially lessening the amount of energy you have to put toward your goals.

Quitting smoking, as with all of the strategies presented in this workbook, is a very personal choice. You may decide to cut back rather than quit. Because of the addictive nature of nicotine, many people find it difficult to do this. Some people, however, are able to accomplish a substantial decrease in their intake through cutting back. Here are some tips if you decide that you wish to change your smoking habit.

Select the date on which you will begin to change your habit before you actually do it. Try to choose a time when your stress level will be relatively low, such as a weekend or a vacation. Choose a vacation when you're going to be away from your usual environment and routine as this removes you from the situations in which you usually smoke. These "cues" serve as prompts for you to light a cigarette. For example, you may smoke while watching television or cooking dinner. If you are not doing those activities, the cue will not be present. Of course, there are a great many instances when you may have a cigarette, whether or not you're on a vacation. You can allow yourself the choice to smoke or not. Even if you smoked after lunch does not mean you must choose to smoke after dinner.

The next step in changing this habit is to decide on the approach you will use. Many people prefer the "cold turkey" approach, deciding that once they quit they will never smoke again. Other people prefer to cut down gradually on the number of cigarettes they smoke until they have quit completely. Others decide to smoke a small number of cigarettes on a regular basis, never actually quitting. Remember, the choice is up to you.

If you decide to quit cold turkey, throw away all the smoking materials and ashtrays in your home, car, and any other area in which you smoke. Get rid of the constant reminders. If you decide to cut back, keep only the number of cigarettes you need for that day. Throw away the rest of the pack or have a friend keep them. That way, you won't be tempted to smoke more than you've allowed yourself.

And finally, if you are serious about quitting, get help if you need it. There are a number of effective smoking-cessation programs available, and the patches, gum, and inhalers on the market appear to be effective. Smoking is a significant habit to change. You must decide if quitting is an appropriate goal for you, and if so, how you will accomplish it. Whether or not you make the decision to quit smoking, it's important to continue strengthening your other health habits.

Willpower and Alcohol

Those who abuse alcohol or other addictive substances (such as marijuana or cocaine) are very familiar with the common definition of willpower. Most treatment programs rely on abstinence as the main component for success. If you are a true alcoholic or an addict, an approach that relies on cutting back in small increments probably will not be effective for you. Controlling how much to drink or how often to use the drug goes to the very heart of the problem for alcoholics and addicts. These individuals are not able to control their use over long periods of time. If you have any questions about the way in which you use alcohol or any other drug, you should seek help. There are programs available to you, such as Alcoholics Anonymous, that are both free and effective. These programs have offices in nearly every city in the United States, and the listings are usually in the telephone directory.

For those of you who do not have a problem with alcohol or drugs, it remains important to minimize your consumption. Alcohol is a powerful depressant. After a few drinks, especially if you are already tired, you will notice a substantial decrease in your energy. One common drinking occasion is the after-work drink. Many people have one or two drinks to unwind after a hard day on the job. Later, they feel depleted of energy and become couch potatoes the rest of the evening, wishing they were motivated to do something else.

Assuming you do not have a serious problem, you don't have to give up drinking in order to enhance your willpower. You should take a look, however, at the effects alcohol consumption has on the energy you have as you pursue your goals. You may wish to reserve drinking for times when you don't plan to do other things, perhaps times when you are with good friends. Notice the reasons why you have a drink. If you use alcohol to unwind, there are other, energy-boosting ways to do that. And that leads us to the next strategy—the role of exercise in your life.

Get Up off That Couch

The American Medical Association reports that fewer than 30 percent of Americans get regular exercise. In the past, people did more physical work, and when they were tired, they rested. Our foremothers and forefathers might have laughed at the idea of running three miles as a way to relax. The fact is, to build energy you need to expend energy. Couch potatoes who seldom exert themselves find it difficult to be physically active. The regular exerciser has little difficulty getting motivated to do the things he or she wants to accomplish.

Paradoxically, to build energy, you have to expend it.

If you are not a regular exerciser, ask yourself why. Are you too tired at the end of the day? Is your morning so rushed that you can't find a slot for your exercise plan? You may not think you can fit one more activity into your crowded schedule. Perhaps you don't know what type of exercise would be best for you. Or, you may never have enjoyed athletics and so believe you would dislike exercising. Consider these suggestions.

There are lots of ways to increase your activity that don't require a great deal of time or planning. If you work in a building with an elevator, take the stairs instead whenever possible. If you have a choice of parking close to your school or office, park far enough away to provide a small walk. On your lunch hour, take a walk after you eat rather than sitting around and chatting. Better still, get your friends to walk with you and talk as you walk. If you work near a mall, on inclement days you can walk inside. Walking is an excellent exercise, and it costs only the price of a pair of comfortable shoes.

Walking is an exercise that you can tailor to your physical stamina. You can walk faster as you become more fit—your breathing and heart rate will be your indicator. Many people prefer to take exercise classes that are taught by an expert and meet at regular times. For the beginner, try low-impact aerobics, water aerobics, or yoga. Of course, with exercise as with all of the strategies in this chapter, if you have any question about their appropriateness for you consult your physician.

Physical fitness should be enjoyable. If it's not, you won't keep it up. Are there sports you enjoyed as a kid that you haven't played for a long time? Getting together with friends for regular basketball games or touch football can be great fun as well as wonderful exercise. Tennis, racquetball, handball, and squash are vigorous games requiring skill but are also highly enjoyable. Whatever you like to do, find a way to do it!

One of the best ways to exercise is to cross train. That is, do not limit yourself to one activity. Do several types of exercise, but most importantly, do what you enjoy. Begin your exercising with small steps, as you have been advised for the other strategies. If you're not accustomed to using your muscles and you do too much at first, you'll discover aches in parts of your body that you didn't even know you had. Despite any strange pains you may experience, the benefits of exercise are great. You will find yourself less stressed, you will sleep better at night, you'll lose weight if you don't increase your food intake, and you will increase your energy to do more of the things you want. So, begin to add physical fitness in small increments to your daily routine—in time you will not want to go a day without some form of exercise.

The Importance of Rest

How do you rejuvenate yourself? When you work hard and lead a stressful life you need a chance to relax, clear your mind of the worries of the day, and refresh yourself. A full night's sleep will usually restore your energy. A surprising number of people, however, either do not sleep well or get less rest than the optimum number of hours they need. There can be many reasons why sleep is disrupted, some of them serious enough to merit a visit to the doctor. Many people, however, simply do not make getting enough rest a priority. Instead, they sacrifice their sleep in order to do other things.

Eight hours of sleep in a twenty-four-hour period is considered the average requirement. Individuals differ on the amount of sleep they need, however, and you may find that seven hours works well for you, or you may require ten. Whatever your personal requirements are, try to meet them. It is while you're asleep that your body recovers from the previous day's activities.

Dreaming and the Sleep Cycle

Healthy sleep can be divided into two general stages, nonrapid eye movement sleep (NREM) and rapid eye movement sleep (REM). The first stage, NREM, occurs just before you fall asleep and in the early, lighter, stages of sleep. The second stage, REM, is your deepest sleep where most rejuvenation takes place. Extensive research has shown that during REM sleep the eyelids move rapidly, which indicates dreaming and thought activity.

REM sleep is necessary and desirable, but is only activated after you have passed through the NREM stage. Because it takes time to reach the REM stage, you need to allow yourself ample periods to sleep. Sleep researchers have linked the absence of REM sleep to various emotional and psychological disorders, including confused thought and psychotic-like behaviors. Furthermore, sleep induced through sleeping pills typically does not produce REM sleep, and so the use of these aids over a long period of time can be damaging to both mental and physical health.

The link between physical exercise and REM sleep has been well established, providing another good reason to work out. Research shows that people who exercise regularly stay in REM sleep longer than people who are sedentary. Since REM sleep is where your body does most of its resting and restoring, it behooves you to maximize this sleep stage as much as possible.

Common Sleep Problems

Most people have trouble sleeping from time to time; it's normal and to be expected. If you are especially stressed or anxious over an upcoming event, you may find yourself waking frequently, worried over what is to come. Unless this happens often to you, you can expect to continue with your good night's sleep once the event is over.

There are physical causes for poor sleep, including snoring and sleep apnea, that can be treated medically. About 20 percent of the population reports having insomnia, and usually this means a difficulty in getting to sleep. To be true insomnia, forty-five minutes should elapse between getting into bed and falling asleep at least three times a week for a minimum of three weeks. If this description fits you, it would be a good idea to consult your physician. For most people, however, some difficulty getting to sleep or staying asleep on occasion is quite normal.

As people age their sleep patterns change. Teenagers need more sleep than adults, and the aged often nap frequently during the day. For the years between adolescence and old age, however, you can expect to need an average of eight hours of sleep in order to refresh and restore yourself for the next day. If you don't sleep well, here are some tips that may help.

Guidelines for Sound Sleeping

Because not everyone requires the same amount of sleep, you must determine how much you need in order to function at your personal best. Once you know how much sleep you need, make it a high priority to get the rest you need every night. Set a regular bedtime and stick to it, except in unusual circumstances. Once you get used to going to bed at a regular hour, you will begin to get sleepy at that time. Your body will become "programmed" for that sleep schedule.

Your exercise routine should be completed several hours before you sleep. Exercise energizes you, and in order to sleep well you should be relaxed and calm. You might try reading, listening to music, or watching a little television, providing these activities are calming and not too stimulating. You might save action movies or suspense novels for some time other than bedtime.

If you use alcohol, caffeinated drinks, or tobacco, don't do so before bedtime. Alcohol may cause drowsiness, but it doesn't help insomnia. Caffeine and tobacco contain powerful stimulants that can keep you from falling asleep. Similarly, don't eat too much before bedtime. A heavy meal can cause indigestion, making it difficult for you to fall asleep.

The best way for you to get the rest and refreshment you need is to make rest a high priority, and gear your evening activities so that you are ready for a sound sleep when you go to bed. A full and sound sleep will start your day with the energy you need in order to be a high-willpower person.

Your Total Health Picture

Without a doubt, your health and fitness are important parts of willpower. You must have a reservoir of physical energy from which to fuel the mental stamina you need to work for your goals. Without this energy, your dreams remain just that—fantasies hidden away in your mind. Let's review the strategies you will use to increase your personal energy.

1. Slowly change your diet to include power-packed foods such as fruits, vegetables, whole grains, lean meats, and low fat dairy products. Lessen your intake of high-fat and high-sugar foods. Gradually, the change will help you maintain a desirable weight, and you will notice an increase in energy and well-being.

2. At the same time you're increasing your intake of healthy foods, you are slowly cutting back on your use of caffeine, alcohol, and tobacco products. As you begin to feel better physically, your need for these substances will decrease.

3. Adding regular exercise to your schedule is going to help you cope with stress, give you an additional energy boost, help you sleep better at night, help you control your weight, and benefit your cardio-vascular system. Start slowly, find an exercise you enjoy, and make it a regular part of your routine.

4. And finally, make sleep a high priority. Determine how much you need, set a regular sleep schedule, and take the necessary steps to be ready for a good night's rest.

Remember to take small steps as you establish each of these energy-enhancing habits. Changing too much, too soon, is a recipe for failure. High-hope people know this, and they plan their moves in advance, knowing that it's important to be comfortable with each step before moving on to the next one. Developing your physical energy as a resource for your mental energy is given a top priority in this workbook. You are urged to begin these changes concurrently with the mental-energy strategies in the next chapter. Don't leave them for "some other time." Make your physical well-being a top priority. The following story is about a woman who has a career, a family, and "does it all." She has been meeting everyone's needs—except her own—until she decided to make some changes.

✳ Marianne—A Woman's Work Is Never Done ... Or Is It?

I grew up in a large and high-achieving family. It was important to me to have an interesting career, but I also wanted to have a large family. In other words, I wanted to "have it all." And why not? I was a strong, healthy woman, intelligent and capable of carving out the kind of life I wanted. Choosing a major that would lead to a career with flexibility was critical to my plan. After exploring a number of options, I chose psychology, with the goal of teaching at the university level.

During my doctoral program I met an attractive young law student. We fell in love and planned to be married as soon as he had his degree and I had completed my internship. All our plans went well until we had to decide which career would take precedence in the job search. He had an opportunity to join a firm in a large Midwestern city, and I had a job offer on the East Coast. We decided that, because I would be having children soon, it would be wiser for him to take the law firm offer. We also reasoned that the Midwest might be a better place to raise children than the urban East Coast.

As it turned out, I was able to obtain a teaching position at a small college in our community. This school had a floundering undergraduate psychology major, where the few professors were of retirement age. I was offered the position of chairperson, and my mission was to develop a viable program that would attract new students to the college. I was excited by the challenge and threw myself whole-heartedly into my work.

After two years, both my husband and I felt comfortable with our careers and it seemed like a good time to start our family. I wanted to do everything right for my new family, so I began by taking classes in natural childbirth and learning about breast-feeding. I planned to set up a small nursery in my office so that I could tend to my child and not miss work. This plan worked well, and my colleagues seemed comfortable with the idea of motherhood at work.

Within five years we had three children, and each child was cared for by me at work. When the children became toddlers, I found an older woman who could care for them at home when I couldn't be there. It was important to me to be the primary care giver and for my children to experience a secure home life. As time passed, the expectation that I would meet everyone's needs became a fact. I took care of the children, my husband, my career, our home, and all our social obligations as well. In addition to those responsibilities, I took on the jobs of Scout leader, room mother, and Sunday school teacher.

My career was blossoming and the department was growing. I was thankful to be in a small college where teaching was valued, because I didn't have time to do research. My annual reviews were excellent, however, and I was praised for being a good role model for women students. My friends also marveled at my energy and organization, saying that they couldn't do half of what I did. While the praise was nice to hear, I had begun to wonder if it was all worth it. Being a superwoman may not be all it's cracked up to be. True, I met everybody's needs, but I wasn't meeting my own. With each passing year, it seemed that I had less and less energy to give to my family.

How long had it been since I had done something that was just for me? How much time did I have during a day that I could call my own? The fact was, I read a bit after the children were in bed and the house was quiet, but by then I was so tired that I usually fell asleep after a few pages. I loved my work and my family, but was this anyway to live a life? I decided to make some changes before I lost my enthusiasm and my stamina.

I needed to pay attention to my own needs for a change, and to do that I would have to free some time. After studying my calendar I realized that there were some changes that I could make that would not be drastic but that would give me some personal freedom. The first thing I did was to call a cleaning service and arrange for them to clean my house once a week. I had never used a service before, because I always believed I could do it better. Now I thought, "So what. The house doesn't have to be perfect."

The next thing I did was to excuse myself from several of the less important responsibilities at the college, and designate more duties to my colleagues and to my secretary. I also decided to keep fewer office hours, to take longer lunch breaks, and to allow myself occasional "mental health" days.

I examined my diet, which was essentially a good one. I had, however, been eating fast food at my desk for lunch. One small change I could make was to bring a more nutritious lunch from home when I planned to eat at school. My husband and I also decided that once a week, we would eat lunch together at a nice restaurant. It would be delightful to have some time together alone.

Alcohol and tobacco were never a problem for me. I didn't smoke and rarely drank, but I did drink a lot of coffee. I decided to make a small change in my caffeine intake by using a half-and-half mixture of regular and decaffeinated coffees. I never even noticed the difference!

The final self-nurturing thing I decided to do was to join a health club. I located one that had a wide variety of activities and decided to begin with a low-impact aerobics class that met three times a week over the noon hour. I could do the workout and eat a nutritious sandwich later.

Slowly, I began to make changes. At first I didn't feel much different, but after a week or so I began to notice a change in my mood and in the amount of energy I had throughout the day. Rather than feeling controlled by others, I felt a renewed sense of personal choice. I began to approach my responsibilities with renewed eagerness and excitement. As I looked ahead at my life, it was with high hope.

⁕

Marianne has been a high-hope person all of her life. She approached each new challenge with enthusiasm and had a lot of energy for the full life she had undertaken. Even a wonder woman gets tired, however, especially if she is constantly meeting the needs of others and rarely tending to herself. Marianne saw that her physical energy, and thus her willpower, was beginning to dwindle under the pressure of her daily commitments. She knew she had better remedy the situation, and, being a high-hope person, she set self-nurturance as a goal. She took stock of the situation, made a plan, and then followed it.

Marianne's high willpower was also based on her positive self-talk. She told herself that she could accomplish the things she set out to do, and that if she ran into stumbling blocks along the way she could find ways around them. Learning to use positive self-talk is the subject of the next chapter.

10

Boosting Your
Mental Willpower

In the last chapter, you learned new ways of viewing willpower that did not involve the common images of a person undergoing deprivation and hardship. You learned a number of strategies that will build your physical energy so that you have a reserve to aid in the pursuit of your goals. You learned that changing your lifestyle is accomplished best by taking small steps. Through these small increments you not only can make permanent changes, but you can make those changes so that modifying your routine does not feel like a struggle.

In this chapter, you will learn techniques to change your thinking and the messages that you tell yourself. Where the last chapter dealt with your physical self, this chapter focuses on your thinking processes—your mind. In chapter 3, you were introduced to hope markers, and you kept a ledger recording them as they appeared in your stories about yourself. Those hope markers are similar to the self-talk that you will examine in this chapter, and we will ask you to record self-talk here as well. The relationship between what you tell yourself and how hopeful you feel will become clear as you continue your work in this chapter. Let's tackle next a topic that you may think applies only to persons with severe mental problems—self-talk. We will show you that, contrary to being the working only of those who are psychotic, self-talk is a fundamental and normal process in most people.

More About Self-talk

The way that you think—that is, the type of self-talk you use, has a powerful effect on how you feel and what you do. If you tell yourself negative things, such as calling yourself silly or stupid, you will come to believe these things and to behave in ways that confirm those labels. If, on the other hand, you say positive things to yourself, you will feel more capable and willing to attempt new things. Identifying the messages that you give yourself and learning how to move these messages in a positive direction is critical to the development of high hope. Changing your self-talk is what this chapter is all about.

Giving yourself messages is something that you learned early on. Children who grow up in households where there are large doses of encouragement and praise for their achievements learn to say positive things to themselves. On the other hand, when children are constantly criticized, they internalize what they hear and learn to be self-critical. Children learn their personal messages from people other than caregivers, too. Teachers, ministers, coaches, and a variety of other influential people can be instrumental in the development of positive or negative self-talk. Likewise, recent theory and research in psychology suggests that a child's peers have far more influence on that child than we ever imagined.

One means for identifying where your critical messages have been learned is to listen to your self-talk. Does it sound familiar? Now, think carefully about this self-talk—these literal "voices in the mind." Who do they sound like? You may identify the words of one of your parents, a sibling, or another relative. These voices become imprinted on your mind, and when you repeat behaviors that brought criticism in the past, you often automatically criticize yourself. On a more positive note, you may have been lucky enough to grow up in a household where negative voices were seldom heard and your successes were praised. In that case, you have learned to praise yourself. Whatever their content, these voices in the mind are powerful determinants of your actions and your other thoughts.

For many families, the puritanical roots of our country have produced an ethic that values criticism over praise, punishment over reward. Biblical teachings, especially from the Old Testament, have had a strong influence here, with such adages as, "Spare the rod and spoil the child." Research over the years has shown conclusively that positive reinforcement is a more powerful teacher than punishment. But common wisdom dies hard, and many people—middle aged and older—were raised in households where praise was thought to lead to conceit, laziness, or other negative behaviors. So, it was fairly common for the criticism to be laid on impressionable young minds by very well-meaning elders. After all, it was the same for your parents when they were growing up, and thus they pass it on through the generations. It's now up to you, if you are the recipient of such negative voices, to decide whether you too wish to continue it or perhaps change it for yourself and for the benefit of your children. We assume that because this book on hope has made it into your hands that you want to have hope make it into your mind.

There are many sources of negative self-talk, but the things that you tell yourself have been learned—they do not spring forth from your mind spontaneously. Fortunately, what you have learned can be unlearned. You can replace the negative things you say with messages that boost your willpower and encourage you to reach your dreams.

To illustrate how both negative and positive messages are learned, let's look at two stories, each of which describes a particularly important event in these people's lives. You may remember Ted, whom you met in chapter 1. Ted's mother and father were hard-working people who typically gave Ted little encouragement for his dreams or praise for his accomplishments. Donna, whom you first met in chapter 4, received a great deal of assurance and approval for the things that she did. Her dreams were encouraged, and her accomplishments were applauded. While eventually Ted learned to enhance his hope and start a landscaping business, he had to overcome the negative messages that he had learned from his parents. Donna, who always was a high-hope person, went on to live an exciting life, unafraid to follow her dreams. Perhaps it may be useful at this point to see how the messages that Ted and Donna heard in their childhoods affected their adult self-talk.

The negative self-talk you have learned can be replaced by positive messages that help you reach your dreams.

✳ Ted—If It's Fun, It Must Be a Waste of Time

I always loved growing plants and would have liked to become a horticulturist. Early on, however, I got the impression from my parents that such a career was difficult, and that it was not something I should try. They seemed to think that working with plants was a waste of time. They thought I should be spending any extra time working with them in their store. I remember one incident in particular that made a really big impression on me.

I had a small plot for growing irises in our back yard and I had several different varieties. All of these flowers were doing very well. The previous year I had cross-pollinated two of the varieties, and I was eagerly looking forward to the flowers they would produce. In the springtime, when they were about to bloom, I asked my parents to have a look at them with me. They were too busy to take the time and said they would see them when they were blooming. Within a week, the flowers had opened, and I was astonished to see that my experiment had worked. There, in a pool of late afternoon sunshine, were three beautiful yellow and lavender flowers. Their colors were perfectly blended together, as only nature knows how to do.

I was overjoyed and filled with pride and rushed into the house to tell my mother. She was fixing dinner and, as usual, preoccupied with the details of the meal. She told me she would look at them later, but by then it would be dark and their lovely colors wouldn't show. My father was still at the store, so by the time he got home it would be even darker. I begged my mother to stop for just a few minutes and look at my flowers. Finally, she snapped at me, "Ted, growing flowers is a waste of time!" Those words struck me like someone had hit me. In fact, I felt my mother actually had—with her words. *"Ted, growing flowers is a waste of time!"* Those words stayed with me all my life. I was humiliated when she told me that she and my father thought that there was something strange about a boy who liked gardening so much.

I still remember the crushed feeling I had inside and the blushing heat I felt on my face, knowing that they thought I was odd. I went to my room and fought back tears until dinner. Even though I was only ten years old, I thought that crying would confirm their belief that there was something wrong with me. Later, my parents did go out to look at the flowers, but of course they couldn't see their brilliance. We never spoke of that incident. We didn't have to. I knew their feelings, but I continued to work silently with my plants. The garden became my refuge away from their critical eyes. My plants rewarded me with their lovely foliage and bright colors. It was as if they were telling me that what I was doing was just fine. More importantly, the plants taught me that *I* was just fine.

Ted's parents were strict believers in "keeping the nose to the grindstone," and "walking the straight and narrow." They did little to encourage him, and they actively attempted to discourage his dreams. Ted never would forget his parents telling him that his flowers were a waste of time. Like so many children, Ted found how to survive emotionally, but the negative messages that he heard limited his hope until he was middle-aged. Then, with the help of his wife, Rita, he decided to go after his longtime dream of landscaping. But, the negative voices in his mind needed to be replaced with more positive, hopeful ones.

✳ Donna—The Puppet Mistress

I was always encouraged to be creative, even when my "productions" caught my mother off guard. She was good-natured, and she always encouraged me to express myself. She made the drinks for my lemonade stands, and she helped me make costumes for a ballet I "produced" with the neighborhood children. I usually knew I had her support, but I also knew that if my ideas were too farfetched, she would tell me. The day I put on a puppet show, however, I almost crossed the line.

It was a rainy morning, rare for summer in southern California, and my friends and I were bored. When I got the idea for a puppet show, everyone eagerly joined in with their suggestions. As usual, I became the director and the producer, allotting jobs to each person.

By midafternoon, we had constructed a stage of sorts, made from old wooden boxes we found behind the grocery store. We even made a curtain that could be pulled when each act was over. We used Shirley Temple dolls for puppets, with our hands under their long skirts. Because I had a doll dressed as Heidi, and we all knew the story, that became the play we enacted.

But what was a show without an audience? The neighborhood mothers were all invited to the performance, which was to be given later that afternoon in my living room. Promptly at four o'clock, seven mothers accompanied by an assortment of toddlers and babies seated themselves in chairs grouped around the makeshift puppet stage. At three-fifteen, just minutes into the show, the front door opened and in walked my mother.

She didn't know anything about the puppet show, of course, and she was thoroughly astonished to see the neighbors crowded into her living room. The mothers, for their part, had assumed that my mother knew what I was up to. There was momentary embarrassment all around, until my mother saved the day. Quickly, she made everyone feel at ease by bringing out cookies and preparing tea. It was a grand party and, once the puppeteers stopped laughing over their lines, the show was a success.

Later that night, my mother and I had a discussion about keeping her informed of my activities. She was proud of my creativity and initiative, but at the same time she preferred to know what was in store for her when she came home from work. I felt good about the puppet show, and I vowed not to surprise my mother with any more unexpected guests.   ✳

Donna's mother might have shown anger at unexpectedly finding the neighborhood mothers in her home. Instead, she explained the importance of keeping her informed while at the same time praising Donna for the afternoon's efforts. Because of her mother's positive and encouraging attitude, Donna felt free to try new things—to use her creativity instead of stifling it.

Donna can still remember a few of the words of praise her mother used that day. She said, "The puppet stage was really clever, and the dolls looked lovely." She also said, "You are an ingenious kid, and I'm proud that you're my daughter." Although Donna recognized that she had almost overstepped the line of acceptable behavior, she went to bed feeling pleased with herself that night.

These vignettes show how parents can influence a child's thoughts about himself or herself. The stories of Ted and Donna represent brief but significant episodes in each of their lives. As adults, Ted and Donna vividly remember the details of those situations along with what their parents told them. Multiply those two episodes by the hundreds that undoubtedly took place in both their lives, and you understand the powerful effect that these negative or positive comments had on the self-talk that Ted and Donna each learned.

How and Why You Use Self-Talk

The messages you say to yourself are, to some extent, automatic. That is, they have been so well ingrained that you don't always notice what you're thinking or saying. For example, suppose you hit your thumb with the hammer when you are hanging a picture, or break a plate while doing the dishes. You may utter an expletive first, but then what do you say? Do you call yourself stupid, or careless? A good time to identify your negative self-talk is when something goes wrong. The next time you catch yourself in a verbal put-down, take note of it and think about how you learned to say those things.

Frequently, self-criticism becomes a way of staving off fault-finding from significant other people. You literally get there first with the criticism or put-down. The reasoning goes, if you point out your own flaws, others won't need to do so. Criticism can be hurtful, and early on you may have developed ways to avoid it. When you point out your own errors before anyone else does, keeping others quiet, you are rewarding and strengthening that behavior.

Another example of how self-criticism is rewarded happens when significant other people tell you that what you have said is not true, or that you are being hard on yourself. While parents and others may be quick to point out your mistakes, they often are ready to placate you when you scold yourself. Each time this happens, it only serves to strengthen your negative self-talk all the more. Does this pattern sound familiar?

Negative self-talk is sometimes used superstitiously, in the belief that it will prevent failure. For example, have you ever told yourself that you will not succeed at something before you even try it? Superstitious reasoning sounds like this: "If I tell myself I will fail, then I won't be disappointed if I do. If I succeed, it will be an unexpected pleasure." Does this description fit you? If so, you are deceiving yourself. You will not escape the disappointment you feel with failure, and you also are dampening the joy that you could feel with your success. Using negative self-talk in this way is another learned type of thinking. Superstitious self-talk goes hand in hand with self-criticism, and they are both ways of coping with negative and hurtful experiences.

High-hope people learn to give themselves positive and encouraging messages.

The messages you learn to give yourself can be positive and hope-inducing, rather than negative and defeating. High-hope people have learned to say encouraging things to themselves, especially when they are about to embark on the journey toward a new goal. High-hope people realize that, because they may encounter external roadblocks on the trip, *they don't want to erect any internal hindrances along the way*. They also recognize that negative thoughts about their prospects for success are handicapping, and part of being a high-hope person is establishing conditions for maximum success. Why make your life even harder? Our point here is that by learning to hear positive voices in your mind, you are giving yourself a break.

Learn to Identify Your Self-talk

The messages you give yourself are so well learned that you may not be aware of what you think or when you think them. Identifying these directives, whether spoken aloud or thought silently, is the first step toward changing them and moving them in the direction of higher hope. Because they are automatic, you will have to be observant and note the things that you think. At the end of this chapter is a self-talk record, similar to the one that you used in chapter 5 where you recorded the hope markers you identified in your stories.

In previous chapters, you have investigated your hope through the stories you heard growing up and your own narratives about events in your life. Now it's time to move into the world of your daily life and examine the self-talk that you use every day. Keeping track of these personal messages is not difficult once you alert yourself to watch for them. We advise a two-step process for best results.

First, obtain a notebook that is small enough to carry with you (you will use the self-talk record in the second step). In the little book, note the actual words you used in your self-talk and the situation in which it occurred. For example, if you called yourself clumsy when you broke the plate doing the dishes, you would note that in your book. Specifically, you will write down the words "I'm clumsy" under "self-talk." Under "incident," you would write "dropped the plate while doing the dishes."

It is especially important to write down the self-talk you use when you are working for a goal. These messages may be less obvious than the ones occurring after an accident, but they can be more insidious, because they truly are self-defeating. These messages, if negative, can set the stage for failure and make developing your willpower extremely difficult. Watch for statements such as, "This is going to be difficult—I don't know if I can do it." Or, "I don't think I'm up to it." Whatever negative statements you thought, write the actual words in your book. Also, note the situations in which the thoughts occurred or the goal you were contemplating at the time.

The second step in gathering information about your personal messages is to transfer what you have written in your small book to the record at the end of this chapter. While this exercise may seem redundant, there is a purpose to it. Rewriting your self-talk gives you an opportunity to review the types of messages you used and when you used them.

Keeping track of your self-talk takes practice. Make this task a goal for the next few weeks before you begin making changes. As with most behaviors you want to change, you first have to know when and how often you engage in them. By keeping a record of the words you use in talking to yourself and under what conditions you use them, you will be able to identify patterns that will help in deciding what to change.

To illustrate this process, let's follow Sarah's self-talk as she takes a horseback-riding lesson. Following is an example of her internal dialogue as she rides. She has not been riding long, and began taking lessons to develop more self-confidence. In this segment, the self-talk is underlined. Notice that only the negative thoughts are underlined, although a few of her thoughts were positive or neutral. Positive statements are important, in fact that is the way most of your self-talk should sound. However, because it is the negative statements you wish to change, those are the ones that you are to note and record.

✳ Sarah—Learning to Jump

The horse I am going to ride today looks huge—in fact, he is a lot taller than I am. <u>I don't see how I can ever get up in the saddle.</u> And that saddle is so small, there is nothing to hold on to. But I wanted to do this, and I've paid for it, so <u>I guess I have to go through with it.</u>

Now that I'm up on top of the horse and trotting around the arena it doesn't seem so bad. I might survive this, as long as I don't <u>fall off.</u> The teacher has just placed a pole in the middle of the arena and I'm supposed to have my horse jump over it. <u>I don't think I can do that.</u> What if he takes off running, or what if he jumps really high? <u>I know I'll fall off</u>. I guess I'll try the jump, but <u>I don't feel ready to do this.</u>

<u>We did it, or rather, the horse did it.</u> I wonder if I will ever be a rider, and <u>not just a passenger.</u> I think learning to ride a horse will give me confidence, but I'm <u>not sure I can do it.</u>   ✳

Notice that Sarah used a number of negative messages. In fact, she nearly defeated herself before she began. By using this negative self-talk, Sarah decreased her willpower and made achieving the goal more difficult. If she had approached the riding lesson with more positive self-talk, then her mental and physical energy would have been directed toward the goal.

During the riding lesson, Sarah wasn't able to record all of the negative self-talk she used. After the lesson, however, she was able to remember a few of the messages, and entered them into her record. It looked like this:

Situation/Goal	Self-talk
Riding lesson/mounting the horse	I don't think I can do it.
While riding the horse	might fall.
Jumping the horse	I'm not ready for this.
After the lesson	I'm not sure I can do it.

Your record for an entire day, however, will be much longer and more complicated. There will be times when it is not feasible to record your self-talk at the time you are having the thoughts, so, as Sarah did, try to reconstruct them later. It's critical to the success of this strategy that you record your negative thoughts. It is also important to focus on what you are thinking and in what situations you are most likely to have these thoughts. Ask yourself if you have self-defeating thoughts when you are trying new things. If you encounter roadblocks on the way to your goal, what thoughts do you have? Remember, first you must learn what messages you give yourself, then you will know what to change.

When you make self-defeating statements, you are placing an extra burden on your shoulders. You must cope with your negative mental attitude as well as any external difficulties you may encounter as you try to achieve your target. The negative messages sap your energy when what you want to do is to increase that energy. Let's rephrase Sarah's self-talk to be more positive. Read the following example of her internal dialogue. This time, the phrases that are changed to be positive are underlined.

✳ Sarah Rides Again—With a Better Attitude

The horse I'm going to ride today looks huge—in fact, he is a lot taller than I am. I see some steps I can stand on so that I can get up in the saddle. That saddle is small, not much to hold on to. I see other people riding in small saddles, though, so I think <u>I can do it.</u>

Now that I'm up on the horse, it looks like a long way down to the ground. <u>It's a little scary, but I want to do this. I can do this. I don't want to fall off, but if I do, I'll survive.</u> Now the teacher has placed a pole in the middle of the arena, and I'm supposed to have my horse jump over it. If he goes too fast, I know how to rein him in. If he jumps high, <u>I could fall off, but I think I'll manage to stay on.</u> Here we go, I <u>think I'm ready for this!</u>

<u>We did it!</u> What a good horse, and <u>I'm pretty good too. I think I'm going to like this, and I feel more confident already.</u>   ✳

In accordance with the small step method that we have advocated throughout this workbook, Sarah has not made drastic changes in her self-talk. One important change she made, however, was to observe the situation as it really was, not how she feared it might be. She saw that there was something to stand on when mounting the horse. She noticed that other people managed to stay seated, even though the saddles were small. She also saw that others didn't fall off when their horses jumped. Such observations helped Sarah base her thoughts on reality rather than just her fears.

Sarah did, however, change one very important message. Rather than telling herself that she couldn't do it, or that she wasn't ready, she told herself that she *could* do the things required of her. After her horse jumped the pole, Sarah could enjoy the pleasure of having accomplished a frightening task. In the first scenario, Sarah accomplished the same goal, but her negative self-talk left her in a low-energy place. In the second scene, she approached the goal with a positive attitude, and so when she accomplished her goal, she felt an extra boost of energy and happiness.

After Sarah reviewed her self-talk record, she was able to identify how the negative messages drained her willpower for accomplishing her goal—riding, boosting her self-confidence. Without the detailed record, she would not have had the information to understand what to change. After you have kept your record for a week, you will be ready to move on to the next step—changing your automatic negative self-talk.

Discover Your Self-Talk Patterns

Now that you have a record of your self-talk, you have an idea of the kinds of statements you use and when you use them. Note the patterns that emerge. Are your messages self-defeating, saying that you won't succeed? Perhaps you call yourself names, such as clumsy or dumb (or worse!) when things don't go right. Because your statements are learned, they will form a pattern that you can come to recognize and predict. By studying your self-talk record, you will be able to recognize the situations in which you are likely to denigrate yourself. Armed with this information, you are ready to begin taking some small steps to change.

From your weekly record, select one situation that is fairly frequent and in which you typically give yourself negative messages. Remembering to start with small steps, select a situation that is frequent but brief. For example, imagine a man who must parallel park his car frequently but is not skilled at this task. Each time he misjudges the distance and has to try again he denigrates himself about his parking ability. This is a good opportunity for him to begin working on his negative thoughts. Instead of deriding himself, he could acknowledge that parallel parking is difficult and that he needs more practice to become better. While a negative thought is self-defeating, recognizing the difficulty of a situation is constructive. Even though it's difficult, there is the possibility that this man may become proficient at parking his car.

As you review your weekly self-talk record, look for the types of statements you make when you begin a new project. Do you encourage yourself? Or, perhaps you approach new goals and situations with the "protective" statements described earlier. Those are the "impending doom" messages that are meant to cushion the fall you believe is inevitable. Of course, those messages only amount to heavy baggage you carry down the road to your goals.

If you found yourself saying self-defeating statements, you will want to change them to more positive messages. If you tell yourself that you cannot do it or that you probably won't succeed, change the statements so that they become positive. The positive version would be that you *can* do it, and that you *can* succeed. Initially, when you frame your statements in a positive way, you may not believe them. You may think you are tricking yourself or that this is a gimmick. This technique for changing thought and behavior is well established, however, and with repetition, you will come to believe what you tell yourself.

Throughout this book, you have been asked to remember details about your life and the positive or negative climate of your family. While these memories help you to understand how you have come to be either positive or negative in your self-talk, it is not possible for you to remember all the instances where you internalized your present attitudes. What is true is that as a child you had no choice about the messages you heard, and you were susceptible to whatever the adults in your life told you. As an adult, however, you do have choices, and you can decide for yourself what messages you want to hear.

Honesty as a Redefining Technique

Be honest with yourself about the difficulty of your task and about the obstacles in your way. Be honest and realistic, but do not let the obstacles intimidate you so that it seems necessary to predict defeat. With high-willpower thinking, your chances of success are much greater than they are when you invoke self-defeating messages.

As a child you were susceptible to whatever the adults in your life told you. As an adult you can decide for yourself what messages you want to hear.

You have seen how Sarah changed her self-talk by eliminating some of her negative thoughts and replacing them with realistic considerations of the difficulties of learning to ride a horse. By including in her thoughts the information about the difficulties she was facing, her willpower did not diminish and she was not tempted to stop working for her goal. On the contrary, *the acknowledgment of those difficulties formed a foundation of truth*, and her negative thoughts were recognized as only assumptions she had learned—not fact. Clearing away the negative self-talk so that the truth became obvious allowed Sarah to choose whether or not she wanted to try for her goal.

Learn to take an honest appraisal of your situation. When you find yourself using negative self-talk, stop those thoughts and consider the reality of the task ahead. Ask yourself what is difficult about this goal? What problems might you encounter? Have you done this or anything similar before? What skills do you already have that will help you with this goal? What can you draw from your past experiences that will help you now? These are important questions, and in your answers you will find the keys to coping with negative thoughts and developing higher willpower.

Learn to Appraise Your Abilities

Deciding whether you have the capability of achieving your goal is difficult for a low-willpower individual. Carrying the extra baggage of negative self-talk for many years will make a realistic assessment of your aptitudes and skills difficult. Learning to dissect a situation into the separate skills required for success is a good place to begin. Remember to start with small goals so that you have fewer steps to consider, gradually moving up to larger and more complicated situations.

Let's examine the parallel-parking situation previously described. This individual uses denigrating self-talk after he has not succeeded, thereby placing the entire situation in a negative light. If he looks at each aspect of parking the car, he may find that he actually possesses most of the skills he needs to be successful. He can drive, he can turn the steering wheel in each direction, he can back the car, and he can probably tell how large a space is required. What he needs to learn is how to gauge the degree of angle as he backs the car into the space. Analyzing a difficult task such as this whittles it down to an appropriate size. Let's see what happens next.

After our troubled driver realizes that he has one skill missing, he can decide to practice until he feels proficient at gauging the angles of his turn. If his goal is to learn parallel parking and in the process to increase his parking options and reduce stress, he will need to learn this one skill. In chapter 10 we discussed waypower, and you learned that there are times in goal pursuit when you must learn a basic skill in order to proceed toward your original target. That is what the parallel parker must do. In analyzing his situation, he has come to realize that he is lacking a skill and not just being stupid.

Back to our driver. On a leisurely Saturday morning he decided to take some rubber garbage cans and set off to a vacant lot to practice. No longer in the rush of the day nor under the watchful eyes of nearby people, he places the cans at an extra wide distance. Next, he makes a few successful runs and practices, remembering to praise himself. Then, much like a high-jumper setting the bar higher, our driver makes his task more difficult by setting the garbage cans closer together. Her knocks them over on a few tries, but finally he has it. *He has it!* He can sense the angle at which he needs to make his cut. Importantly, throughout this practice he makes positive, affirming self-talk. He then uses this positive patter on Monday morning when he successfully pulls into a tight spot in front of his pals at work.

An honest appraisal of your abilities in a difficult situation will enhance your willpower thinking. By engaging in this exercise, you can provide yourself with choices to make about how to proceed. An appraisal of your abilities, along with redefining situations and rephrasing your messages, are the keys to unlocking enhanced willpower, and thereby, higher hope.

Putting the Strategies Together

A number of effective techniques have been suggested in this chapter. Here is a list for you to review:

1. You have learned to keep a record of your self-talk and to analyze that record for patterns in both the situations and the content of your messages.

2. You have learned to rephrase the words you use from negative to positive statements.

3. You have learned to redefine the situations in which you denigrate yourself, so that you understand the actual difficulties that may be involved.

4. You have learned to break down difficult situations into their component parts and to determine the areas that are the most troublesome.

5. You have learned to make an honest appraisal of your abilities so that
   you can make realistic choices and learn new skills.

To enhance your willpower thinking successfully you must start with
small steps. All of the strategies suggested in this chapter are effective, but if
you try to change too much at first, you may become confused and discouraged. Begin with the record of your negative self-talk. You need that information before you can implement any of the other techniques. After you
understand the pattern of what you say and when you say it, choose another
strategy to help you begin making changes. Choose the strategy that feels the
most comfortable to you and implement it in limited contexts. We offered the
example of parallel parking because it was a clearly defined situation, and yet
it was important and relatively frequent. Try to identify situations that meet
those criteria as you begin changing the messages you give yourself. Don't
become discouraged if your self-talk doesn't change immediately. Remember,
you have spent many years learning to think negative thoughts, and you cannot expect rapid change.

Practice Doesn't Make It Perfect, But It Does Make It Easier

How does change take place? Changing your self-talk in small areas starts
slowly, but each positive habit you acquire builds on the others, and the subsequent steps become easier. Practicing each step is the key to success. Once you
have decided on the change you wish to make, practice your new self-talk
every time you have the opportunity. The more you practice, the faster your
new way of thinking will become habitual.

It's also important to learn to reward yourself for a job well done. While
your positive self-talk will be rewarded with an increase in willpower, it is also
good to give yourself a verbal pat on the back as you are working on your new
habits. At the end of the day, review your self-talk record to see how the negative messages are decreasing in frequency. Tell yourself you did a good job.
Remind yourself that even though it may seem slow, you are heading in the
right direction, and you are making progress.

You may wish to set some tangible rewards for yourself. For example,
when you have reduced your negative self-talk by a specified amount, give
yourself a special treat. Increasing your willpower and achieving your goal is
the greatest reward for your efforts, but those results are often in the future.
Make sure you have little incentives along the way to give yourself short-range
rewards for accomplishing the small steps. You have the control; you can
choose to reward yourself.

To illustrate the strategies described thus far, let's return to Sarah, who
has struggled most of her life with low hope, lacking the confidence to pursue
many of her dreams.

✳ Sarah—A Significant Accomplishment

I'm not sure how I happened to doubt myself so much. I do remember that I was too tall, too gawky, and too skinny as a child. My hair was long and thin, I wore glasses and braces, and because I grew so fast, my clothes were always too short. Everything about me felt ugly, and I got teased so much that I came to believe what was said. The one good thing about me that no one could take away was that I was smart. In elementary school my brains were a liability, though, and I got teased for being the "teacher's pet" or a "nerd."

My mother told me the story about the ugly duckling, but hearing that in the future I might be a swan did little to help me at the time. I believed I was an ugly duckling who would grow up to be an even uglier duck. For comfort I retreated into books and the schoolwork in which I excelled. Although I had wonderful daydreams about exciting things I might do later in life, each day of my childhood cemented my low self-esteem.

As an adult I look back on the taunts, teases, and my mother's attempts to help, and realize where my lack of confidence was learned. Having this information is important, but learning how I keep those negative thoughts and feelings alive in my life is critical if I am to change them. People don't tease me anymore, of course, and when I look in the mirror I see a tall, slender woman who is no longer awkward. In fact, I am often complimented on my grace and attractiveness. My outsides have changed nicely—now it's time to work on my insides.

I understand that the negative thoughts I have about myself were learned long ago. I also understand that, because they were learned, they can be relearned, taught by a more sympathetic and positive teacher—me. My first step is to see what those negative thoughts are as I use them in my life. I have been keeping a record of them as they occur to me during each day and discovered that they seem to occur most whenever I attempt to do physical activities.

This pattern makes sense to me, because it was for my physical awkwardness that I got the most teasing. I can still remember the agony of always being selected last for any team, and the groans of the other team members when they got stuck with me. I have tried to avoid sports all my life, and I suspect that I have deprived myself of potentially fun and healthful activities. It's time to change that pattern and find out what I can do.

In my childhood dreams I had a repeating image of myself riding a wild horse through fields, jumping over walls and streams. In those fantasies I was free and brave. The horse and I moved as one. We were graceful and nearly capable of flight. Perhaps I would never ride a wild steed, but I could at least learn to ride a tame one. I decided to take English riding lessons where I would learn to jump my horse over small hurdles.

When I saw the size of my horse at that first lesson I almost quit on the spot. He was taller than I, and I'm tall. I was assured, however, that he knew what he was doing and had a mild disposition. Getting into the saddle was a challenge and staying up was an even greater one because there was so little to hold on to. We started slowly, however, just walking and trotting. When the teacher told me to trot over a pole on the ground, I was apprehensive that I might fall off. Throughout the lesson I warned myself of dangers and catastrophes that could happen and prepared myself for the worst. It wasn't until later that day, while entering my thoughts into the self-talk record, that I realized how I had nearly sabotaged my success. I made a decision to change my negative messages to more positive ones for the next lesson.

I also decided to examine the skills necessary for learning to ride to see if I already had any of them. At first I thought there were none because I was inexperienced with athletic activities. On deeper reflection, however, I discovered two competencies that might apply: I knew how to ride a bicycle, and I liked to hike. The bicycle riding meant that I had a sense of balance, and the long walks had given me strong legs—both essential to horseback riding.

Taking a realistic appraisal of my abilities and being honest about the difficulty of the goal helped me see that I had undertaken a challenge that was possible for me to achieve. I *could* learn to ride a horse, and it would help me feel more self-confident.

I approached my next lesson fully aware that I needed to say encouraging things to myself. It was helpful for me to develop a type of mantra that filled my mind and blocked out the negative thoughts. I said over and over, "I can do this, I will succeed." As the lessons continued I began to focus more on the activity of riding the horse and less on my mental processes. I no longer had automatic negative self-talk, and I began to experience the success of accomplishing my goal. Learning to ride and to jump my horse was a significant accomplishment. I believe now that I can do many other things that I have never had the courage before to try.   ✳

Sarah used all of the strategies to tackle her negative self-talk about learning to ride. She found that turning one positive statement into a mantra, which she repeated over and over, had the effect of blocking her negative thoughts. She also discovered that as she became less absorbed in her negative mental processes she was able to focus more of her mental activity on riding the horse. Her thoughts changed from low to high willpower, and her hope increased substantially.

Your assignment in this chapter is to keep a record of your negative self-talk, first in the book you carry with you, and then on the form provided in this workbook. Practice the strategies in this chapter and you will find your willpower increasing just as Sarah's did.

In chapter 11, you will learn to increase your willpower thinking even further by visualizing your goals. You will also learn about the advantages of finding high-willpower people who have accomplished goals similar to yours, with whom you can identify and from whom you can learn.

Self-talk Record

Goal/Situation   **Self-talk**

11

Imagine Yourself

Previously in this section, you were introduced to a variety of ways to increase both your waypower and your willpower. Beginning with the concept of holism, that there is a connection between the mind and the body, you were encouraged to examine your lifestyle and apply techniques to enhance your physical energy. You learned about health habits that would help you build a reservoir of stamina, from which to draw as you pursued your goals. To increase your willpower thinking, you kept a record of your negative self-talk. You learned ways to redefine situations, change negative thoughts into positive ones, appraise your existing skills, and practice each step along the way. By combining the strategies that work best for you from both the waypower group and the willpower group, you will see an increase in your overall hope.

Reminders

A few of the guidelines you have learned so far are worth repeating here. Consider each strategy that you tackle as a goal to be accomplished. While your large goal is to increase hope, implementing each of the techniques constitutes a somewhat smaller goal. Each step you master while acquiring these new habits constitutes an even smaller step on the path to your large goal—enhanced hope. *The first reminder is to break your goals down into small, manageable steps.* We have made this point time and again throughout this workbook.

The second reminder is to start with small steps, working up gradually to larger ones. Focus only on the small goals you're working on and don't allow yourself to be distracted by all the other things you will have to do to reach the larger goal. The ability to focus your energy on the task at hand is the third reminder. Focusing increases your willpower, and allows you to reach your goal faster. High-hope people know how to direct their energy and exclude other distractions.

The third reminder is that all important changes take time to accomplish. If you don't see immediate results, be patient. You have spent years establishing your health and wellness habits as well your habits of thought. You cannot expect these to change quickly, and to have that expectation is to court negative results. High-hope people have learned patience and know that for changes to last, they must be acquired slowly. In modern time, people are in hurry—fast foods, convenience stores, etc.—but acquiring hope is not something that is purchased at the convenience store.

Enhancing your hope should be a pleasurable process. Learning ways to heighten your physical energy and incorporating more positive habits of thought into your existing system need not be a struggle—you are not making drastic changes. Goal setting, finding ways to accomplish what you want, and then doing it are such basic parts of life—which means that you have more skills than you may think. This workbook shows you how to enhance the skills you already have, and to focus your actions and thoughts in directions that will increase your life satisfaction. *The fifth reminder is that you already have the basic skills of waypower and willpower thinking.*

About the New Strategies

In this chapter, daydreaming, visualization, and modeling are added to your reserve of hope-enhancing strategies. Through your daydreams you will discover which goals are the most important to you, and you will learn to increase both your waypower and your willpower by visualizing yourself meeting these goals. You will also learn to observe others who have successfully accomplished the things you want to do. These role models demonstrate your goals in action. From noticing the specific things these successful people do, you can tailor many of your own behaviors to increase your chances for success. These strategies, detailed in the next pages, are established methods for enhancing hope and promoting effectiveness in reaching your dreams.

When you are asked to visualize yourself pursuing an objective, you will see yourself in your mind's eye taking the necessary steps for success. The actions you visualize will be the actual steps you would take as you work for your goal. Daydreaming adds an element of wishful thinking to your picture. Dayderams often have a bad reputation as sort of silly, lightweight constructions that people indulge in when they are bored or have too much time on their hands. On the contrary, we believe that daydreaming is a normal part of successful goal-directed thought. Daydreams are creative endeavors in which you can envision yourself doing virtually anything. Both are valuable and play a role in the enhancement of hope.

Modeling is an established method of learning that people use throughout their lives. For example, learning to dance is almost impossible without someone to show you the steps. Learning to speak a foreign language requires that you hear someone else pronounce the words. Your life is replete with examples of things you have learned to do through watching and listening to those who already knew how to do them. Interestingly, most people are not even very aware of the process of modeling, though it's an important tool you can use to learn hopeful thought. If you can learn such a variety of new skills through modeling, why not add that method to those you already employ for enhancing your hope?

Dream a Little Dream

Daydreams are your opportunities to discover what you would like to do if you had no limitations. Your images don't have to be realistic, and you need not .be constrained by a lack of money, education, beauty, or any of the other "advantages" you can think of. Engaging in daydreams is pleasurable, and it can be healthy—unless it takes the place of living in the real world. In our work with clients, we sometimes ask, "What would you like to do, if you could do anything?" The answers rarely reflect the impossible. In fact, they usually contain the seeds of possibilities that can grow into realistic goals. This type of question taps into the daydreams people have but don't share with others.

Daydreaming helps you to identify the goals you really want but may be reluctant to pursue.

You can ask yourself this question in many situations. For example, if you have a problem, ask yourself, "If I could solve this however I wanted, how would that be?" If you cannot decide what choice you should make, ask yourself, "If I could make any choice I wanted, which would it be?" The purpose of tapping into your true desires is to clear away the roadblocks that you imagine will stop you, so that you can see the goal you really want.

Do you allow yourself to daydream? Perhaps you discard your daydreams as simple fantasies that have no relevance to your daily life. If you daydream, do you share these secret goals with others? Or, do you keep them to yourself, believing that they are impossible to achieve? Examine your dreams for the elements that might come true, and ask yourself what you really want your goal to be. The story of Miranda illustrates how powerful a daydream can be and how one important question brought it to light.

✳ Miranda—Rock Bottom but Climbing

She was only twenty-two years old, but she already had three young children and a crack habit she hadn't been able to shake. Miranda received Aid to Dependent Children because she was a single parent with no way to support her family. She had no skills and no education, having dropped out of school in the tenth grade. Miranda's family, with the exception of an aging aunt, lived in another city, too far away to be of any help. Although her aunt took care of the children on occasion, the older woman was not well and it was not a satisfactory arrangement.

When I first met Miranda, she had just been admitted to a chemical-dependency rehabilitation program. Her treatment was mandated by Social and Rehabilitation Services because she had used her children's welfare money to buy drugs. During our first interview Miranda was hostile and resistant to treatment. As the days wore on, however, and as the drugs wore off, Miranda and I developed a congenial relationship. She began to open up and share her dreams.

She often mentioned that she didn't want to be on welfare. She thought it was demeaning, but she also felt trapped. Having quit school when she was pregnant with her first child had left her at a disadvantage she had been paying for ever since. I asked her, "If you could have your life the way you want it to be, what would it be like?"

I expected that she might say something about getting rich quickly, or meeting a man to save her from her troubles. Instead, she gave the question serious thought and replied that she wanted to be able to support her children and not use drugs anymore. Her dream career was to be a secretary. She had a lot of strikes against her, certainly, but her goal was not impossible. Her answer gave us a place to begin planning her future.

Miranda was taking the first step toward reaching her goal by being in treatment for her drug addiction. The program she was in was good, and if she followed the guidelines and stayed motivated, she had a chance of success. The route to becoming a secretary and earning enough money to support her children, however, was not so clearly defined. But there were ways to reach her goal—they just had to be discovered.

Miranda and I worked out a plan that had a number of steps to reach her goal. The first step was for her to study for, and pass, the General Educational Development test so that she would have the equivalent of a high-school diploma. This step actually required a number of smaller steps, such as locating the test site and determining the bus route, both of which she accomplished while in treatment. The next larger step was to discuss with her social worker what funds were available for secretarial training. With that successfully done, she would need to locate a secretarial school and make an application. Finally, if she were accepted, she would need to arrange for child care and then begin her program of study.

When we began charting her course, Miranda was dubious about her success. As she obtained more information, however, she became increasingly excited and eager to begin. At times I would ask her to envision herself going through each step. This technique not only gave her confidence but helped her to identify any steps about which she felt anxious. When she felt uncertain about what she would do or how she would cope, we were able to discuss that step in greater detail. Although there were setbacks, Miranda was finally able to achieve her goal, a dream which might never have materialized if the critical question about her future had not been asked.

As Miranda's story shows, dreams are important sources of information about your true desires. Ask yourself what you really want to have happen in the area you're contemplating and then allow yourself to dream. Write you dream down or discuss it with someone you trust. Consider ways you might make your dream come true; it may be more achievable than you think. This leads to our next step—imagining yourself taking the steps necessary to reach your goal.

Visualize Yourself . . .

When you decide on a goal, how clearly do you envision yourself succeeding? If your goal were to make a birthday cake, can you visualize what it will look like when it's finished? Can you see people eating and enjoying it? Perhaps your guests comment on how pretty it is and how delicious it tastes. Or, perhaps your goal is to buy a new car. You may imagine yourself driving a number of cars, until you find the one that suits you best. When you have a clear image of the cake or the car, you can begin to take the steps required to achieve the final goal.

If you did not use a visualization process to some extent, your actions would be unfocused. For example, without mentally trying out different cars, you might have to test drive hundreds of makes and models before you found the right one. Visualizing yourself driving first one type of car, and then another, helps you narrow the field and helps focus your attention on the features you actually want.

Without visualization, your goals will remain unfocused.

Some of the goals you achieve each day are routine and you may not be aware of visualizing them. You may not imagine yourself taking a shower or brushing your teeth, but you probably visualize how you want to look and what you will wear. At times, these small goals can be problematic and visualization can help. On those mornings when you're having trouble getting out of bed, try imagining yourself going through your morning routine. After a few minutes of "mentally" getting yourself around, you will find that you actually become energized to get up and get going. This simple experiment, which you can try, shows that visualizing yourself in action has the effect of revving your motor and getting you ready to go.

In addition to energizing you for the tasks ahead, visualization clarifies your goals. If you cannot envision the goal clearly, and see yourself achieving it, your chances for success are diminished. The more often you imagine your goal and see yourself in action, the more real it will become.

Another purpose for visualizing is to help you troubleshoot, that is, discover roadblocks that may lie ahead. As you see yourself taking the steps to reach your objective, you can spot problems that may come up. Let's use the example again of visualizing yourself getting ready for work. You may envision all the steps going smoothly until you realize that you haven't planned what to wear. At that point you can mentally review your options and decide on the outfit, all from the cozy comfort of your bed. When you get up and follow your envisioned steps, you will not encounter any surprises—perhaps even no surprises at all because you've thought it through in your mind's eye.

Visualizing your large goals is especially important for success. With a long-range, larger goal, there will be many small steps and many opportunities for unexpected hindrances to occur. Visualizing the steps and charting your course in writing as you learned in chapter 7, helps you to be prepared for the road ahead. The story of Rachael illustrates the way visualization helped bring together an unfocused collection of goals and pointed her in a direction that eventually led to success.

✳ Rachael—Focused on Success

You may think that having a Ph.D. and working in a large university is the be-all and end-all of success. Let me tell you, in some ways it's only the beginning. When I went through graduate school, the route to success was clearly defined. There were few choices for me to make because the classes I had to take were predetermined. As long as I made good grades, passed the comprehensive examination, wrote a dissertation, and completed an internship, I was certain to achieve my goal.

When I finished my training I was offered a tenure track position at an excellent state university. Once I obtained tenure I would have job security, so that became my next goal. The road to tenure was not as clearly defined, however, as the path to the Ph.D. To begin with, more duties were expected, and the way to succeed in each of these tasks was not always clear. For example, I had several undergraduate courses to teach every semester. Each aspect of the course, the content, the textbook, the teaching method, even how grades would be assigned, was totally my decision. The teaching I had done as a doctoral student had given me some preparation, but a professor who was responsible for those choices had always supervised me.

Serving on committees was another duty required in order to be awarded tenure. Again, the expectations were not clearly defined. How many committees did I need? Which ones were the best? How important was committee work in the overall picture? When I asked my colleagues, everyone had different answers. This certainly was not as clear as was graduate school. I remember as a graduate student fully expecting my professional career to be far simpler. Oh, how wrong I was!

One thing became clear very early on—publishing was the most important aspect of obtaining tenure. I had been a research assistant throughout most of my doctoral training, and I enjoyed scientific projects. My dissertation had been based on my advisor's ideas, and it seemed that now I needed to develop some theories of my own. I had a lot of good ideas, perhaps too many. I spent my first year pursuing one notion and then another, never following through with any of them. It felt like I was spinning my wheels . . . and I was. As anyone knows, spinning wheels don't get you anywhere at all.

During the summer between my first and second year as an assistant professor, a colleague gave me a manuscript of a book he had written that was about to be published. I began reading it and was captivated by its message. Here was a theory I could envision using to research ideas of my own. This theory could be helpful to people with many different problems. Finally, I had a way to focus my ideas and develop an ongoing program of research.

There were so many ideas to investigate, and I felt energized and eager to begin. My colleague was also excited at the prospect of these research ideas and instructed me to write them all down. He advised me to select the ones that were most interesting to me as our starting point. Once I had made the selection, he encouraged me to visualize not only the end result, but also each of the things that I would have to do to get there. Each aspect of the research design was clearly spelled out in my mind, as well as on paper. I could see myself carrying out each step along the way, from testing the subjects to the final published document.

My visualizations kept me motivated and helped me to anticipate potential problems. The first research project was a success and was only the beginning of many more. My colleague's advice was good, and together we designed projects that were interesting to both of us.

※

Rachael had the goal of becoming tenured, but she had a difficult time envisioning a clear path to achieve that goal. She knew that, although teaching and committee service were somewhat important, publishing research was what counted most. When Rachael began to focus on an interesting research project, she could see the steps that she would need to take more clearly. The process of promotion and tenure finally became manageable. Essentially, Rachael had been focusing on the large goal and ignoring the smaller goals in between. When she could see the smaller goals, she could visualize herself taking each step as it came.

Visualizing yourself moving along the path to your goal is the best way to inform your actions. As you go through each step mentally, you can often foresee problems and make necessary corrections in advance. If you've never pursued your selected goal, however, how do you know what the path will be like? One way is to observe someone else who has done what you wish to accomplish. Seeing how someone else has reached the goal provides you with a role model on which you can base your own actions.

Modeling—A Basic Method of Learning

How do babies learn to talk? How do children learn to write their names? How do teenagers learn to dress the way they do? More behaviors than you can imagine are learned from watching or hearing others do them first. Think of the various things you have learned through the years from watching or listening to others. Perhaps you learned to sing, draw, or play a musical instrument. Think of the many skills that you have. Perhaps you sew or knit, do woodworking, or even change the oil in your car. Someone probably showed you how to do these things when you were first learning.

The things you have learned in the past will help you learn new things in the future.

If you are learning something that is totally new for you, you will almost certainly need to have an idea of how it should be when you are finished. The idea that you carry in your mind is a type of model. To illustrate this point, let's use the cooking example. If you are trying a recipe that you've never made before, you must have a general idea of how it will look and taste when it's finished, otherwise you won't know if you were successful. While you don't need a chef watching your movements in order to produce the new dish, you do need an information source. In this case, the source is your own previous cooking experience, as well as all the foods you have eaten.

When you select a new goal, here are some questions to ask yourself before you proceed:

- Is this goal brand new to me, or have I done similar things before?

- If it is new, how will I determine what steps to take?

- If I have done things similar to the things required for my new goal, what information and skills did I learn in the past that will help me now?

If your goal is unlike anything you have done before, and if you have no related skills or information to use, you will need an example to show you the way—a role model.

Learning new behaviors from others who have special abilities is a smart technique, even if you have some familiarity with the task at hand. When you observe people who are very good at what they do, see what you can learn from their actions. Avoid becoming jealous—that just makes it very hard to learn from the other person because your jealousy may cause you to want to find faults in that person. It's perfectly normal, healthy, and hope-inducing to admire another person's skills and talents, and other people enjoy serving as role models. After all, imitation *is* the sincerest form of praise. Such admiration opens the door to your learning from this other person. And, you will note that your role model may be quite delighted to teach you. Note the special qualities that make them outstanding, and then practice these until they become natural for you to use. Learning a sport like horseback riding is an example where modeling is useful. Verbal instruction gives you some information about using your hands and how to sit, but seeing an expert demonstrate these skills is far more meaningful. The expert provides an example you can imitate—this is what modeling is all about.

Not all learning through the observation of role models involves physical activity. It is also possible to learn new ways to speak, even to think, from others who inspire you. Most actors or newscasters, for example, have learned to speak without regional accents, no matter where they were originally from. Learning a professional role, such as being a doctor or a lawyer, is also done largely through modeling. Let's go to medical school next and follow Erin as she learns to ne a physician.

☀ Erin—Baby Doc

Becoming a doctor was not a life-long dream for me like it is for many people. In fact, I'd planned on being a physicist or a mathematician until the thought of helping people in pain and suffering began to seem like a better goal. I came from a family of college professors and lawyers and being a doctor was an unfamiliar professional role. I realized quickly, however, that learning the doctor's role would be no problem.

From the first day of medical school we were encouraged by our professors to feel and behave like doctors. The year began with a ceremony at which we were each given our white coats. Just days into the coursework, we were each assigned to work with a preceptor—a physician who teaches the student to be a doctor.

I was very lucky to get my preceptor, because he believed in giving his students a great deal of responsibility. His teaching philosophy was to show me what to do and then have me do it. The first day I watched as he gave a young man a physical examination. The next patient was an older man, and I was instructed to do his examination. With each new type of procedure, my preceptor modeled what was done, and then I learned by imitating his behavior. This "see one, do one" is our mantra for learning.

The entire medical school experience strikes me as one of learning to act like a doctor. In the emergency room, patients respond to me as if I were already a fully trained physician even though the identification I wear says that I am a student. In the free clinic where I see indigent patients two weekends each month, I'm given the responsibility for initial diagnosis and determining the necessary treatment. Of course, a licensed physician makes the final determination and writes the prescriptions. The patients, however, do not care that my name-tag says "student": they respond to me as if I were the doctor.

When we aren't seeing patients, we are in classrooms or laboratories learning basic information about the human body. It's clear, however, that one of the most important parts of medical school is learning to act the part of a doctor, and I'm learning to do this by watching and emulating what I see. It is no coincidence that, from the first day of medical school, they do not call us "students," but rather, "baby docs."

※

Erin's experience demonstrates the adoption of a career role through the observation and modeling of others who are successful in the profession. Role modeling is a valuable and necessary component of achievement in most occupations, as it is for success in many other life arenas. In order to have succeeded in college and mastered the science courses for medical school, Erin had to be strong in both waypower and willpower. How then can the modeling technique help you to increase either component of hope, if you start out as a low-hope person?

An established observation in psychology is that your thoughts or beliefs will change to become consistent with the actions you take. The song "I Whistle a Happy Tune" from *The King and I* is a good example of this point. If you pretend you are not afraid, and whistle a happy tune, you will find you really aren't afraid after all.

In social psychological research there are a number of studies demonstrating that people's attitudes about others or about situations are influenced by the way they behave. To illustrate this, imagine that you must give a speech to a large group of people, and that you're very anxious about your performance. Your low-hope belief is that you will not do a good job and that it will be a negative experience. If you will "pretend" to be a competent, self-assured speaker, you will find that you can deliver a self-assured speech. If you have watched other people deliver excellent speeches to large audiences, you may find yourself "role-playing," as if *you* were one of those speakers. In order to do that, you will emulate their style of delivery, mannerisms, and so on. Even though you had low hope about your public-speaking abilities in the beginning, if you use the technique of modeling to achieve your goal, your hope in that area will be enhanced.

Modeling is a technique that can be used to great effect in many areas of your life, for long-range as well as smaller, short-range goals. Much of what you already know how to do has been learned through the observation of others. To use this valuable learning strategy to enhance your hope now, you must purposely identify other individuals who demonstrate the skills you want to acquire, observe them closely, and then emulate the things they do that have led them to achieve the goal.

The story of Toni is an illustration of the effectiveness of modeling, as well as daydreaming and visualizing, in helping an individual reach a long-range goal—going to college and becoming a nurse.

✳ Toni—Achieving a Lifelong Dream

My name is Antonia—Toni for short. I'm now in my third year of college and plan to become a nurse, which is a dream I have had for a long time. Getting to this point has not been easy. I was born in Mexico, but my family moved to California when I was a baby. We moved to East Los Angeles, to the barrio, where nearly everyone was Mexican, poor, and uneducated. No one in my family had ever considered going to college, and the teachers I had were not especially encouraging about my chances for success.

I worked hard, though, and I made good grades in high school. Sometimes I think it is an achievement just to have graduated from high school, because most of my friends dropped out. When I graduated, my father wanted me to get a job and help support the younger children, and it was difficult to make him understand that being a nurse was better in the long run. I'm still not certain that anyone in my family understands why I want to do this.

I have even asked myself why I would want to become a nurse, but I know where I first got the dream. When I was a young child I had a series of ear infections and other ailments. My mother took me to a clinic for treatment, and there was a wonderful nurse who saw me every time we visited. I remember her as beautiful and young, and she spoke Spanish, so she could talk to my mother and me. I knew then that when I grew up I wanted to be just like she was.

Of course, I didn't know then how difficult becoming a nurse would be, especially for someone with my background. I worked hard in school and made good grades, and when I applied for college I was able to get a scholarship. But that was only the beginning.

Nothing in my previous schooling, and certainly not in my family, had prepared me for the role of a college student in a nursing program. To begin with, the course material was much more difficult than anything I had ever encountered before. To cope with the deficiencies in my knowledge I took advantage of a tutoring program designed for people like me. That helped, but I continued to feel out of place and inadequate. Somehow, I just didn't belong.

When I envisioned being a nurse, I saw myself doing the things my early role model had done. But what I needed at this point was a role model for becoming a nurse, not already being one. To find the model I needed, I observed the other students until I found one particular girl who seemed to be admired by students and professors alike. She dressed and acted in a professional manner, and when she spoke in class it was with a self-assurance that I envied.

I decided to emulate as much about her as I could. She wore dark-colored skirts or slacks and white blouses, which I began to wear also. Her hair was always pulled back in a ponytail or a twist, instead of the long loose curls that I wore, so I changed that too. With each adjustment I made to my appearance I began to feel more professional. The next step was to learn to sound self-confident when I spoke.

This was more difficult than changing the way I dressed, and it required a closer and more detailed observation of my role model in order to identify the elements that signified self-assurance. After observing her for a few weeks, I noticed that she spoke fairly often in class, where I spoke very seldom. She also spoke with a louder voice than the soft one I used. I observed that, where I tended to sit in the back of the class, she sat in the first or second row, always appearing attentive to the lecturer. And finally, I saw that she smiled often, which gave her a friendly and approachable look.

I began slowly to emulate each of the details that I observed my role model doing. Sometimes things were uncomfortable, such as sitting at the front of the class rather than remaining anonymous in the back. But I took each step slowly until I could do as my role model did and feel comfortable with the changes. At this point, in my third year, I feel good about myself, and I can envision even more clearly the way I will be as a nurse.

While Toni was not an extremely low-hope person, it would have been very easy for her to abandon her goal and get a job after high school. She had a dream, however, that drove her to achieve something more. Throughout her life, she envisioned herself in the shoes of the nurse who had impressed her when she was a child. Once in college, she needed a model to help her learn her new role in life, that of being a successful student. Nothing in Toni's daily environment had prepared her to be what she wanted to become, and her role model helped her envision the steps to her goal.

Putting It All Together

In this chapter you have added three new techniques to your reserve of hope-enhancing strategies. Daydreaming, visualizing, and modeling are skills you already possess. The task is to learn to apply these techniques purposefully and for your specific goals. Each story in this chapter depicts an individual who is using these techniques with knowledge and forethought, and in each case the strategies have added to the individual's success.

As this section concludes, remember that for the most effective hope enhancement you must do each assignment and practice the new habits until they become part of your everyday routine. Remember that this will take time. Important changes will not last if they are made quickly. You need to start with small goals, focus on each thing you are doing, and practice patience with yourself.

Section III addresses the need for hope enhancement in specific groups: women, men, ethnic minorities, the elderly, and the physically disabled. Individuals in these groups often encounter unique situations that can severely diminish hope. The next chapters describe many of those situations and show how hope can alleviate their negative effects.

SECTION III

Hope for Special Groups

In section I, you learned about hope and how to measure it in yourself. You discovered that writing about your life was one way to tap into your current level of hope, and that examining your family background gave you even more information. You remembered family stories, writing them down, and looking for the hope markers they revealed. These exercises gave you a background from which you could determine any changes in your thinking and behavior that you wished to make.

In section II, you learned a number of strategies to enhance your hope. You were given suggestions for improving your physical well-being and thereby increasing the energy reserves you have to draw upon when working for your goals. You were shown how to restructure your thoughts and the automatic messages you use so that you can infuse your life with positive self-talk. We also advocated daydreaming, visualizing, and using role models as efficacious methods of increasing your hope.

Each of these strategies should be undertaken in small steps and with patience. You already have the basics of hope, but enhancing your hope through the introduction of positive changes will take time and practice. Treat each strategy as an objective that you set out to accomplish. Tackle each new step after you've become comfortable with the previous step. Paradoxically, you are using the strategies to learn the strategies. Work on them, and they will become your own.

In section III, we address the need for, and application of, hope enhancement in specific groups. While there are a number of groups that could have been chosen, we have selected several that encompass a large number of individuals. The section begins with a chapter on gender and addresses the issues of men and women that can diminish hope. Next, there is a chapter about the needs for hope enhancement in ethnic minorities. The ethnicities chosen are African American, Latino, Native American, and Asian American, because those groups encompass most of the ethnic population in the United States. The last chapter in this section deals with the elderly. Because of problems that multiply with aging, it can be easy to lose sight of the hope process. There are numerous facets to each group which could be discussing points of departure for hope. We have chosen the areas of role expectations and stereotypes because these concepts include experiences that are common for many of the members of each group. For example, the role expectations of being female dictate which behaviors are appropriate and limit the choices for many women. If you are a member of a minority group, the stereotypes and perceptions held about members of your race may limit your possibilities and serve to diminish your hope. If you are elderly, the views and expectations for people of your age can have subtle and sometimes not-so-subtle influences on your life.

As you read about these groups and the individual stories that emerge, remember that each tale is about a specific person and is not meant to represent all of the individuals within that group. Some generalizations are necessary whenever groups of people are the topic of discussion. It is impossible to represent all of the unique detail embodied by individuals in a group. As you read this information and the various hope narratives, however, you probably will find individuals with whom you can identify and through them you can begin to see ways to enhance your own hope.

12

Gender and Hope

Women and men share many events in the normal course of life, but the actual experience of these events is different for each gender. One might argue that each person experiences life in a unique way, and of course that would be correct. It is also a fact, however, that there are different experiences, based on whether you are a man or a woman, that can be generalized to other individuals within the given gender group. Some of these gender-based experiences can have a powerful impact—positively or perhaps negatively—on your hope. This chapter details some of those experiences, specifically how you have learned to be a man or a woman, and the effects that these gender lessons may have had on your own level of hope. True stories help to illustrate the points, and perhaps you will recognize yourself in some of the narratives.

A Woman's Place

The women's movement that began twenty-five years ago, as well as the civil rights movement of the past fifty years, brought the role of women and minorities into the public arena with dramatic consequences. Legislation was passed making discrimination on the basis of gender, ethnicity, age, or physical disability an illegal act punishable by a loss of federal funding. Until these powerful movements, however, the public often ignored the social conditions of these groups. Currently, controversy reigns about how much change actually has occurred in the daily lives of individuals in these groups.

If you are a woman, your life is no doubt vastly different than that of your mother and even more different than that of your grandmother. Not only do you have access to machines that free you from many of the time-consuming household chores with which they once had to contend, but you have other types of freedoms as well. Many women work outside the home, either by choice or necessity. More women prepare for professional positions such as law and medicine, or hold important jobs in industry and commerce. Women are found in virtually all careers that formerly were available only to men.

As a woman, you have many more options available to you than your mother or grand-mother did, so use your options to enhance your hope.

Along with these freedoms, however, are different problems and concerns than those that your mother and grandmother experienced. At one time it was expected that a woman's aspirations for a life-career choice were remarkably simple—wife and mother. Women's work was in the home, rearing children and keeping house. If women worked outside the home, the work was usually temporary, and considered a "job" rather than a "career." How has this situation changed? How have the changes affected the potential for hope in women?

The changes that have occurred over the past thirty or forty years have affected the potential choices available to many women, *but the expectation that women will continue to be the mainstay of home and family is still present.* Many women put in what is termed "the double day," indicating that they work a full day at work outside the home, and then a full day of housework and child care once they get home. For women trapped in the double day, choices are as limited as their mothers' and grandmothers' options had been. Whenever choices are experienced as limited, there is the possibility of low hope.

Your age group influences the options you can envision in your life. If you were raised in the 1940s or 1950s, a baby boomer, chances are you have been influenced by the traditional role expectations for women. Women of this generation were taught that their worth was determined by their success in relationships with men. Achievement was to marry well and to have a happy family. Women were expected to devote their lives to their husbands and children and having a career was considered self-serving.

The process of discovering that your sense of self-worth comes from you and not through others is a difficult and often painful journey. With a divorce rate of around 50 percent, many women who might have elected to remain married are put in the position of discovering their worth outside of the role of wife. While this can be an opportunity for renewal and personal growth, there is frequently a great deal of grief and anger to be overcome before progress can be made. Learning to be alone and to find a personal identity that is not the reflection of someone else is a difficult but worthy goal.

Not all baby boomers divorce, of course, but even if you have remained married and have spent your adult life raising children, the "empty nest" may prompt you to reconsider your personal worth and your future goals. You may find yourself seeking hobbies or volunteer work outside the home. You may decide to go back to school to develop a new career, to pick up where you left off before you got married. Whatever your choices, you will need high hope to achieve your goals.

You may be a stay-at-home mother and experiencing challenges that may diminish your hope. The role of wife and mother carries with it the expectation that you will devote your energy to the care of others. While meeting the needs of others can be highly satisfying, you may find that you experience guilt when you take time away to meet your own needs. Learning to cope with the guilt that you have internalized through generations of traditional role expectations is a first step in raising your level of hope.

Learning to be an independent woman is an often painful but worthwhile journey.

If you are a young woman just entering adulthood, you may be freer of some of the traditional role constrictions, but your role identity may not be as clearly defined as it was for your mother. You have more choices from the outset, but you may still feel the pressures to incorporate the traditional role with a career. If you decide not to marry, or if you marry and decide not to have children, you are very likely to experience pressures from parents who want grandchildren. The challenge for you may be to do it all, to have a home and family as well as a career. Unless you and your partner have a truly equal approach to housework and child rearing, the decision to do it all frequently leads to the double day.

For women of any age who decide to pursue careers there are special concerns that have an impact on hope. Even though much progress has been made in the area of equality for women in the workplace, men continue to fill more high level positions than do women, and men in all types of jobs are paid more for their work than are women. Affirmative action laws have done a great deal to further equality in both hiring and work conditions, but there is still a long way to go. Knowing this and experiencing it firsthand can make sustaining high hope difficult.

The majority of women who work are not in a position to choose between a career or home and family. Economic conditions have dictated that two income earners are necessary for the family to succeed financially. Therefore, many women hold either part-time or full-time jobs for which they did not necessarily plan. If you are in that situation, you are among the majority of American women. You may be lucky enough to be engaged in work that is satisfying and interesting, but the chances are that what you do is just "a job," with little or no prospects for the future. If you find yourself going through each day longing for quitting time, and if you are too exhausted after work to do the things you would enjoy, you may be on a low-hope track.

Expectations and Demands as Challenges to Women's Hope

Not all challenges to hope in women involve work and career identities, of course. Women have other pressures that impact hope, such as maintaining their youth and attractiveness. A woman's worth may not be based as much on whether she has romantic partners or is married as it once was, but there continues to be pressure on her to achieve nearly impossible standards of beauty. Do you find yourself fighting the weight battle? Are you satisfied with your hair, your complexion, or your features? The battle of keeping up appearances can place a strain on hope, especially if you do not believe you are winning.

If you are a woman, the difficulties of developing high hope and of maintaining it often are rooted in society's long-standing attitudes about women. In many subtle ways, and despite the gains that have been made, women still have less status than men. When you are examining the messages that you have been taught as a child, especially the ones that have influenced your self-talk, look for the subtle indications that girls are less important and perhaps less intelligent or competent than boys.

Low hope can be rooted in traditional sex-role expectations that can limit your choices.

Such discouraging messages are not necessarily communicated by parents—there are many other sources from whom you may have learned negative beliefs about being female. Teachers, for example, may call on boys more often than girls for answers in class. Another example is when adults praise boys for their intelligence, while commenting on girls' attractiveness. These are not-so-subtle messages that communicate the superior intelligence and competence of boys. If you are struggling with low hope, make a ca4reful inventory of your beliefs about women in general and yourself in particular. Identify, if possible, where you developed the beliefs you have. Do these messages tell you that you are capable? Or, perhaps they encourage you to be passive and not try for large achievements.

Our point is that even though the place of women in society has changed over the past thirty years, there continue to be messages that discourage high-hope behavior. If you have dreams and goals that you have not pursued, and if you feel mildly or greatly dissatisfied with the way your life has gone, developing your waypower and your willpower will help you reach your objectives.

How Do You Regard Your Gender?

An important starting place is to examine your views of women. Do you generally hold men in greater regard than you do women? Do you believe that certain professions, such as law or medicine, are best practiced by men? Do you generally seek the advice of men over women? If your answers are "yes" to any of these questions, it's likely that you do not hold your own gender in high regard.

As a woman, you must consider how your beliefs affect your thoughts and feelings about yourself. You may hesitate to set high goals, you may not see many routes to your goals, and you may lack the mental energy to go after what you want. In other words, your internalized attitudes about your role as a woman may have contributed to your low hope.

In section 1, you wrote stories about yourself as a way of discovering where the self-talk that influenced your hope level originated. You may not have considered your gender self-talk previously. However, you do have thoughts and beliefs about your role as a woman, and those beliefs influence what you perceive yourself as being able to do. These perceptions can be empowering or disabling, but remember, they are perceptions. You might, for example, believe that as a woman you could be a nurse but not a neurosurgeon. You might believe that you could be a school teacher but not a physicist. In reality, at present there are a few women who are physicists and neurosurgeons, but there are many more who are nurses and teachers. The point is to identify your *perceptions* in order to discover how these beliefs may have affected your hope.

Your assignment is to write a story about yourself becoming a woman, and here are some points to serve as guidelines. Search your memory for answers to the following questions. The answers will help you examine the limitations you may experience now as you select goals and enhance your hope.

1. What messages did you get, directly or indirectly, from your parents or other significant people in your life, that told you how to be a woman?

2. What were the peer pressures you felt as you began to become a woman?

3. What behaviors did you engage in that were rewarded?

4. What behaviors were either ignored or punished in some way?

5. What influence did your gender have on your life plans?

Here is the story of Linda, a fifty-year-old woman who has a successful career as a teacher. She recounts what it was like to grow up as a woman in the 1940s and 1950s.

✳ Linda—The Tomboy

I was born in 1946, just as World War II was ending. My mother had worked for a few years in an airplane plant while my father was in the Navy. When they were reunited, they decided it was time to have children. I was born first, followed quickly by a brother and sister.

My mother always said she was glad to be able to stay at home and raise us; she hadn't liked working on airplanes very much, although the pay was good. When my father got out of the Navy, he went back to his job as an insurance salesman, which meant he traveled quite a bit. My mother didn't like the times he was gone, although she was able to carry on quite well without him.

She probably would have had an easier time dealing with his absences if I had been more ladylike. The truth is, I was a tomboy to the core. I hated playing with dolls and having tea parties. I wanted to play "war" in the vacant lot with the boys on my block. I wore shorts or jeans when the other girls were wearing dresses, and my hair was always in long braids rather than hanging down in curls. In school I was always the captain of the kick ball team, and I loved to play softball and touch football.

I remember my mother clucking over my skinned knees and muddy clothes, telling me I should act like a girl. She said I was not setting a good example for my younger sister, but I didn't care—I was having too much fun. When I was in the sixth grade, however, and we saw a movie about menstruation, my life began to change.

We girls did a lot of whispering amongst ourselves about how our bodies were going to change and what we might look like. Some of my friends got brassieres, had their ears pierced, and began shaving their legs. I wasn't ready to give up my tomboy clothes, but if I were to continue being popular, I knew I would have to start dressing more like a girl. My mother was delighted! She took me shopping and acted as if I were a new doll she had just been given.

One of the changes I could see was that boys were beginning to act differently toward me. Boys with whom I used to play rough games no longer wanted to include me and acted as if they didn't want me around when I suggested things to do. It was time for me to start the process of becoming a woman, and that meant giving up many of the things I had really liked to do.

My adolescent hormones helped the process along when I began to get crushes on boys in my classes. My mother was more pleased when I got my first boyfriend than she was with the good grades I was getting on my math tests. When I overheard her bragging to my aunt about how popular I was with the boys, I understood that having boyfriends was very important. When I went to my first dance, my mother hovered over me, fixing my hair and putting on my makeup; you would have thought I was Cinderella.

When I joined a girls club that had monthly dances with the boys club, my mother spared no expense to buy me an assortment of pretty formal dresses. The message was clear: looking feminine and pretty was the most important thing I could do. I made good grades, and I was good in sports, but to my mother, it was my looks and my boyfriends that were praiseworthy.   ✳

Linda got the message loud and clear that being a girl meant being pretty and attracting boys. This was the hallmark of success for women of her generation, but are things so very different for women today? If you have any doubts, scan the magazine racks and notice the television commercials that crowd the airwaves. There are many products and a great deal of advice about how to look and how to please your man.

Looking pretty and being sexually attractive is a double bind, however. The prettier and more feminine you look, the less capable you are thought to be. The sexier you are, the more suspect are your successes. Did you get that promotion because you slept with the boss? Did you get that good grade because the professor liked to look at you? Even if you know your behavior was beyond reproach, you may come to doubt your own abilities and internalize the attitudes of others.

As capable and assertive as Linda had been as a child, the expectations of femininity and the behavior of others began to grind down her belief in herself. Let's continue with her story as she leads her adult life.

❋ Linda—The Young Educator

I did very well in high school by making good grades and of course having lots of dates. When I went to college and announced that I was going to major in mathematics, my mother was pleased because she thought I would meet many eligible men in that field. Her intention was that I should get the "Mrs." and not bother with the B.S. degree. My intention was otherwise. I wanted to teach math at the high school level, and I wasn't so concerned about getting married.

I had developed into a very attractive woman, and my appearance always drew attention from my male peers. I did nothing to diminish my looks, thinking that they should be an asset. What I found instead was that while all the men wanted to date me, none of them wanted to discuss math with me. At study groups where I was usually the only woman, the men all spoke to each other and seldom did they make eye contact with me. It was as if they didn't take me seriously. I began to think that perhaps I wasn't as intelligent as I had thought, or that I didn't have anything important to say.

Later, after I had graduated and was teaching, I met a young man, fell in love, and married. He was also a math teacher, and we were in the same department. At departmental meetings in our school, I had the same experience of being ignored that I had as an undergraduate. My husband told me it was my imagination, but I noticed that he usually addressed his comments to the other men. I concluded that either they thought I really didn't have anything worthwhile to say, or they were not in the habit of discussing math with a woman. Whatever the explanation was, I always left those meetings feeling unimportant, as if my presence just didn't make a difference.

❋

Linda was beginning to feel the subtle consequences of the behaviors of her male peers. Her second conclusion, that they were not in the habit of discussing math with a woman, was probably correct. These men were most likely unaware that they were not speaking to her, and if she had mentioned it, they would have been quite surprised. Her husband's surmise that it was her imagination was indicative of that stance. However, any woman who has been in a similar situation knows the debilitating effect being ignored can have, regardless of the intentions of others.

A first step in counteracting the negative effects of your own beliefs or the behaviors of others is recognition and understanding. Examine the way others have responded to you in your adult life, especially when you have pursued a goal that might not have been usual for a woman. At times, when you have stepped out of the gender-appropriate role, remember the comments and reactions of others. Write those responses down—they are the key to understanding how your hope has been influenced by your gender.

Linda became aware that her thoughts and feelings about her competence as a math teacher were being influenced by the reactions of her colleagues. She began to examine other areas of her life and discovered that she sometimes limited her own goals because she didn't think they were appropriate for a woman. For example, she had considered going back to school to get a Ph.D., but because her husband was against it, she abandoned that goal. She didn't think it was appropriate for a wife to be better educated and make more money than her husband. Let's continue with Linda's story as she moves into middle age.

※ Linda—An Equal

In the long run, I decided to go back to school and work on a master's degree with the possibility of getting a Ph.D. My husband decided that he would rather be married to someone who was not in his field, and so we got an amicable divorce. By the time all of this happened, our children were in high school and college, and I was free to do what I wanted with my life.

One of the first things I did was to join a support group for women who had recently been divorced. In that group, I met women who were articulate about their experiences, and who felt free to express their emotions. I found that I shared many common experiences with these women, and that gave me the courage to tell them what my life had been like. When I spoke, everyone looked at me and listened. When another person spoke, she made eye contact with each of us. After each group meeting I felt valued and respected, a feeling I was not used to having with my male colleagues.

My support group talked a great deal about men and about how to have good relationships while maintaining your own identity. There were women of all ages in the group, and this appeared to be a common problem for each of us. No one in the group was blaming men, nor were we angry. It was simply important to recognize what was happening and not allow ourselves to be diminished.

I decided to change my own behavior, and I set a goal of appearing to be more confident when in a group of male colleagues. I began speaking up and offering my opinions, whether or not anyone was looking at me. The more I participated in the discussions, the more the others began listening to me. I was not pushy, I just acted like an equal. After a few months, my colleagues got accustomed to my participation, and I felt included and respected.

❋

Linda's story illustrates many of the pressures and demands that being a woman can place on you. Linda was born into a generation in which the role of women was more traditional than it is at present, but many young women of today experience similar pressures. Having a career or working outside the home is now perfectly acceptable—60 percent of American women hold jobs. Combining a career and family is not easy, however, and constant choices must be made about which partner will perform which duty. When major choices must be made, it is still most often the man's work that takes precedence over the woman's. It's a rare man who chooses to be a house husband.

To determine the effect being a woman has had on the types of goals you have set in your life and how you envision your future, detail the messages you have gotten from the comments and behaviors of others. If you are not happy and satisfied with the goals you have set and achieved, determine whether the role you believe a woman should play is part of the reason. Have you imposed limitations on your goals because of your gender? If so, set a goal for yourself to understand the basis for your limiting beliefs and, as Linda did, find ways to counteract them. You will find that the more you understand about how you have learned to be the woman you are, the better equipped you will be to enhance your hope.

Men Need Hope, Too

The previous discussion has been about how the traditional gender roles for women can have a deleterious effect on hope. Men, of course, have traditional gender roles, and to a great extent those roles are even less flexible than those for women. The women's movement brought sex roles into prominence but did little to effect changes for men, for whom fixed roles also constitute a threat to high hope. Although a men's movement is beginning to attract some participants, it hasn't touched the lives of the majority of men, and the potential impact of the expectations placed on men is difficult to recognize.

There are generational differences in role expectations for men, just as there are for women. Generally speaking, the older you are, the more traditional your goals and choices will have been. If you are a baby boomer, even if you were influenced by the nontraditional 1960s, the chances are that you married and had children. Your wife may work, but you probably considered yourself the primary breadwinner. If you are a young man coming of age in the 1990s, you may expect to share household and child care responsibilities with your wife, who may have a career of her own. Even if you are in the young group, the chances are that you still experience pressure from your older relatives to have a more traditionally male life.

When you think of the term "manhood," what connotations does it hold? You may think of power, responsibility, success, or sexual prowess. Traditionally, adult men are expected to marry, have children, and support their families. In our culture, the type of home you have, the clothes you wear, and the car you drive—all external markers—are the usual measures of your success. In addition, you're supposed to be brave, physically strong, and emotionally contained. These expectations constitute a large order for a young man approaching adulthood.

The traditional role expectations of "manhood" can limit your choices, and thus, endanger high hope.

Just as girls are instructed on being women, boys are taught how to be "real men." From very early in your life you may have been told not to cry but instead to be brave. If you cried, you may have been called a sissy, or worse yet, a girl. If you played football or were in the military, your manhood was questioned if you did not perform up to expectations. The rules are specific, and breaking them can lead to humiliating consequences.

While each person experiences unique expectations about how to be successful, the common expectations for men carry a great deal of responsibility. As you were growing up, you probably heard messages about what type of job or career would be best, how much education you should get, and even how much money you should make. For most young men, the messages are unambiguous, and they carry with them a frightening amount of responsibility.

Your sexual prowess is another expectation that may place pressure on you. You are expected to have romantic relationships with women and, because you are a man, you are supposed to do the pursuing. Do you remember the agony of learning to ask someone for a date? Do you remember the fear of being turned down? You may have been shy, or perhaps you were not interested in dating—yet your identity as a man may have been dependent on your romantic success.

Although male sex roles are changing to some extent, it's important for you to determine how your beliefs about what is appropriate male behavior may be diminishing your hope. Write a story in which you describe the messages you heard about being a man as you were growing up. Think of specific incidents, if you can, in which significant people instructed you to be brave, strong, or not to show tender emotions. Remember the games you played, the books you read, even the messages in the music you liked. What did your parents tell you about your future? What did they want you to do? Which of your accomplishments got you the most praise? Which got ignored? How did your peer group influence you? The questions in the section on women's hope will also provide guidelines for you.

Darrin's narrative provides an example of growing up male in the 1980s. Although he is a young man, he was raised by conservative and traditional parents who believed that it is the man's responsibility to support his family.

✳ Darrin—All Boy

We could have been on television as the all-American family. My mother prided herself on being a model homemaker, and she excelled at all the domestic arts. My father, the breadwinner, was a successful business executive who provided well for his family. My brother and I played football and basketball, we were in Boy Scouts, and were even altar boys in our church. We did all the things that were expected of good, upstanding young men.

Busy as my father was, he managed to be involved in our activities. He came to all our sporting events and was the assistant Scout leader of our troop. It was during a meeting at which we were building our Pinewood Derby cars that I remember one important lesson on manhood that my father taught me. I had been using a sharp knife to whittle the wood on my car, when I cut myself quite deeply. I was frightened when I saw the blood covering my car, and I began to cry. My father's first response was to tell me not to cry and to act like a man. He became exasperated with me when I continued to whimper and told me that if I didn't stop he would give me something to cry about. I suppose I was more frightened of my father than the blood, so I managed to stop crying. That was a lesson I have remembered all my life.

It seemed as if all the men in my life were tough and strong. The coaches I had in middle school and high school yelled at us if we weren't playing hard enough, and even Father Thomas encouraged us to be stoic when life was hard. We were a rowdy group of boys, we played hard, teased each other, and when we got old enough we chased girls. The message I got was that strength, power, and loyalty were important. Being part of a group was also important, because it was from the group that we got our identity.

I made average grades in high school but that was alright with my father. I was on the football team and had become an Eagle Scout, and those were the things he admired. As long as my grades were good enough to get me into college, my parents were happy. ✳

Darrin was rewarded for playing sports and achieving in other action-oriented activities. He was threatened into containing his emotions, which proved to be a powerful lesson. Darrin's father, coach, and priest were his main role models and sources of information on how to become a man. As you write your narrative, describe your role models and the lessons they taught you.

The next phase of Darrin's life involved college and then the business world. The messages were similar to those he had received as a child, but as a young adult he was able to discard those that did not fit with what he wanted in life.

✳ Darrin—Student and Businessman

I decided to go to the state college near my home because that's where all my friends were going. I moved into a residence hall and went through rush to join a fraternity. Everyone I knew was joining a frat, so naturally I wanted to do that too. Because of all the social life, I nearly flunked out the first year, and my father really became angry. While it had been alright to do poorly in high school, it wasn't alright to make poor grades in college. Grades were suddenly more important than they had ever been, so I decided to buckle down.

The first thing I did was to stop going to the fraternity parties every weekend. There was always plenty of drinking, which meant that I wouldn't get any studying done if I went. My friends started calling me a nerd, but that was okay, I was acting like one. The next thing I did was to get some help learning study skills, the habits I hadn't formed in high school. My dedication to coursework was new to me, but it felt good. I felt responsible, like I was finally growing up.

As part of my new image, I bought some clothes that were more adult—shirts and khakis, rather than baggy jeans, sweatshirts, and a baseball cap. I was beginning to look and feel like a man, not a teenager, and, as a plus, I attracted the attention of more girls.

My parents were glad to see the new, adult me, and my father began introducing me to his business acquaintances. With my father's encouragement, I decided to major in business administration to please him, even though I was not attracted to the type of work I would do. Nevertheless, I made good grades and obtained an entry-level position with a large company. My parents were both pleased, my father because I was following in his footsteps, my mother because she thought I would get married and give her grandchildren. I guess I was well on my way to being the traditional American male.   ✳

In college, Darrin was secure enough in his identity as a man that he was able to leave the partying and teenage behavior of his friends behind. He continued, however, to follow in the path forged by his father, who had been his primary role model throughout childhood. An important part of being a man in American culture is being independent, and Darrin was beginning to demonstrate his ability to be his own person by making choices that were different from those of his peers. As Darrin continued his adult life, he made more independent choices, as we see in the next portion of his story.

✳ Darrin—Student Again

I worked for two years in the corporation, but the work was boring and stifling. Surely, I thought, there must be a job that would be challenging and interesting—if only I knew what it was. I had never explored my career options when I was in college, so I decided to do that now. I started by going to the career center at a local community college and taking some interest inventories. The counselor helped me see that my interests suggested that I might be happy with a career in law, and my undergraduate major would qualify me for admission to law school. Of course, I still had to take the LSAT, the law school admissions test, and then find a school that would accept me.

As it turned out, I scored well on the test and was accepted to the law school at our state's university. My father was not pleased when I told him about my change in careers, but he accepted it. I was, after all, a man now. I was able to finance my education with loans and money I had saved from my job, and that meant I could remain independent.

During the second semester of law school, I met Karen. She was a year ahead of me and was on Law Review, a coveted honor only reserved for the best students. We married the following year as she was getting ready to graduate and then interview with firms. I still had a year to go, but we decided that wherever Karen got a job was where we would locate. My parents were critical of the fact that I was deferring to my wife's career. That was something they would never have done. For us, however, it was a reasonable decision.

Karen was a brilliant student and had excellent recommendations from her professors. She was hired by the top firm in our city, and I wondered if I would be able to do as well. I had never before considered having a wife who had more status and made more money than I, and it caused me to question my worth as a man. I had set my goals, however, and I was achieving them. My value and male identity did not depend upon having a wife who was subservient in order to boost my ego. I had already expanded my role to include many chores that were not part of the typical male role, and when Karen and I had children, we planned to share the child care. My parents didn't understand our relationship, but that was because they were from a different generation. I was much happier and far more fulfilled, knowing that I could make decisions in my life based on what I wanted and not based on a traditional idea of what it meant to be a man.

※

Darrin had finally broken free of the role expectations that had limited his choices, and thereby diminished his hope. Once he allowed himself to consider options that were different than those that he was given as a child, he was able to structure the life he really wanted. He married a woman who also had made choices that were different from those that most women choose. Together, they worked out a lifestyle that provided them both with a strong foundation for building high hope.

Recognize Your Role Limitations

Recognizing how your role expectations are limiting you is not always easy. Begin by asking yourself, "If I could have my life anyway I want it to be, what would it be like?" Question your choices. Are you limiting yourself in order to stay in tune with your internalized vision of what a man or a woman is like? Your sex is a characteristic with which you are born, but the cultural ideas that constitute gender, what makes you a man or a woman, are concepts you can choose to accept or reject. The first step in this process, however, is to examine what you believe is appropriate for your gender. That is the purpose of the writing assignment you are to do for your work in this chapter.

The cultural ideas that constitute gender, what makes you a man or a woman, are concepts you can choose to accept or reject.

As you write your narratives, review the writing you have done in previous chapters. You may find in them the seeds of your role expectations. Allow the memories that were stimulated when you wrote about your childhood to stimulate your recollections for this assignment. Think of the characteristics of your childhood role models. What were the values they exemplified? What was it about them that you admired? How did these role models demonstrate hope in their lives?

As you do this writing assignment, take your time and write as much as you wish. The stories in this chapter are brief, but yours can be as long as you want to make it. Again, don't worry about your grammar, punctuation, or spelling; no one will read your narrative unless you allow it. You will find that studying your role expectations allows you the possibility of setting new, nontraditional, goals for yourself. The more you expand your goal possibilities, the more you will be able to enhance your hope.

The role expectations detailed in this chapter are based, to some extent, on those determined by the dominant culture—that is, white and middle class. While many of these expectations hold for men and women of other socio-economic classes and other ethnic groups, there are differences based on the subculture in which you were raised. The next chapter describes the expectations, and most importantly the stereotypes, that may limit your hope if you belong to an ethnic minority group.

13

Ethnic Minorities
and Hope

This chapter focuses on the effects that negative stereotypes and beliefs held by the dominant culture have on members of selected ethnic minority groups. Although social conditions, racism, oppression, and numerous other factors have a powerful influence on the development of hope, it's not possible within the scope of this book to cover them in detail. We mention only a few briefly before proceeding to the hope-diminishing factors of stereotyping.

As an individual who is a member of an ethnic minority, you may have risk factors that can diminish your hope. Ethnic minorities in the United States tend to have lower incomes than people in the dominant culture (Caucasian), frequently have higher unemployment, less education, more illness, poorer nutrition, and the list goes on and on. You may not have any of these risk factors, or you may have one or two, but it's likely that you have acquaintances and family members whose quality of life is lowered because of them.

It is more difficult to develop hope when these risk factors are present. Our research with minority children shows that in the early years, children of all ethnicities have higher hope than do the adults of their group. They believe they will do well, and that they can find ways to do the things they want. As these children enter adulthood, however, they are confronted with the reality that their ethnicity, added to any risk factors they have, may make it difficult to maintain their hope.

Despite the gains made by the civil rights movement, minority individuals are still subjected to prejudicial actions in housing, employment, education, and numerous other facets of life. All of these incidents of subtle and not-so-subtle discrimination create an environment in which hope does not flourish. There have been many books and articles written about the plight of minorities, and therefore we won't be focusing on those risk factors in this chapter.

A Comment About Stereotypes

As a minority person, you are subjected to both good and bad stereotypes held by the dominant group about your culture. While stereotypes are based on some small degree of reality, they characterize groups, and rarely are they totally true about the individuals in that group. There are many problems with stereotypes, but two are especially problematic in terms of hope. The first problem is that other people may respond to you in terms of the stereotypes they hold about members of your group. One example is the belief that all Asian Americans are good at math and have high academic expectations. Acting on this stereotype, the school counselor may place you, as an Asian student, in math classes, when you may or may not have any talent or interest for this topic.

Stereotypes, whether negative or positive, can diminish your hope because they limit the goals that you set for yourself.

Some stereotypes are negative and racist. If you are a young African American man, you may be accustomed to women crossing the street or hiding their purses when you approach them. Or, when shopping in a department store, you may realize that you are being watched by the store security in case you try to steal something. Despite the fact that you are a law-abiding person, when others respond to you in this way, you may be left with anger and a sense of having done something wrong. The way other people treat you, which can be largely based on the stereotypes they hold about your group, has a powerful effect on the way you feel about yourself.

The second major problem with stereotypes is that you may internalize the beliefs others have about you. By this we mean that you may come to think about yourself according to prevalent stereotypes. For example, a negative stereotype many people have about Native Americans is that they are lazy. If you are a Native American, you may find yourself questioning your work ethic and wondering if you work hard enough.

When you know others have stereotypes about your group, you may try to compensate for the image you believe they have. When this happens, you may drive yourself beyond healthy and normal bounds to prove that you are exceptional and that the stereotypes do not fit. At other times, the fight may become so tiresome and your energy so drained, that it's simply easier to give up. Whether you find yourself reacting to or accepting the stereotypes, your goals and choices can be limited by the negative beliefs that other people have about your group.

As a member of an ethnic group that has experienced oppression, racism, and denigration, your choices in life are defined by others to a greater extent than they would be if you were Caucasian and a member of the dominant culture. Not only can your choices be more limited in actuality, but your perception of what is available to you also may be more restricted. For the majority of individuals born into conditions of poverty and discrimination it's this *perception* of fewer choices that can diminish hope. For example, if you have never known anyone who has attended college, you may not consider that as a choice you could make. If many of your friends are having children while they are in high school, you may feel pressure to demonstrate your adulthood through that route. You *can* choose to do things differently in your own life, however. Your roadblocks may be more daunting, and it may be more difficult for you to sustain the physical and mental energy needed to achieve your goals, but it is possible to pursue your dreams. Don't let the stereotypes held by the dominant culture define what is possible for you to accomplish. Don't be afraid to set your sights high. Go after what you want, and you will find there are others there to help and encourage you.

About the Ethnic Groups

The ethnic groups we have chosen for this chapter are African American, Latino, Asian American, and Native American. We recognize that within each group there are many subgroups. For example, as an Asian American you could be Chinese, Japanese, Korean, Indian, or from one of the Southeast Asian countries. Even within those groups there are distinctions amounting to recognizable cultures. It is not possible, however, in the scope of this workbook to discuss all of the distinctions among groups that might influence hope. Rather, you will read about general stereotypes and how these beliefs can limit your hope. A true story will accompany the discussion of each ethnic group, illustrating one individual's struggle with the effects of stereotyping.

The assignment for this chapter is for you to examine the stereotypes about your group that you may have internalized. One way to do that is to write a story about yourself that illustrates how your ethnicity has affected the goals you have set, the roadblocks you have encountered, and the energy you have had to work for your goals. Even though you may not consider yourself to be representative of the ethnic minority to which you belong, stereotypes may have been applied to you by those who do not know you as an individual. It would be difficult, given the emphasis and interest in ethnicity and race in this country, not to have experienced the results of stereotyping and prejudgment. For this reason, and in order to maximize your hope, it's important to examine how you have been influenced by your minority group membership.

To help you conduct this examination through your story, here are some questions to serve as guidelines. Remember to take your time and write as much as you wish. Don't worry about the style of your writing, because no one will read it but you. Allow your memory to roam over your past, as you have done with the other stories you've written. Memories of these experiences may be painful. We suggest that you find someone who has had similar experiences and talk to them. Talking about your experience with someone who truly understands can help to lessen your pain. The extent to which these experiences are painful, however, may be a measure of how much they have diminished your hope. Therefore, it is all the more important for you to look closely at these memories.

Guidelines for Personal Stories

Ask yourself the following questions as a way to begin thinking about stereotypes in your life. Use the thoughts the questions bring up in your narrative.

1. Have you selected major goals in your life either in accordance with, or in reaction to, the stereotypes others have had about you?

2. Have you experienced difficulties reaching your goals because others responded to you as "typical" of your group, rather than as a unique individual?

3. Have you found it difficult to believe you could reach your goals when you knew that others thought that people of your ethnicity were not capable?

4. Have you, at times, believed the negative stereotypes others held about your group, rather than thinking of yourself as an individual?

5. Have the reactions of others to your ethnicity made it difficult for you to sustain the energy needed to reach your goals?

Use these guidelines to help you get started. Explore as many memories as possible to help you realize the powerful effect your experiences have had on the development of your hopeful thinking.

African American Stereotypes

In the past and continuing into the present, negative stereotypes about African American men and women have been prevalent in the Caucasian culture. If you are an adult African American, you are familiar with a number of these stereotypes. Many of the commonly held beliefs are negative in nature, such as depicting African Americans as lazy or criminal. Other beliefs are seemingly neutral, such as having rhythm or being good dancers. Examples of positive beliefs are that African American are good athletes, or that Black women are the strength of the family. Of course, even "neutral" or positive stereotypes can be limiting if the dominant culture believes that *all* you are is a good dancer or athlete, and that you're unable to excel in other areas. It is important, if you are not going to allow stereotypes to influence your hope, that you examine how you've been treated in the past and what that treatment caused you to believe about yourself.

In the previous chapter, we asked you to write a story about yourself that described the messages you heard as a child about how to be a man or a woman. If you are an African American man or women, your assignment here is to write about the lessons you learned in childhood about being a member of your ethnic group. As you do this, you are to look for the messages that contained hope-diminishing thoughts. These are messages that may have limited your choices—lessons that told you what was possible to accomplish or appropriate for a person of your ethnicity. For example, if you are a Black man, were you ever told to avoid looking directly at Caucasian men? This was a common message designed to keep Black men safe from the anger and hatred of Caucasians, yet avoiding eye contact also can have the undesirable effect of placing you in a subservient position.

In chapter 12 you learned that many of your beliefs about your options stemmed from the role models you saw when you were young. As you write your present story, consider what those role models were like. What choices did they make in their lives? What were the examples they set? Did you model your behaviors after what you observed? Or, perhaps you've done the opposite of what your role models have, because you believed their lives were too hard or unhappy.

Examining the messages you heard and the role models you had is one way to see how your hope may have been limited by the proscriptions imposed upon you. Marion's story shows how her life was circumscribed, for a time, by the lives that her mother and grandmother had led.

※ Marion—The Early Years

My early life began in a small town in Mississippi where my grandmother and grandfather lived. My mother had moved to Chicago when she was in her late teens, and when she became pregnant she moved home to be with her parents. I don't remember the earliest part of my life, but I know my mother stayed with us the first year and then moved back to Chicago. She got a job as a waitress and sent money to my grandparents to help support me.

When I was five years old my grandfather died, so my grandmother and I moved to Chicago to live with my mother, who had an apartment in a housing project. Our neighborhood was a scary place to live, and my grandmother walked me to and from school every day. She told me not to talk to the older boys, and she kept me busy with church activities.

My mother, however, had a boyfriend, and soon I had a baby brother. My mother didn't want to get married, because she said he didn't have a job, and she didn't want him hanging around the house. I saw that both my mother and my grandmother were strong women and were very capable of taking care of themselves. My mother was a beautiful woman, and she loved to go out and have a good time. She never seemed to want to get too attached to any man, however, and she said she was waiting for Mr. Right. My grandmother had been married for fifty-one years to my grandfather, but she never pressured my mother to get married. She said that a woman had to be strong and believe in the Lord to show her the path.

Our church had a big influence on my life. Throughout high school I went to church several times a week, sang in the choir, and participated in the youth group. I learned that the Black community could be counted on to help each other. I also learned that as African Americans, we had many trials and hardships, but that God would take care of us in the end. Whenever things were difficult for us, my grandmother prayed that much more.   ✳

The messages Marion learned in her early years were that women needed to be strong, and that it was not necessary to have a man in her life in order to be happy, raise children, or support herself. Marion also learned that other members of the Black community could be relied upon in times of crisis, rather like an extended family. Church played an important part in her life and the formation of her values, teaching her what was expected of her as a young African American girl.

How did the messages she received and the life she had lived influence Marion's hope? Because she was born into an economically marginal family, Marion never had the special lessons, opportunities to travel, or access to cultural events that enrich the lives of wealthier children. The absence of these opportunities limited the scope of options and choices from which Marion had to choose. Marion's role models were her mother and grandmother, neither of whom had achieved success in the academic or economic area. If she were to set her sights on college and a career, Marion would have to break away from the pattern she had seen. This is not an impossible task, but it is a difficult one. Let's follow Marion through her young adulthood and watch as she develops more hopeful thinking.

✳ Marion—Breaking New Ground

My life began to change when I started high school. For one thing, I realized that I was pretty when the boys paid attention to me and said I was "hot." There were a lot of fun things to do after school, and I stopped going to church with my grandmother quite so often. I joined the choir at school, and I also got selected for the drill team. I started dating a young man who was a member of our church and who played the drums in the school band. We spent a lot of time together on road trips with the football team, but I didn't want to get pregnant like my mother did, so I was very careful.

Because we lived in a project, most of our neighbors were either Black or Latino. Most of the people I knew had never thought about going to college—in fact, most of my friends didn't have any plans at all. The thing to do if you were a man was to be in a crew or gang, and get high. If you were a girl, having a baby was a cool way to become an adult. I saw that scene as a trap, and I didn't want to fall into it.

I began thinking about what I was going to do with my life. I didn't want to be a waitress, but I didn't know what I could do. Some of the women in our neighborhood worked in stores or in the beauty parlor, but those jobs didn't appeal to me. There was a lot of pressure from my friends to drop out of school and just "hang out." I certainly didn't want to go down that road. My boyfriend said he wanted to go to college, so I decided to talk to the school counselor about my chances of doing that, too.

I was surprised and pleased by what I learned from the counselor. I found out that I could go to college on a grant, and that if I worked hard there were many opportunities. First, of course, I had to stay in school and graduate. This meant not getting pregnant, not doing drugs, and passing all my classes. I figured that I could do those things, even though it might mean not having as good a time in high school as it seemed my friends were having. Since my boyfriend was trying to get ahead, too, we could keep each other company.

Attending college was a new and frightening experience. The school was in Chicago, but I didn't know anyone in my classes except my boyfriend. Although my mother and grandmother were very proud of me, they had no advice to offer. Our pastor was the most helpful person, and he encouraged me to stay out of trouble, study, and ask for help when I needed it—the things I was already doing. Going to college was like moving into a different world. Almost all of the teachers, and most of the other students, were white. I didn't feel accepted by them, or rejected—it was more like I was invisible. They even spoke a different dialect than I did, and I felt sometimes as if I was in a foreign country. But I wanted to succeed, so I kept trying.

In order to pick a major and decide what kind of a career I wanted to have, I sought out a counselor at the career center. With his help, I decided to major in social work. Although we had never had a case worker, many of my friends did, and I was somewhat familiar with what social workers did. I thought my knowledge of the projects and the poverty and crime that is found there would be an asset. I certainly had firsthand knowledge.   ✳

Marion rejected the images she saw around her of unsuccessful young people. She had examples of hard work in her mother and grandmother, and she had the support of her pastor and congregation. It may have been fortunate that she did not have many occasions for contact with the dominant culture, otherwise she would have encountered stereotypes and prejudices that depicted young people from the projects as failures.

Marion's counselor proposed a route to success, but it took courage on her part to take a different path than her peers. Growing up in the Chicago projects might have meant dropping out of high school, having a baby, and leading a dead-end life. Marion was able to step out of the stereotypes and prejudices about her race and set goals for herself that would lead her to a high-hope life. Her road was not easy, but she found ways to overcome the difficulties and each small success fueled her energy for the next step. Marion was well on her way to creating a high-hope life.

African Americans continue to have a great deal to overcome, regardless of the socioeconomic group into which they are born, and despite how successful they have become. As a successful Black person you may feel that you need to prove yourself in each new situation and with each new group of people you meet. Developing and maintaining high hope may be harder for you than for other people. When you set high goals, you may find that people frequently discourage you, either out of a lack of belief that you can succeed or because they know how hard the road to success will be. In addition, there may be many more roadblocks ahead of you than for other people. Equal rights is not yet a fact, and that means it may be difficult for you to gain access to the resources you need to reach your goals. And finally, with the difficulties facing you, it may be hard to keep up the mental energy you need to reach your goals. You *can* do it, however, and each success you have can make working for the next goal a little easier. Furthermore, each successful African American person is a role model for others beginning their hope journeys.

Latino Stereotypes

If you are Latino, your cultural origin could be Mexican, Cuban, Puerto Rican, Spanish, Central or South American. The stereotypes held by the dominant culture, however, may not distinguish between the values of each subcultural group, and this can be a cause of frustration. Furthermore, these stereotypes, like those held about African Americans, are often negative.

The length of time you and your forebears have been in the United States may make a difference in how closely you identify with your culture, and consequently, how affected by the negative stereotypes you will be. If your family has recently immigrated, the probability is that you are very close to the culture of the country from which you came. If, on the other hand, your family has been in the United States for a long time, you may identify with the dominant culture and therefore assume the stereotypes do not relate to you.

What are some of the images of Latinos that are limiting? Many in the dominant culture believe that Latinos are lazy, that they do not wish to learn English, that they are dishonest, and that they do not value education. The basis for these stereotypes may be that Hispanics, as is true for most immigrants, come to this country to make a better life, and they come with very little. Initially, all immigrants settle in areas that are populated by others of their culture, and it's more comfortable to speak their native language rather than to learn English. It may be difficult to find work, especially without speaking English and being unaware of other American customs. While the Statue of Liberty welcomes people who are tired and hungry, the rest of America is not always especially cordial.

How do the stereotypes held about Latinos diminish hope? If others hold negative beliefs about your potential for success, it will be more difficult for you to achieve your goals. There will be more roadblocks on the pathway to achievement, and it may be harder for you to envision solutions to these problems. Furthermore, it may be more difficult for you to maintain the high willpower it takes to achieve your goals in the face of the negative beliefs others hold about you.

There is also the danger that you will come to accept the negative beliefs others have about Latinos, as being true for you in particular. It's important for you to be aware of these stereotypes and to examine the ways they influence the goals you set, as well as your outlook on life. The effects of stereotypes are insidious, and they can influence your beliefs about yourself without you being aware of it. The negative beliefs become internalized, and you may find yourself acting as if they were true.

An effective way to combat the effects of negative stereotypes is to conduct a thorough inventory of your personal beliefs. To do this, we ask you to write a narrative about your life, your goals, and your beliefs about yourself. This assignment is similar to the story you wrote in chapter 3; however, here you are examining beliefs about yourself that may have come from negative and limiting stereotypes that others hold about your group. As you remember events of your life, select one or several in which you were especially aware of being Latino. How did your ethnicity influence the outcome of the situation? How did the reaction of others influence your self-image? What lessons or messages did you learn from the event? Use the suggested questions at the beginning of this chapter to jump-start your creative processes.

The story of Luisa illustrates one woman's struggle to develop a comfortable ethnic identity and still be a success in the Caucasian world. As her story begins, she is twenty-five years old and has recently moved to Kansas City from a small town in Texas on the Mexican boarder. Luisa has obtained a job as a secretary for a small law firm, and she is the only Mexican-American woman on the staff.

✳ Luisa—So Much to Learn

After the interview I didn't think I would get the job. When I walked into the law offices and saw the beige wallpaper, the dignified pictures of judges on the walls, and the expensive leather furniture, I knew I was out of place. There I was in my short red plaid suit, my four-inch heels, long hair, and large earrings. The other secretaries were dressed for success the Anglo way, muted tones, skirts below the knees, and none of them had long billowing curls.

I was surprised when I got a call saying I had the job. I had wanted to be a legal secretary for some time, and this was a great opportunity. The only problem was how could I be a success, fit in, and still be myself? Where I came from in Texas, nearly everyone was Mexican and I never felt that I didn't belong. And here in Kansas City, I live in a community of Mexican Americans, but outside of that area I feel different.

When I was growing up we always spoke Spanish at home, and now I speak English with an accent that is a combination of Mexican and Texan. Perhaps this made me appear uneducated, because the other secretaries treated me as if I didn't know anything. It's true that I had not worked in a law office before, so I had many questions about how things were done. Each time I asked for help, the explanations were given slowly and in simple language, as if I was not capable of understanding. After a while I was beginning to feel stupid and dreaded asking questions. If I didn't ask, I made mistakes, and then I felt worse.

I really wanted to be a legal secretary, so I decided to talk to the other women about what was happening and how I felt. They didn't seem to dislike me, so I thought it must be that they had misconceptions about me. I decided to clear the air.

I waited until it was time for a coffee break and then, when the other secretaries were all together, I told them how I felt and asked them what was going on. At first they were confused and denied that they treated me differently. Finally, the head secretary said that she had thought, with my background, that I would be difficult to train. Then, another woman blurted out that she thought I was hired because it looked good for the firm to have a Mexican American. The others agreed, and I felt mortified.

I went to the man who had hired me and confronted him with this rumor. He assured me that they had hired me because I had excellent references from my previous company, because I had attended a community college (and was better educated than most of the other secretaries), and because I could speak Spanish. Now I had new information but, although it bolstered my self-esteem, I still had to deal with the other women.

My next tactic was to invite the head secretary to lunch and ask her what she meant when she referred to "your background." She was not angry and readily confessed that she had stereotypes about Mexican Americans. For some of my people there was an element of truth in those stereotypes. Many Mexican Americans do not finish school, live in poverty conditions, and do not strive for the values of the dominant culture. I was not living in poverty, of course, and I had completed two years of college, so she must not have been seeing me as a unique individual. As for the acculturation part of what she said,

I suppose I was straddling the Anglo and Mexican American cultures.

After my confrontation and subsequent conversation, things got better for me at work. The women began asking me questions about my culture and how to say different words in Spanish. Since they seemed interested, I decided to ask them to attend the Cinco de Mayo fiesta in my community and then come to my house later for a big Mexican meal. It was a pleasure to share my culture, and I began to explore more of theirs. I learned to eat many different types of foods and to appreciate art and music that was different from that of my own culture. I also discovered that I had many stereotypes of my own about Anglos and dispelling those was helping to broaden my choices and goals.

＊

When Luisa moved to Kansas City, she had already achieved a great deal. Graduating from high school and attending a community college was more than her mother or sisters had done, and so she was confused when her coworkers responded to her as if she was uneducated. Her high hope enabled her to confront the situation and deal with their attitudes as a roadblock on her road to success.

When Luisa lived in the small boarder town in Texas, she seldom came into contact with the dominant culture. Until she began working in a situation where everyone else was Anglo, she was unaware of the stereotypes they had of her, or of the beliefs she had about them. When she began to feel less competent because of their behavior toward her, she knew it was time to confront the situation. If you find your choices and goals limited and there is a possibility that the limitations are related to your ethnicity, it's important for you to examine the stereotypes applied to your group.

Write your own story about an event in which you believe your ethnicity played a role. Luisa identified her language as one important factor contributing to the negative reaction she experienced. Try to identify the characteristics that trigger the negative stereotypes in your situation. Notice that Luisa did not try to become Anglo, although she allowed herself to appreciate aspects of the dominant culture. Respect your culture and nurture it in yourself. It is a large part of who you are, but do not let negative stereotypes about this culture delineate your goals and lower your hope.

Asian American Stereotypes

As an Asian American, you are probably aware of being part of a "model minority." Because the values in your culture of origin, especially the work ethic, are closely aligned with those of the dominant culture, your group is used to illustrate the possibilities of success for other ethnic groups. There are problems with this stereotype, however. To begin with, not all Asians have the same experience in the United States. Groups that have been in this country for some time, such as Chinese, Japanese, or Korean, are generally better educated and financially more successful than those groups that have recently immigrated.

Many Southeast Asians who came in great numbers after the Vietnam War have not been well received. As is true for all groups that have immigrated to this country, they initially moved into enclaves populated by others from Southeast Asia. The older people do not learn to speak English readily. The language difference, along with unfamiliar religious practices and a perceived clannishness, has promulgated negative stereotypes.

The stereotypes and beliefs about Asians, therefore, are both positive and negative. Any view that does not recognize your individuality, however, can decrease your hope. No matter how "positive" a stereotype may be, if it does not fit you, it sets up conditions for failure. Previously we mentioned the belief that all Asians are good in math. A number of our university students have told us that they have suffered from this stereotype. These students were not mathematically talented and believed that their other real talents were overlooked.

The consequences of negative stereotypes are documented in many places and have been the subject of numerous books and articles. To detail them here is beyond the scope of this workbook. What is important is that you have a method to recognize any ill effects on your life and the ways in which these stereotypes may have diminished your hope. Again, we suggest that you construct a story about your personal experiences, identifying situations in which you specifically felt the effect of the dominant culture's beliefs about your ethnicity. As you write your story, detail the specific ways in which it has been difficult for you to maintain high hope. Review the questions at the beginning of this chapter, and use them as your guide.

The story of Sue Ann, a Chinese American woman, documents her struggle to be her own person. Her teachers had expectations that she would go to college and become a scientist. She was an excellent student and showed promise in chemistry and physics. On the other hand, her parents, who had both been born in China, expected her to help manage the family import business. She wanted to choose her own life but was torn by the expectations of others and the values of respect for her elders and family loyalty.

✳ Sue Ann—A Life of Her Own

I know that American girls decide for themselves what they want to be when they grow up. Chinese girls, however, must listen to their fathers and older brothers; it is a matter of respect. My oldest brother has done what my father wished, and he has become a doctor. The whole family is very proud of him. My youngest brother will probably be a scientist, and my parents are willing to borrow the money to send him to college.

We live in Chinatown in San Francisco and have an import business. Even though my parents came to this country from China twenty years ago, they still have very traditional ways, and neither of them speaks English very well. That is partly why they want me to work in the shop. They also say that I will get married, and that I don't need to have a career. They say I have an obligation to help the family.

I have done very well in school, but I don't want to have a profession like my brothers. My teachers keep telling me that I should be a scientist of some sort, because I make good grades in subjects such as chemistry and physics. They think all Asians are going to be either scientists or mathematicians, but they are wrong. We don't all do that well in those subjects, and even if we did, it doesn't mean we enjoy them.

There is something I not only love, but that I can really do well. I can dance! Ever since I was a small child I have taken dance lessons, and now I am very good at it. I can do ballet and modern dance, folk dances, and even tap. Early in middle school I was given a scholarship to the school that trains dancers for the San Francisco Ballet Company. Receiving the scholarship was quite an honor and, while my parents seemed proud of me, I could tell that they regarded my dancing as frivolous. My father said that dancing would never bring honor to the family.

I want to be a ballet dancer, and I have worked very hard to become a good one. Sometimes it seems as if I am fighting everyone to be able to do what I want to do. If I am offered a chance to do ballet, I am going to accept. I know I will feel badly disappointing my parents, and I feel badly now disappointing my teachers. Everyone seems to know what a Chinese girl should do, and no one listens to what she wants.

※

Sue Ann is experiencing a common dilemma for young Asian Americans. She is caught between two worlds, the traditional Asian and the modern American. In this case, she is contemplating choices that go against the expectations of both cultures, but because she is a high-hope person, she will probably succeed no matter what choice she eventually makes. Sue Ann's story illustrates how the traditions of a culture can place as many, or more, limitations on an individual as the stereotypes held by the dominant culture. As an Asian American man or woman, it's important for you to identify how you have been affected by tradition. While many of the values of the Asian cultures are consistent with those of the dominant American culture, one very important value conflicts. Individuality, a cornerstone of western values, violates the Eastern assumption that allegiance to the family or group is more important than pursuing your own will. Examine the extent to which your goals, waypower, and willpower may have been shaped by your reluctance to act as an individual. If you find that your hope has been hindered, you are in a position similar to Sue Ann's, which requires you to make the choices that feel the most comfortable for you.

Native American Stereotypes

The dominant culture holds many stereotypes about Native American culture, some of them are negative, and many of them are quite romantic. A love-hate relationship exists between the dominant culture and Indian people. As long as Native Americans do not remind Anglos of their shared and tragic history, the romance can continue. There is a fascination with Indian rituals and spiritual artifacts such as dream catchers and medicine wheels, but the reality of poverty among Indian people is ignored far too often. The dominant culture loves Indians, as long as they do not get too close. A joke among Indian people is that when Caucasians claim Indian heritage it is usually Cherokee (a very advanced people), and they are usually descended from a great-grandmother who was an "Indian princess." Such a claim, of course, shows a lack of information about Indian people and can be insulting.

If you are a Native American man or woman, you are probably well aware of the negative stereotypes about your group. Indian people often are seen as being lazy, having problems with alcohol, and being dishonest. The truth is that Native Americans do not necessarily place a value on being either competitive or acquisitive. Instead, an emphasis is placed on cooperation, and Indian people do not appear to be driven by the need to compete as many Caucasian people are. Acquiring "things," which is an important indicator of success for the dominant culture, is supplanted by the value of sharing in Native American culture. These two major cultural conflicts have led to negative stereotypes that can severely diminish hope in Indian people.

The major threat to hope in Native Americans, however, is the poverty and desperation in which many in this group live. In our research on hope in children, Indian youth score the lowest of any group on the hope scales. Native Americans perceive few options available to them for careers and education. At least 50 percent of the Indians in the United States live on reservations where there are few opportunities to work, go to school, or have a social life that does not include alcohol.

Many Indian people live in nonreservation areas, however, where there are many opportunities to build a successful and happy life. Enhancing your hope, if you are such a person, is one way to help yourself. If you raise your hope through the strategies in this workbook, you will be in a better position to help your children and others in your community to enhance their hope. It works. Hope is infectious.

To determine how your hope has been affected by the images others have of you, write a story about yourself that describes how being a Native American has determined your choices and goals. Choose one or more incidents—events that stand out in your mind. Refer to the questions at the beginning of this chapter to guide you through the process. Bobbi's story illustrates a journey toward higher hope that took her down a bumpy road.

☀ Bobbi—Who Am I, and What Do I Want?

I was born in Montana on the Black Feet Reservation nearly fifty years ago. When I was five years old, the Bureau of Indian Affairs sent me to a Catholic boarding school miles away from my home. Once there, I had to learn to speak English and was never permitted to speak my native language again. Although the nuns were kind, I was lonely for my family, and I felt cut off from everything that had been familiar.

Each summer I was allowed to go back to the reservation for a month. As the years went by, however, I felt less like I belonged to my tribe, and more similar to the nuns who were raising me. Eventually, I converted to Catholicism, and after high school I received a scholarship to college. Everyone said I was lucky because I had escaped the poverty of my home, but I wasn't so certain it had been a fair trade.

In college I was a good student, so good in fact that I was accepted to law school after graduation. With all my achievements, I should have been happy, but there was something missing in my life. I wasn't sure what it was, but I thought it had something to do with being an Indian. In law school, I began to go drinking with my friends. I discovered that I liked the feeling alcohol gave me—it filled the empty space that continually plagued me.

I remember one incident, after a weekend when I had drunk far too much, when the dean of the law school called me into his office. I will always remember his words. He said, "I know you Indians like to drink, but you had better watch it or you'll get yourself thrown out." I was floored. I knew I was an Indian, but I'd never thought of myself as a "drunken Indian."

Even though I continued to drink, I became a lawyer and went to work in the counsel's office at the university. From time to time people made reference to my ethnicity, but I felt detached from my culture. I heard veiled references about how much I had achieved (for an Indian), or that I didn't seem like a "typical" Indian. The stereotypes were beginning to bother me, so I decided to see for myself what being an Indian was really like.

I decided to spend my vacation going back to the reservation where I had been born and looking up my extended family. When I arrived, I was shocked at the poverty of the homes, although the country was beautiful. I spent hours speaking with the elders, learning about the broken treaties of the past and the legal problems of the present. I was beginning to see that my training and talents might be useful to my people.

While I was in Montana, I spent time with a spiritual healer—a medicine man. I talked with him about my burgeoning alcohol problem, and he explained to me how my life was out of balance. I had become alienated from my true self, and I needed to heal the rift if I was to feel whole again.

When I returned to my job, I had many things to think about and many new choices to consider. I wasn't sure if or how my life would change, but I felt certain that I was an Indian, and I was proud of it.   ✳

Bobbi, like so many of her generation was forced into a mold that was not her true nature. Caught in the cleft between two cultures, she developed low hope, which led to her potential alcohol problem. When Bobbi became aware that she could choose an Indian identity, a new world opened up for her. She could set goals based on what she wanted for herself or her people, and she could use her legal expertise to find ways to reach those goals. As her will-power increased and she could actively pursue her goals, she was also able to stop drinking. Eventually she divided her time between a private legal practice and doing pro bono work for her tribe. She even began to learn the language that was forbidden so many years ago.

Stereotypes Can Affect Anyone

Throughout this chapter, we have stressed the difficulties you may have encountered in pursuing your goals and developing your hopeful thinking due to your minority status. Race and ethnicity is a big issue in the United States—this is a country divided between a desire for acceptance and unity on the one hand and a call for cultural pride and continuance on the other. We do not believe it is very likely that a person can grow up as a member of a racial minority and not experience fallout from stereotypes and negative beliefs held by many in the dominant culture. Our research with hope in young people and adults demonstrates that as ethnic minority children grow into adulthood, their hope diminishes.

In this chapter, we specifically have addressed the issue of stereotypes for minorities. As a white woman or man, however, you also may have been oper- ating under the influence of stereotypes. White ethnic minorities, such as the Irish, Italians, and Jews, have experienced oppression because of their cultural backgrounds. You may wish to write your own story examining the influence that your white ethnicity has had on your development of hopeful thinking. Follow the same guidelines you have used previously and answer the ques- tions provided earlier in the chapter. You may discover some interesting infor- mation that will help you in your quest for higher hope.

High-hope Role Models
for Minorities

If you are discovering that being a minority individual has had a diminishing effect on your hope, what can you do about it? The strategies detailed in sec- tion II of this book will work well, and, as you incorporate them into your daily life, you will see your hope increasing. You will find yourself setting your sights higher, finding more ways to cope with problems, and experiencing more energy and drive to pursue your objectives.

A strategy that will be especially helpful to you is to identify successful role models from your ethnic group with whom you can identify. Look for stories that depict high hope. They do not have to be factual to give you inspiration. We have selected a sampling of stories, both fact and fiction, for each ethnic group including Caucasian. These are described in the Recommended Reading Section along with other resources that will provide helpful information for increasing your hope.

The next chapter describes the challenge of having high hope in old age. Age, like gender, cuts across all ethnicities and lifestyles. Even if you are not approaching old age now, you will find the information and suggestions in the next chapter helpful. Remember, few of us look forward to growing old, but it is far better than the alternative.

14

Growing Older with Hope

✳ **Not for the Faint of Heart**

My mother died last year. She was ninety-one years old, and until the last two weeks of her life, she was in good health. Like so many older women, she was widowed, and she had lived alone for the last twenty years. Her days were spent doing housework, gardening, playing bridge, and going to various club and church meetings. Because she had worked her whole life, she didn't enjoy volunteer work, but her many activities kept her busy.

We spoke on the phone every day, and I came to know her physical ailments well. Her every ache and pain was related in great detail, and I accompanied her on all her visits to the doctor. Because she was basically a healthy person, I believe my mother was surprised each time her body acted like an old person's. She hated to hear the doctors say, "You're just getting old." My mother was going to go kicking and screaming into old age. She always said, "Growing old is not for the faint of heart."   ✳

Perhaps growing old takes courage, but it also helps to have hope. As you will see in this chapter, the lessons you have learned in this workbook will help you cope with the problems you encounter as you age. This chapter is for everyone, not just the elderly. The truth is that everyone ages—if they are lucky—and the guidelines covered here will smooth the process and help you age with high hope.

Age is both a biological fact as well as a social construct. The biology of aging begins the moment you are born and finally ends in death. This process is inevitable and, depending upon your unique genetic makeup and unforeseen accidents, it will follow a predictable course. The social construction of age is neither predictable nor inevitable. What it means to be elderly, and who the elderly are, have changed significantly over the years, as has society's view of them and how the elderly are regarded.

Who Is Old?

Whether you are fifty or ninety, it is generally true that you feel younger on the inside than you look on the outside. Have you ever caught a glimpse of yourself in a store window and wondered who that person is? And then, with some dismay, you realize it's you. Do you remember the first time a younger person called you "sir" or "ma'am"? Suddenly, you were aware that you were seen as an older person, you belonged to another generation.

To a large extent, the experience of aging is determined by external reminders. If you teach in a university, as we do, the students seem to get younger each year—a visible reminder of our own encroaching age. Watching our friends grow gray or bald and seeing their figures spread is another external reminder. There are so many reminders that it would be impossible (and depressing) to list them here. The point is, however, that we often *do* need reminding. For most people, it would be easy to forget how old they are, because they still feel young inside. Perhaps that's why the slogan "you're as young as you feel" is so meaningful.

Classifying people as "old" according to their chronological age makes little sense. Certainly most people in their nineties are old by all standards, yet there are exceptions to any rule. Many individuals stay very physically active well into their nineties, while others become couch potatoes early in life. There are certain events and life stages, however, that can be identified as more common to certain age groups. For example, people in their fifties face different psychological and physical challenges than do people in their seventies. For this reason, the ten-year periods of the fifties, sixties, and seventies, and then the over-eighties, are each treated separately in this chapter. The guidelines for aging with hope are suitable for people of any age. The tasks for each of these periods, however, are somewhat different.

As you read through the challenges for each decade, remember that these events could happen earlier or later in your life. What we have detailed is typical for many people, but your life is unique, and thus may not fit this pattern.

Fifty to Sixty—The In-between Age

This is the fulcrum decade, the turning point in the aging process for many people. It is a generation of in-betweens. People in this age group are between middle age and old age, between their children and their parents, between their productive years and retirement, and often between focusing inward or looking outward.

In your earlier years, you probably devoted your energy to caring for your family, while now you may be taking care of elderly parents. There are times when your own age identity may feel like a ball being bounced back and forth, as you spend time with your parents (who see you as young) and your children (who see you as old).

During this decade you may become aware for the first time of the social reminders of your age. Your fiftieth birthday can be traumatic, and those "over-the-hill" cards may seem insensitive and not so funny. Younger people begin to treat you with more respect and often assume that you have different ideas and tastes than they do. This is a time when you take stock of the clothes you wear, the slang you use, your taste in music, and many other signs of your generation. You evaluate whether you want to "look your age," what that phrase actually means, and what the implications may be of identifying with a younger age group.

Your body may also serve as a reminder that you're getting older. It is natural for the ratio of body fat to muscle to increase, so your shape will probably change to some extent. Your hair may begin to gray or to thin, and your eyesight will likely change. Even if you have never worn glasses, you may need them for reading at this age. You will begin to notice a change in speed, agility, and strength, although if you are a regular exerciser, these may be minimal.

One of the most important challenges you face during this decade is that of learning to value yourself as an older person. Even though the number of older people is increasing with each generation, the dominant culture continues to place an inordinate worth on youth. Science, usually an ally of the elderly, has contributed to the emphasis on youth with its quest for remedies to prevent aging. While people are living longer and healthier lives, they—especially women—also are encouraged to look as young as possible while doing it. The message is mixed—live to be old, but don't *look* old.

As a woman, the decade between fifty and sixty may be especially difficult. You will probably experience two major changes in aspects of your life that may have been very important to your feelings of self-worth—the end of childbearing and the empty nest. Menopause can be difficult, but with the hormone treatments now available, it can be made much easier. While most women do not want to bear children after the age of fifty, the indication that it is no longer an option may be difficult. Menstruation is fraught with many personal and symbolic meanings, and if menopause is difficult, those meanings should be explored with the aid of a counselor.

The empty nest may come as a relief to many, but it also can mean the loss of part of your identity. If you have seen your primary role in life as being a mother, you may no longer feel needed as those you love begin to care for themselves. You will need to set new goals and discover your worth outside the role of the family caregiver. In chapter 13 we mentioned the guilt that many women experience when they take time away from their families to do things specifically for themselves. To avoid depression when your nest is empty, it's vital to develop a life of your own by setting goals and using hopeful thinking.

Being in your fifties also has its benefits, and it is important to recognize and value them. You are in a position to evaluate your life and plan the things you want to accomplish with the time that is left. You have the wisdom that comes from accumulated experiences, and you can see life from a larger perspective. You may wish to rearrange your priorities, planning to accomplish things you have wanted to do but have delayed because of other obligations. This decade offers you opportunities and perspectives you have never had before. It's an ideal time to use your hopeful thinking to enrich the rest of your life.

Donna, whom you first met in chapter 4 and have followed at other points in this book, is in her fifties. A continuation of her story illustrates some of the challenges and gifts of this age.

✳ Donna—A Time for Reflection

Turning fifty was pretty traumatic for me. I was never one of these people who was reluctant to tell her age, but I looked younger and people were often surprised when they knew. My feelings caught me off guard, when a group of my friends hung a banner at the office party saying "Congratulations on your fiftieth birthday." It was there, staring me in the face. I was fifty!

Although that was nearly a year ago, I have done a lot of thinking about aging since then. I may look younger now, but that won't always be true. How will I feel about myself? How will other people respond to me? There are so many questions that don't have answers. It is time to do a retrospective on myself. I look back on the things I have done in my life, and I am pleased with my accomplishments. I have helped a lot of people, and I have accomplished many of my personal goals.

The dilemma I face now is accepting myself as the older person I am becoming. It feels strange to be one of the older members of the firm and to realize that others look to me as wiser and more experienced. It feels good, but sometimes I want to look around and say, "Who me?" These years are going to take some getting used to. I have the time and freedom to plan what I want to do with the rest of my life, and there are so many options available to me. I don't have to be young to have a wonderful life.   ✳

Donna always has been a high-hope person, so we would expect her to greet the prospect of getting older as a challenge to be met. She will set new goals within realistic bounds, but she will never say she is too old. She will spend her fifties valuing the person she has come to be, and looking forward to the person she has yet to become.

The Challenges Between Sixty and Seventy

As you enter your sixties, it is virtually impossible to avoid the fact that you are getting older. The word "senior" that you might have been avoiding in your fifties now definitely applies to you. You get senior discounts at the movies, restaurants, on your prescriptions, even at some veterinarians and doctor's offices. Social Security and Medicare loom on the horizon, and even if you are not ready to retire, the prospect is "in your face."

This is a decade of other reminders as well. Your own parents may die, leaving you as the oldest family member. While your parents were alive, you were always the "younger" generation. After they are gone and there is no longer a cushion of age above you, you must confront the fact that you are the oldest generation.

You are likely to have grandchildren who also serve as a reminder that you are getting older. When you are with them you cannot help but realize your position in the generations of a family, and know that you are at one end and they are at the other. For women who suffered from the empty nest when their children became adults, grandchildren help to assuage that longing. Even if you are a devoted grandmother, however, your entire family will benefit if you establish interests of your own. Learn to enjoy your empty nest.

During your sixties, you are more likely to experience more aches and pains, and sometimes serious ailments, than you did in your fifties. These serve as further, and annoying, reminders of aging. Even if you have never exercised before, remember that it is not too late to begin. There is ample research showing that exercise begun at any time is beneficial. A quote by James Herbert Blake, who lived to be one hundred, provides a humorous forethought. He said, "If I had known I was going to live this long, I'd have taken better care of myself." Take good care of yourself to make your long life wonderful.

Retirement is an issue with which you must deal in your sixties, even though many organizations have no mandatory retirement age. You may ask yourself whether you are still productive and still respected by the standards of the younger employees. Your coworkers may start asking when you plan to retire and what you will do afterwards. These are questions you should begin to ask yourself, because planning what you will do with your leisure time can determine the success of your retirement.

There are very few role models that people in their sixties can refer to for how to be as they age. In the past fifty years, the concept of old age has changed drastically. Where a sixty-year-old person was considered old by nearly every standard in the past, now he or she may be thought to be in late middle age. Seniors are encouraged to do everything from running marathons to climbing mountains. Whole communities, such as Sun City and Leisure World, have been established to cater only to the needs of seniors. Organizations such as the American Association of Retired Persons (AARP) are strong advocates for the rights of seniors. What does it mean to age? What can aging people truly expect of themselves? There is a wider range of choices and options than ever before in history. It's a good time to grow old *with hope*.

George is a sixty-three-year-old man who retired three years ago from a middle-level management position in a large company. He had been a valued employee, he thought, but when the company offered to buy him out and replace him with a much younger man, he wondered what he was really worth.

✳ George—A New Beginning

I had heard of this happening to other men in my company, but I didn't think they would do it to me. They pushed me out, more or less. Yes, the deal was sweet, a good retirement package. I just wasn't ready to stop working. But that was three years ago, and I've changed a lot since then.

Sixty years old used to seem ancient when I was young. I guess it was pretty old fifty years ago, but it isn't old anymore. Why, even though I'm called a senior in some places, I am also considered late middle aged. There are years of productive time ahead of me, but when I first retired, I didn't see it that way. At first I puttered around the house driving my wife nuts. Then I became lethargic, and all I wanted to do was sit in my recliner and doze.

After a year of that, my wife became concerned about me and suggested that I visit a psychologist. I was told that I was depressed, and medication was suggested. Before I resorted to that, however, I decided to try to make some changes on my own. The first thing I did was to begin exercising again, something I had stopped during my year of malaise. That helped, and soon I felt like investigating other things to do with my time. I had always been handy at small carpentry jobs, so I volunteered for Habitat for Humanity.

Now my life is full of rewarding activities, and my marriage is better than ever. We are looking forward to doing the traveling we put off when we were younger, and I feel like I have the energy to pursue whatever I want.   ✳

George had worked hard during his middle years and felt discarded when he was asked to retire early. He slipped into depression, a common reaction in his situation, but was able to pull himself out of the doldrums by setting goals and pursuing his dreams. George used hopeful thinking to salvage the years ahead and go on to lead a fulfilling life.

The Decade of the Seventies

By the time you are in your seventies, you probably will be into your retirement. If you are healthy and financially secure, this can be a wonderful chance for you to do things you only dreamed of when you were younger. You might travel, explore hobbies that interest you, or you might volunteer to do things that will help others. Keeping active after you retire will help you live longer, as well as happier.

Many people, however, are not enjoying their retirement because of poor health or financial insecurity. If you are one of those individuals, then you are especially in need of hope enhancement. There are many things you can do to improve your situation and your well-being that do not require money. The last section of this chapter gives a list of goals that you can establish for yourself that can make your later years more satisfying and filled with hope.

The seventies often are filled with reminders of your advancing age, as well as your mortality. As in your past decades, you see your age reflected in your friends. These reflections may show weakening physical conditions and infirmity, as well as the appearance of age. Peers begin to die, and the number of deaths is bound to increase as you outlive your friends. As you near your eighties, the task of reconciling yourself to death becomes more salient. While this picture may seem bleak, especially if you are a younger person, the seventies can be a wonderful time to come to terms with yourself and how you have lived your life.

All of the strategies you have learned in this book have stressed self-knowledge through introspection. From the vantage of the seventies, you have the opportunity to see your life spread out before you. What do you still want to do? What do you want to learn? What new goals will you set for yourself to make your life complete? Your life may be far from over, so fill your days with high-hope thoughts and high-hope actions.

The story of Thelma illustrates a woman who was widowed in her mid-seventies. After a long period of grieving for her husband, she decided to reshape her life, setting goals she had never considered before.

✳ Thelma—A Time to Mourn, and a Time to Move On

Ben and I had such plans for our later years. We were going to move to Florida to live in one of those nice senior citizens' communities. We had always enjoyed fishing and camping, and we wanted to do some deep-sea fishing and explore the Everglades. Then, when he got sick and we knew it was terminal, all our plans just evaporated.

That was several years ago, and I have spent a lot of time mourning him and wishing he were still with me. For a time, I made a shrine to him in the living room, with his pictures surrounded by flowers. Every time I saw it, I cried and sunk further into my depression. Fortunately for me, I have two daughters who live nearby, and together they pulled me out of my grief.

Ben's illness drained our finances, which made it even more difficult for me to live in comfort. My daughters had their own financial problems, so asking for help from them was out of the question. I decided to sell the home we had lived in because it was much too large for one person and move into a small apartment that would not have the upkeep a house required. I made a substantial profit from the sale of the house and invested it in an annuity program. With Ben's Social Security and the monthly annuity payment, I had enough money to live comfortably.

Moving to a new apartment was difficult because it meant leaving memories behind. I had always been an inventive homemaker, however, and I enjoyed fixing up my new surroundings. I also began to attend church more frequently and join in more of the activities. One group was especially for older people, and I found there were many women in my situation. I made some new friends, and of course there were the old friends Ben and I had, so I developed a busy social life.

When I look back on it, the time I spent grieving for Ben was very important. By the time I sold the house and made other changes in my life, I was ready to move on. I had a wonderful fifty-two years of marriage, but I was ready to have some more years as a woman on my own.

⁕

Thelma had lived her life centered around her husband, and when he died she was bereft. A high percentage of women outlive their husbands, and their situations may be similar to Thelma's. It was important for Thelma to begin making changes only when she was ready, allowing herself enough time to grieve. Selling her home was a major change, but for her it was a way to obtain the money she needed to live comfortably, and it was not an impulsive decision. Thelma was demonstrating high-hope thinking with each step she took toward establishing a life that was her own.

The Eighties and Older

Your life expectancy, if you are young now, is that you will live well into your eighties. These truly senior years can be filled with activity and satisfaction if you are healthy and have developed high hope. There are many challenges for these years, however, such as illnesses and the death of friends. Decisions must be made about where you will live and with whom you will live as you get older. Most women are happiest if they can continue to keep their own homes, while men who are widowed seem to be the most satisfied living in a retirement or assisted-living community.

Even into your eighties, there are many goals you can set and options from which you can choose. If you have maintained your mental alertness, managing your own affairs and remaining in control of your life will help you cope with aging. It can be difficult to convince others that you are able to do things for yourself, however, and the more you allow others to do for you, the less capable you will become. Ask for the help you genuinely need, but do as much for yourself as you can.

Once you have made it through the seventies and are into your eighties, there are normal concerns that arise. Fears of disability and illness requiring long-term care are the most common. Alzheimer's disease has become a dreaded affliction, prompting many to fear the slightest sign of memory loss. Many people develop hope in their spiritual arena, even if they have not done so before. You may find this is helpful for you.

If you have developed high hope in your younger years, you will find your later years to be more pleasant. It can be difficult to learn new ways of thinking when you are in your eighties, and if you have not been a hopeful person prior to that age, you will need to be very patient with yourself. The changes you make in your approach to hopeful thinking may be very small, but they will be worth the effort.

Fern is an eighty-eight-year-old woman who has been an assisted-living resident for the past three years. When her children insisted that she move from her apartment into the nursing home, Fern was quite resistant. Even though she knew she needed care that her children could not provide, she had not wanted to give up her independence.

✳ Fern—Making a New Adjustment

Whoever coined the term "the golden years"? They certainly weren't my best age. I can't say I am enjoying myself these days, but I'm making the best of it. When I moved from my own apartment to this nursing home I felt ornery and mean. I think I gave everyone a hard time because I didn't want to be here. I'm a little sorry about that now, because, considering the care I need, it isn't such a bad place.

I have my own room—actually it's two rooms because I have my own bathroom and my bed is in a little alcove. I brought some of my favorite pieces of furniture and my pictures and knickknacks to put around. I have my privacy, but there are also people to talk to and a few things to do. Everyone eats meals in a big dining room, where you can order from a menu just like a restaurant. We can play bingo once a week, and there is a big television in the lounge where we can watch videos. All in all, it isn't so bad.

I think the problem with getting old is that you have to give up so much. When you've been used to having your own home, and could go anywhere you wanted and do what you wanted, you miss that freedom. The only way to live with the restrictions is to value what you can do and the choices you can make. I can choose to watch television, read, crochet, visit other residents, or participate in one of the activities that are available each day. I go out at least once a week with my children and grandchildren, and they can join me in the dining room for dinner. It has been important for me to stop thinking about how things used to be and to start focusing on today—the here and now.   ✳

Fern's adjustment was a difficult one to make, and it was high-hope thinking strategies that helped her through the process. The key to her success was to focus on the moment, and let the past be in the past. Once Fern got over being angry, she was able to look around her, and make the best of a situation that was not ideal. Had Fern continued to be angry and as she said, "ornery," the nursing staff and her family would have been far less supportive. Because Fern was able to regain her high hope, she was able to adjust to her new situation and live her last years in comfort.

The information and the stories you have just read are examples of the dilemmas and challenges that you may face as you grow old. The way you age and how satisfied you are in your senior years depends, to a large extent, on the way you lived your younger years. It's true that people usually become more fixed in their attitudes and behaviors and less willing to change. But the adage "you can't teach an old dog new tricks" doesn't need to be true. With the strategies in this book, you can make important changes to increase your hope.

As a younger person using this workbook, the messages are obvious. Develop your hopeful thinking and learn to live your life as a high-hope person now, and you will have an old age filled with high hope. You should go ahead and save money, investing in your financial future so that your retirement will be comfortable. Consider that developing your hope is also an investment for the future, as well as an asset you can use every day of your life.

Guidelines for Aging with Hope

The first section of this workbook taught you to explore important facets of yourself as they influence your hope. In the second section you learned a number of strategies to increase your hope. The guidelines suggested here help to keep you active and feeling better about yourself as you age. At the conclusion of the chapter, each guideline is presented as a goal to which you can apply the strategies you learned in section II.

Take some exercise every day. It's never too late to begin an exercise program, but start with short periods and easy activities. Walking is a wonderful way to get the circulation going. In inclement weather you can walk inside your home, and if you have stairs, you can climb them for an added benefit. Ask your doctor about the right exercise for you.

Good posture helps you look better and younger, it helps your breathing, and it helps prevent back problems. Stand or sit straight and keep your head held high. Look proud, and feel proud! And smile, too!

Eat nutritious foods, eating enough, but not overeating. If you live alone it can be difficult to fix a full meal for yourself. However, it is important to eat well. Treat yourself as well as you treated others in the past, and learn to cook real meals just for you. If you do not know the best foods for you, there are many resources to help. Ask your doctor or a local bookstore.

Learn to breathe. As simple as this sounds, many people take short and shallow breaths, not filling their lungs and brains with the oxygen they need for clear thought and energy. Learn to take deep, long breaths, especially as you exercise and practice good posture.

Sleep patterns change to some extent as people age; however, it's still very important to *get enough of the right type of sleep.* Many older people nap frequently during the day and then find it difficult to sleep through the night. Staying active will help you regulate your sleep, and if you have trouble getting the sleep you need, review the guidelines in section II that pertain to sleep. It is not normal, even for an older person, to sleep most of the day. If you believe you sleep too much, ask your doctor about it—you may be depressed. Regulating your sleep habits is possible, and depression is treatable.

Keep yourself mentally active, as well as physically active. Keep learning new things. If your eyesight is good, read books. If your eyesight is poor, you may qualify to receive the Braille Institute talking books and tape player. These are complete books on tape that are sent to you through the mail at no charge—a wonderful service.

There are many ways to keep yourself mentally active, even if you do not enjoy reading. You can join interest groups, play mentally challenging games such as bridge or chess, or take classes through your parks and recreation department. Try new things, even if you do not find them especially interesting in the beginning. Give new activities a chance—you can always quit if they really fail to hold your interest. The point is that to stay mentally active and alert you must make the effort. Continuing to learn and develop new interests is probably the single most important thing you can do, next to exercising, to have a satisfying old age.

Keeping yourself clean, neat, and attractive will help you feel better about yourself, and it will make you a more pleasant person to be with. Older people can sometimes have unpleasant odors, but these are not inevitable and they are controllable. Don't neglect your personal habits, and learn ways to take care of the additional hygiene problems that occur in old age.

Making your surroundings comfortable and attractive is an important part of feeling good in your later years. Even if you have had to move to a care facility or to a smaller home, furnish it with your most cherished possessions, surrounding yourself with items that you love. Older men who may not have been accustomed to decorating and furnishing a home may need special help in this area. Living in a pleasant space, one that is clean and comfortable, is important for all people.

Research has shown that having a pet is good therapy for older people. If you live in an accommodation that allows pets, *consider getting a dog or cat to keep you company.* Cats are generally easier to care for, but they are also more independent than dogs and may not always want to be cuddled. Both types of animals give unconditional love and affection that is missing in the lives of many older people. Be sure, however, that there is someone who will take your pet if you become unable to keep it.

Try not to be unnecessarily frugal. Many older people live in fear of poverty, even though they have plenty of money. Consequently, they deprive themselves of pleasures that would make their lives comfortable and interesting. Learning to spend your money can be difficult, and habits of thrift are hard to break. Consider, however, if you have enough money to treat yourself well, why not do so? It's your money—use it.

If at all possible, continue to drive. Having the mobility and freedom of wheels will make it easier for you to keep active. If you question your ability to continue driving, take a driving test at the motor vehicles department. They'll let you know if you should be off the road.

If you cannot drive, locate a shuttle service for seniors to take you to your various activities. Nearly all cities and many small towns have these services now, and they are either free or minimally expensive.

Along with your interests and activities, be sure *to keep up with current events.* Listening to or watching the news at least once a day will keep you abreast of what's happening in the world. Simply because you're getting older doesn't mean you have to abdicate your participation in local or national affairs. Form opinions of your own, speak your mind, and be willing to work for what you believe.

Be of service to others. There are many ways to volunteer in most communities, and doing so will help you feel needed and valued. If you enjoy children, you can work as a foster grandparent. Many hospitals need volunteers to visit with patients, or provide the little services the nurses have little time to do. One of the authors had a Scottish aunt who, at age eighty-five, used to make regular visits to a nursing home to "visit the old folks." Volunteering can give your life a sense of purpose because your services are needed. Making a contribution to the lives of others repays you manyfold in personal satisfaction.

If you have, or suspect you have, a medical condition that warrants treatment, *see your doctor.* Don't avoid finding out what may be wrong, and definitely comply with all of the doctor's instructions. Write down what he or she tells you, and don't necessarily trust your memory. Take a friend or relative with you if you don't think you will be able to understand the instructions. A surprising number of people, young and old, do not follow their doctor's orders, and of course, this lessens their chances of recovery.

Finally, *have courage* as you get older. As my mother said, "growing old is not for the faint of heart." You have many challenges ahead of you, and some of them may be very trying to your hope. Always do the best you can do, take each situation as it comes, and cope with it in small steps. Stay focused on today, and tomorrow will take care of itself. It is possible to have a long and enjoyable old age.

Goals to Set for Your Later Years

Each of the guidelines you have just read can be translated into a goal you can set for yourself. As you choose to work on these goals, remember to follow the strategies you learned in section II. Remember also, take small steps, practice each step until it's comfortable, and be patient with yourself. The changes will come, and they will make a difference in your life.

1. Exercise regularly—stay physically active.

2. Develop or maintain good posture.

3. Eat nutritiously.

4. Learn to breathe correctly.

5. Develop good sleep habits.

6. Stay mentally active.

7. Stay clean, neat, and attractive—keep up your personal hygiene.

8. Make yourself a comfortable nest.

9. Consider getting a pet.

10. Spend money on yourself.

11. Keep mobile, continue to drive, or find other ways to get around.

12. Keep up with current events.

13. Find ways to be of service.

14. See you doctor regularly—comply with doctor's orders.

15. Have Courage!!

With high hope you can have a wonderful life. You can pursue your dreams, expand your horizons, and be a joy and inspiration to yourself and others. Hope is a carousel—from childhood to your senior years. Enjoy the ride.

Section IV

Hope Is a Relationship

In section I, you learned about hope and how to measure it in yourself. You also explored your early life, family stories, and other sources from which your hope may have developed. In section II, you refined your knowledge through the examination of specific life domains, and went on to learn strategies for enhancing your hope. Section III allowed you to explore the stereotypes and expectations of being male or female, growing older, and belonging to an ethnic minority, and how these stereotypes could affect your hope.

In this section, we consider relationships—relationship to self, and relationships with others. A healthy relationship with yourself is primary and precedes any good relationship with others in your life. In essence, if you do not love yourself, how can you love others? The first chapter in this section, therefore, deals with the way you love and care for yourself. Hope is an important part of having a good relationship with yourself. Research has shown that people who have low hope also have poorer self-esteem than those with high hope. Low-hope individuals do not take care of themselves as well, nor do they meet their own needs as well as do high-hope people. Low-hopers generally are less satisfied with most aspects of their lives, including their relationships. For this reason, it's important to shine the light of the hope development you have practiced in earlier sections on your relationship with yourself.

In chapter 15, you will explore some of the reasons why taking care of yourself can seem like a daunting task. You will read suggestions to remedy this situation, and find a list of goals you can use to focus your hope enhancement on yourself. You'll read that making yourself a high priority, without guilt, is one of the most difficult, but important lessons you will learn. You are all you have, and you are worth every effort you can make.

Chapter 16 focuses on your relationships with other people. These include your romantic relationships, and relationships with your family and friends. In this chapter, you will see how your thoughts and feelings about yourself can color your relationships with others. You will read guidelines for having better relationships, which then translate into goals you can use for your hope enhancement work. Stories illustrate the use of hope-enhancing strategies by people who are developing better relationships with self, lovers, family, and friends. You may see yourself in a few of these scenarios.

Relationships are a vital part of life satisfaction. Low-hope individuals have been shown to have fewer and less satisfactory relationships than do high-hope people. Thus, enhancing your hope in this life domain is an important part of your success in developing overall high hope. If you have learned the lessons of hope to this point, you are in an excellent position to apply them to your relationships. Remember to take small steps toward your goals, use you waypower and your willpower, and be patient with yourself. Learning to be patient is one vital key to having good relationships.

15

Hope Is Loving Yourself

Can you honestly say that you love yourself? What does that mean, to love yourself? Self-love is a concept fraught with meanings, both good and bad. The term "self-love" encompasses everything from masturbation to egotism, and somewhere in between is the notion that you can actually care for and nurture the person who is you. For a number of reasons, this is a difficult thing to do.

While dictionary definitions of self-love consider it to be the instinct or desire to promote your own well-being and survival, dictionaries of quotations give no such positive ideas. Self-love, according to history's greatest minds, is considered vanity, conceit, and selfishness. Some have considered self-love to be based on delusions, and still others thought of it as folly.

Religious teachings suggest that self-love is dangerous and sinful. According to the Bible "Seest thou a man wise in his own conceit? There is more hope of a fool than of him" (*Proverbs*, 26:12). Religion, influential in child rearing practices for centuries, may have negatively tainted the concept of loving oneself. Emphasis has instead been placed on the idea of loving others and self-sacrifice. It is clear that the concept of self-love has become confused with negative and potentially destructive outcomes rather than the adaptive and beneficial aspect of assuring one's own survival.

Cultural and religious proscriptions aside, you probably grew up being more self-critical than self-loving. Modern psychology has given self-love a somewhat better reputation. It's now widely recognized that, in order to love others, you must first love yourself. Psychotherapists, such as Carl Rogers, have built psychotherapeutic models based on the negative effects of not learning self-love. People grow up feeling bad about themselves because of the way they were taught to view their own behavior when they were young. You have learned that critical messages from adults can be internalized, and from those internalizations you learned to be self-critical. Self-criticism, along with the cultural ethos that warns against the dangers of self-love, creates a situation for many people in which attending to their own needs is difficult and guilt inducing.

It is a positive and hope-enhancing definition that we use in this chapter. Loving yourself means treating yourself at least as well as you treat the others whom you love. It means recognizing what your needs are, and most importantly, being willing to meet them. It means being able to put yourself first and doing so without guilt. It means giving yourself time and attention. This definition has nothing to do with vanity, conceit, or egotism. It is about positive growth and giving yourself the things you need to be a happy and productive person who, in turn, can truly love other people.

On the surface, loving yourself seems like an easy and evident thing to do. It isn't. Many women have an especially difficult time giving to themselves. The traditional roles of wife and mother stress that her primary function is to take care of others. When this emphasis on caretaking is combined with negative cultural beliefs about loving yourself and religious teachings about self-love, it's no wonder that so many women put their needs last.

Men can have problems with self-love as well, but the roles of husband and father may permit more latitude in their ability to meet their own needs with less guilt. Traditionally, the husband/father worked outside the home to support the family, while the wife/mother took care of the household and played the major part in raising the children. Men were more accustomed to controlling their own time and the family's resources, and therefore had a greater ability to meet their own needs than did their wives.

Traditional roles for men and women are changing. Large numbers of women work outside the home, and more men share housework and child-rearing duties. For women, however, this has not necessarily meant a shift in perspective about self-nurturing. What has happened, in many cases, is that women simply have added their careers or outside jobs to the work they already did in the home. By accepting a double work load, these superwomen virtually have eliminated any time that they might have spent doing things for themselves.

Does this description fit you? What does it all have to do with self-love? The ability to give to yourself and to put yourself ahead of others at times is a manifestation of loving yourself. Here is the story of Bonnie, who played many roles well. She took care of everyone and everything—except herself. You may see yourself reflected in Bonnie.

✳ Bonnie—I Want to Do It All

I'm not sure when I decided I wanted to be both a mother and have a career, but I know I have always felt that if I didn't have both I would be missing something. I'm lucky to have a lot of energy, because I'm on the go from early in the morning until late at night. Let me describe my life:

I have three children, ages seven, nine, and thirteen. Each of them has different activities and interests, which means that after school they are all going in different directions. Juggling their schedules, as well as my own, is a real trick. Fortunately my career (real estate sales) allows me the time to be an involved mother. I'm a soccer mom, a Girl Scout leader, a room mother, I teach Sunday school, and I help one of my daughters show her horse.

My days start early, getting everyone ready for school. My husband leaves before the children get up, so I'm the one who holds them to their schedules and gets them on the school bus. I'd like to collapse after they leave and the din quiets down, but I usually have appointments with people interested in buying new homes. I love my work because I love to help people get happily situated in the home that's just right for them. It's a career, but I think of it as also a public service.

I usually work until school is out, at which point I become a chauffeur. I car pool with other moms who have children in the same activities, and between us we manage to get each person where he or she needs to go. In the evening there is always a big family meal where we each tell our adventures of the day. My husband usually gets home by 6:30, in time to have a drink and relax a little before dinner. After dinner the children have homework, and I often have chores to do, such as baking or laundry. My husband putters in his shop, or works in his home office. We're not much of a television family—too busy I suppose. When everyone has gone to bed, I manage to sit down for a little while and read. The only problem is that I invariably fall asleep after a page or two.   ✳

Does Bonnie's life sound familiar? Your life may not be quite so full, but this picture fits many women who put in the double day. Bonnie's husband is fulfilling the traditional role of the primary breadwinner and thus doesn't participate in many household and child-rearing obligations. Bonnie enjoys her life and will tell you she finds it fulfilling. There are times, however, when she realizes she has needs of her own. There are things she would like to do for herself, and if she does not allow herself to make time for her own dreams, she may begin to resent those persons whom she loves.

While many men structure their lives as Bonnie's husband has done, there are increasing numbers of men who also perform a double day. These men, usually young, realize that those who live in a home should share the upkeep of it, and that it's unfair to place all of the responsibility on one person, especially if she also has a career. Many men also wish to be a larger part of their children's growing years than was encouraged in earlier times. These men may remember absent fathers and may have determined to give their own children more of their time. Ken's story shows that men also may have difficulty taking time to nurture themselves.

✳ Ken—Being a Responsible Father

My mother and father were divorced when I was very young, and I was raised by my mother and stepfather. Both my own father and my stepfather were busy men who had little time for a growing son. All the nurturing I received, I got from my mother. I decided that when I had my own children, I wasn't going to be an absentee father.

My career as the branch manager of a bank is very time consuming, and because I would like to be promoted to a general manager soon, I don't feel free to take time away from work for family obligations. The world of finance does not want to play second fiddle to anything else; it requires dedication to make the climb to the top. Often I feel torn between advancing in my career, and thus increasing our income, or taking the time to be with my children, which is also very important to me.

I reconcile my dilemma by putting in long hours each day and taking very little time for myself. My wife has a career as well, and we decided before we had children that we would share all of the responsibilities. So, each morning we work together to give them their breakfasts, make their lunches, and get them off to school. My wife's position is somewhat more flexible than mine, and so after school she picks the children up and takes them to their lessons or home. At night, she usually fixes dinner while I help the children with their homework. I do the dinner dishes and then help put them to bed, which is a lengthy process with baths and bedtime reading. After that, exhausted though we are, my wife and I have a chance to get caught up with all the events of the day.

The weekends are the time when I relish my role as a father. Even though I have to spend half of two Saturdays each month at the bank, I usually arrange a fun outing with the children for each Sunday. We also do household maintenance on the weekend, but we typically make those chores group projects. I never had an opportunity to work beside my father, to learn to do the things he could do. That's something I want to pass on to my children, both the boys and the girls.   ✳

Ken is a nontraditional husband and father, but he is paying a price. He has elected to put in the double day, alongside his wife, so that he can reap the rewards of a close relationship with his children. Both Ken and Bonnie want to do it all—Superman and Superwoman. They do the things they do out of love, but they are shortchanging themselves along the way. It is doubtful that either Bonnie or Ken ever take the time to think about loving themselves though, if asked, they would probably say, "Of course I do."

To the extent, however, that Ken, Bonnie, or *you* feel less than fulfilled with your daily routine, you're not taking care of yourself as well as you are taking care of the other people in your life. While you may be willing to say that you love yourself, if you do not give your own needs the attention they deserve, then you are not acting toward yourself in a loving way. You know you are loved, after all, through the actions of others. You feel loved when you are cared for, when people do nice things for you. In order to show yourself the love you are worth, you must take care of *yourself*, and do nice things for *you*.

Can You Learn to Love Yourself?

The first step in learning to love yourself is to give yourself permission. This is the hardest part because, as we have mentioned, so many of our cultural values make it very difficult. To give yourself permission for self-love, you must value who you are. Do you believe you are important? Do you have intrinsic worth as a person, just because you are you? Or, perhaps you believe that your value is based on what you do, especially the things you do for other people.

Try this little exercise. On a sheet of paper, write all of the qualities that you believe constitute your value as a person. Your list might include such items as your intelligence, experience, wisdom, beauty, and so forth. On another piece of paper, write a list of the things you do for others whom you believe make you valuable. The first list constitutes those qualities that, although may benefit others in an indirect way, are mainly valuable to you. The second list, which undoubtedly gives you a sense of personal worth, is where others see your value. Which list is longer? It is highly probably that your second list is far longer than the first, if you have many items on the first list at all.

In our experience as psychologists with adult clients, listing qualities they value or like about themselves is a difficult task. Recognizing your good points and coming to value them is a first step in learning to love who you are. As you think about the qualities in yourself that you are fond of, focus on those that have their greatest impact on you rather than another person. For example, your life experiences have given you a great deal of wisdom. The primary beneficiary of your wisdom is you, even though you may share it from time to time with others. Being a great cook, while it probably gives you pleasure, is usually done for other people, and the pleasure comes from their enjoyment.

The first assignment of this chapter is for you to create a list of personal attributes that show your worth. The first list you made can serve as a beginning for this longer, permanent list. This list is to be used to affirm your positive characteristics. Make the list as long as you can. Take your time to examine yourself, then make your list even longer. Read the list several times a day for a week, telling yourself that these attributes are valuable, and because of them, you are able to love yourself.

Listen to Your Needs and Your Wants

New mothers learn immediately to waken at the slightest sound their babies make. Parents can pick out their own children's cries from a noisy crowd. Can you recognize your own needs when they "cry" to you as well as you can hear your children? When you were young, if you had attentive parents, you probably expressed your needs and received satisfaction. Part of growing up, however, is learning to put your needs on hold; and so you learned to delay your gratification. You may have learned that lesson so well, in fact, that you forget how to gratify your needs at all.

When you were young you often had needs confused with wants. "I need a new dress." Or, "I need to have a boyfriend," are common refrains in young people. Another part of growing up is learning to tell which is a need and which is a want. The problem with stressing this distinction, however, is that it minimizes the importance of "wants." You come to believe that you can justify meeting real needs, but not the things you want.

Because this is so often true, you may label things you want as things you need so as to have a reason for doing them. For example, a man who really loves his work may spend twelve hours a day at the office. When his wife complains, he says he *needs* to spend so much time at work because the family *needs* the money. His reasoning may or may not be true. The point, however, is that needs can get confused with wants to such an extent that you have lost track of what is important.

Loving yourself means learning to listen to both your needs *and* your wants. It also means learning to be honest about what is a real need and what is something you prefer. Understand that both are important to a balanced life and to valuing yourself. The second assignment for this chapter is for you to identify your needs on a sheet of paper, and then, on another sheet of paper, identify the things you want.

Your list of needs will include the basic requirements for human survival, but it also may include other items unique to you. Examples of these might be time spent alone, a chance to exercise on a regular basis, or esthetic activities like listening to music and visiting museums. These last examples are not simply wants, but they may well be needs you have that you are currently not allowing yourself to satisfy.

Your list of wants is likely to include the more material aspects of life, such as a new car or a better washing machine. It also may include expectations that you have for someone else. For example, you may want your children to get better grades, or you may want your spouse to spend more time with you. Your wants are important, too, and they also should be heard.

It's important for you to be able to identify those things that you really need and to be able to fulfill them. It is also important to be able to ask for what you want and not feel you must justify it as a need. You are worth having your wants heard, but, as the Rolling Stones advise, "You can't always get what you want."

Honoring Your Needs

After you have examined your needs, and distinguished them from your wants, ask yourself how well you're meeting them. Notice that the question is how well *you* are meeting them. As an adult, the responsibility is on you to see that your needs are met, but this may involve asking someone else to help you. Living is usually a cooperative venture—you help others, and they help you. Asking for help is sometimes difficult, however, especially if you see your primary worth as being the one who meets the needs of others.

Both Bonnie and Ken found a great deal of their self-worth and their love for themselves through the things they did for their families. For both of these people, asking for time away from these commitments in order to meet personal needs probably would induce guilt. Bonnie might have to hire someone to help her with her children's schedules, and Ken might need to ask his wife to fill in for him. While these solutions might work, it's probable that neither Bonnie nor Ken would seek to employ them. They would not feel right about taking time for themselves.

Do you find it difficult to take time away from others in order to meet your own needs? Do you tell yourself that your needs can wait? Perhaps you tell yourself that something you need is really only something you want and therefore unimportant. Turning your needs into wants, and then discounting them is an old trick used by many people who find it difficult to ask others for help. Learn to identify when you do this, and learn to be honest with yourself.

At this point, you have made a list of characteristics that you value about yourself, and you have reviewed this list often. Your task then was to make lists of your needs and your wants, learning to distinguish between the two with the caveat that they are both important. Your next assignment is to select one need that is not currently being met and determine what will have to happen so that you can satisfy it.

When you were acquiring high-hope strategies, you learned to ask yourself, "If I could have (do) what I want, what would that be?" You were learning about goal setting, and your work here involves seeing the process of satisfying your need as a goal that you can accomplish. Now, rephrase the question slightly to read, "If I could meet my need, what would have to happen?" Seeing the satisfaction of your need as a goal and using your waypower and willpower thinking strategies can make this task manageable.

Let's see how this process works, using Bonnie as an example.

✳ Bonnie—Asking Permission

My life appeared to be wall-to-wall commitments with no time left over for the things I might want or need to do. I love my family and valued myself for the things I am able to do for them, but I was beginning to feel as though I was ignoring my own needs. I decided to construct a list of needs and wants, which I then prioritized, determining that my strongest need was to find time to exercise. I had never shed the extra pounds I gained with the last child, and I felt somewhat dumpy and out of shape.

In order to create time for this activity, I would have to take time away from another responsibility. At first, each time I thought of something I could do differently, I discarded the idea because I believed my children would miss my participation. Finally, I decided to speak to my family about my need to exercise and ask them to help me think of a way I could fit it in. In part, I realized I was asking for permission, but I also saw this as a good place to begin looking after myself.

I called a family meeting where we discussed schedules. Initially, no one wanted to do anything differently, which meant I would have to stick up for myself a little more firmly. I explained that I did things for everyone else, and this was something I needed to do for myself. I also went on to explain that staying physically fit would give me more energy to meet my other responsibilities. Put in that context, my children and husband agreed that they wanted to help me make time for exercise.

I was able to arrange for someone else to pick up the children after school three days a week while I went to an exercise class. I found that I was still able to attend most of the children's activities after my class, missing only the initial part. The solution to my need was not nearly as difficult as I had anticipated. The next step would be to meet other needs without asking permission and without feeling so much guilt.   ✳

Bonnie took the first step in taking care of herself and showing self-love. Her experience may sound familiar to you—the initial hesitancy in asking, followed by guilt. Her family's reluctance to change anything in their lives is also a common reaction. Bonnie was persistent, however, and the honest presentation of her needs was honored. Making changes in your life to meet your needs is difficult, but it's important to make a start.

You have now made your lists, isolated at least one need to tackle, and attempted to find a way to achieve your goal. Was your experience similar to Bonnie's? If you were not successful on your first try, rethink what happened and try again. Do you firmly believe that you have the right to have your needs met? If you are wavering on this basic assumption, you're probably not being as assertive as you need to be.

Go back to your list of personal qualities, and try to include as many items as you can think of. You might find it helpful to ask good friends and family for their contributions. Sometimes others see our value better than we do. Spend the time it takes to convince yourself that you are worth caring for.

Without this fundamental regard for yourself, it will be difficult to expect others to care for you and especially difficult to take care of yourself.

If you were successful in your efforts to meet the need you established as your first task, it's time to move on to the next step. After you're comfortable with the arrangement you have made to get your particular need met, try tackling another of the needs on your list. Think about the importance of this need to your overall life and what it will take to satisfy it. If it is going to require other people to accommodate you, change their schedules perhaps, or do some of the things you would normally do, you will need to discuss the arrangements with them.

Be prepared with a plan for getting this need met, and be prepared to discuss your reasoning. If you understand and believe the importance of what you are asking, it will help you feel more confident and less guilty. It is important for you to present your idea as reasonable, and with the understanding that you have every expectation that it will be honored. Remember, you are not asking for permission, as Bonnie felt that she was doing—you are simply stating a reasonable request. You are acting as an adult member of a family who has every right to expect the same privileges as any other person in that family. When you are comfortable with that belief, you're ready to move on to the next step.

Asking for What You Want

You have now distinguished between wants and needs, and you have now tried asking for some of the things you have termed needs. Needs may be somewhat easier to ask for than wants, because they can be viewed as reasonable requests that are necessary to your well-being. It is in the interest of a family to preserve the well-being of each person, and you, of course, play a very important role.

Wants can be seen as frivolous, less necessary, and therefore may take more courage on your part to request. The things you want, however, can be very important to your happiness. Consider how many times you have given others not only what they needed, but what they wanted. Do you have the right to expect the same in return? We believe the answer is an emphatic "Yes!"

If you experienced some amount of guilt when you asked to have your needs met, you probably are going to experience more guilt when you ask for what you want. It may be more difficult to justify these requests in your own mind, and therefore you may not feel the same degree of certainty that you have the right to ask. An important part of taking care of yourself, of showing yourself love, is learning that you are entitled to ask for what you want.

Your next task is to examine your list of wants and select one that is important and for which you feel safe in asking. What do you need to do to get what you want? Do you need to clear it with anyone, as you do when it involves others? Perhaps you can simply do it, or get it on your own. If what you want involves spending money, what kinds of thoughts and feelings do you have about that? Spending money on yourself can create guilt feelings as well as anxiety, even if it is money you have earned. You may feel you are being selfish or self-indulgent, which is another quality, along with self-love, that is misunderstood and is frowned upon in our culture. Again, we ask you to consider whether you're worth giving yourself what you want. How many times have you given to others? It's your turn now. Enjoy it without guilt.

Let's follow Ken as he asks for something he wants that will involve both spending money and changing the routine he has worked out with his wife.

✳ Ken—The Ball's in Your Court

One thing I have always wanted to do was to learn to play tennis. Somehow I never found time in college, and then, after I married and we had the children, it just didn't seem possible. An opportunity has come along, however, that is too good to turn down.

One of my regular clients at the bank is a professional tennis instructor. He offered to give me lessons for a reduced fee and get me a discount to purchase a membership at the tennis club where he teaches. He could give me lessons every Thursday evening, and, of course, I would also needed time to practice.

Here was something I had wanted to do for years, but it would take time away from the children, and my wife would have to pick up some extra responsibility. Did I have the right to take this time for myself? I knew a lot of men who played golf every weekend, who went to poker parties, and spent far less time with their families than I did. But we had worked out this arrangement before we had children, and I questioned how fair it was for me to ask for a change now. On the other hand, I wasn't getting any younger, and it would never again be as easy for me to learn tennis as it would be now. What a dilemma!

Because what I wanted to do would require the accommodation of my wife, I needed to discuss it with her before I could make a decision. As I feared, she wasn't too happy about the extra work she would have to do. She knew how much I wanted to play tennis, however, so she suggested I give it a try. If the work was overwhelming, I agreed to quit.

This was not the blanket approval I had wished for, but it was better than a refusal. I still had decisions to make and guilt to cope with. While her suggestion seemed reasonable at first, it meant that every Thursday evening when I was finished with my lesson I would half expect her to tell me the work was too much. I felt as if I couldn't throw myself into learning tennis. I kept holding back because I thought I might have to stop.

After a month, I brought the subject up again. I managed to put my guilt aside and tell her I wanted to either make a commitment to learning tennis, or I would stop. I also stressed that I was enjoying myself, and that I knew this would be a long-term and satisfying activity. To my surprise, she told me to continue. She said the work wasn't as overwhelming as she had thought it would be, and, in fact, the children were learning lessons in responsibility by doing more for themselves.

✳

Ken's story illustrates the guilt that you may feel when asking for what you want. In his case, learning to play tennis meant that he was changing an agreement he and his wife had about sharing responsibilities. There can be many reasons why you may experience guilt; the most problematic one is founded on your belief that you're not worthy of asking for what you want when it involves being accommodated by another person. If this is true for you, it is a sign that you do not care for yourself enough. Continue reviewing your list of positive personal characteristics, telling yourself that you are valued by others, and that you are valuable to yourself.

A Room of Your Own

One of the needs that most people experience is to have some privacy, a place where you can go and know that, for a period of time, you will be undisturbed. Do you have a space that is just yours? A place where you can be alone, or at least keep private personal things that are important to you? Having an area that belongs to you and you only is an important part of caring for yourself—demonstrating your self-love. If you live with other people, especially children, you may not have considered the importance of your own privacy. You may think that having a space that is off-limits to others is another sign of selfishness. Not so.

Why is it important to have your own space? To be a happy and emotionally healthy person it's important to have boundaries, and these can be represented by having this private place. Boundaries are barriers to parts of yourself that you do not share with other people unless you choose to do so. If you find it difficult to ask to have your needs and wants met, there is a good chance that you also have problems establishing and maintaining firm boundaries.

The relationship between establishing boundaries and being willing to meet your needs is clear. Both require you to stand by your belief that you are a valuable and lovable person. You must be willing to take the risk that you may annoy or anger someone who is important to you. Loving yourself means trusting that you are also lovable to someone else. *Anger or annoyance should not equal a loss of love.*

If you do not have a space that you can call your own, your next task is to create one. Your personal place does not have to be an entire room, it can be a closet, a chest of drawers, or a table. The point is that this place is for you only. You can put anything into it you wish, and you should be able to know that, when you return, it will be exactly as you left it. Declare that this is your space. Tell the others in your household that you don't want anyone touching it.

If you're lucky enough to have an entire room of your own, what kinds of things do you have in it? Is it furnished with things you love? Or, is it furnished with the leftover furniture no one else wanted? Maybe you have the ironing board there, or the vacuum cleaner. You should be able to use your space for anything you wish. You can use it for your hobbies, you can use it for your home office, or for a reading and relaxing room. Don't allow other people to use it for their purposes, because this is an infringement of your boundaries. Use the creation of your space to show your love for yourself. Make it a reflection of the good things you enjoy, and the positive things you feel about yourself.

Give Up Perfectionism

If you are like Ken or Bonnie, a do-it-all superperson, you are probably a perfectionist. Do you believe you are valuable because of all the things you do? Would people love you less if you didn't do everything? Would you love yourself less? If you were not a perfectionist, in fact, you would probably be far more accepting of yourself and treat yourself better. Having perfectionist standards may seem like a productive way to live, but these standards really only give you a way to be more critical of yourself.

It can be difficult to let go of your high expectations when you're surrounded by images of what the "perfect" wife, mother, husband, career person, etc. should be like. The message is that you are supposed to be able to "do it all." The flaw in the picture is, if you do it all, you don't have time for you. Who are you being perfect for?

One way to let go of perfectionism is to challenge your ideas of what is necessary. How clean does the house really need to be? How often does the grass have to be cut? Think about the reasons you expect the things of yourself that you do, and question their validity. Try not doing something you have always done and see how it feels to you. For example, Bonnie always turned her husbands undershirts right side out when folding the laundry. This got to be a time-consuming chore. She decided to fold them as they were and let him reverse them before he put them on. This simple act helped Bonnie to let go of some of her perfectionism.

Perfectionism seldom has to do only with oneself. The expectations you have of yourself generally involve others and are based on what these people will think of you. Bonnie took the chance of annoying her husband when she stopped reversing his shirts, and it took courage and trust to take the risk. If you drop some of your perfectionistic expectations, what repercussions might there be? Do you love yourself enough to cope with them? If the idea of not being perfect causes you anxiety, you need to continue reinforcing your self-worth.

The Self-Love Mantra

One of the strategies you learned for increasing your hopeful thinking was to change your self-talk. You learned that you could alter the way you thought by altering the things you said to yourself. If the previous information and arguments haven't convinced you that you are a person who is worthy of care and attention, someone who is worthy of loving yourself, you may find the self-love mantra to be useful.

A mantra is a word or phrase that is said over and over to oneself. One effect a mantra can have is to calm you in high anxiety situations. However, if your mantra is a phrase that is positive about yourself, whether or not you originally believe it, you will gradually begin to accept it as true. Here are a few examples of effective mantras.

- I am worthy of care and love.

- I have a right to have the things I need.

- I have a right to have the things I want.

- I love myself.

You can create your own phrases, adding some of the characteristics that you value about yourself. The key to success is repetition. Find activities that do not require much mental attention, and use those times to repeat your mantra. If you are a jogger, say your mantra in rhythm with your steps. You can use the times when you're doing housework, gardening, or taking a walk to do this self-loving activity. Do it privately, and do it often. It will work.

Learn to Nurture Yourself—Aggressively

The assignments up to this point have been designed to help you take charge of meeting your own needs and pursuing what you want. Nurturing yourself will be easier if you have successfully negotiated the previous tasks because you will be ready to make yourself a high priority. Learning to take care of yourself is difficult, however, and you still may be struggling with some of the earlier tasks. Nurturing yourself not only shows your self-love, but you will find that, as a result, you have higher hope to meet your needs and wants.

In chapter 9, we discussed ways to increase your physical energy to help you enhance your willpower. Those strategies are a few of the methods you can use to nurture yourself. If you are a parent, think of the good care you take of your children. You feed them nourishing foods, keep them clean and well-clothed, making certain that they get enough rest and stimulating their minds. You comfort them in times of pain, and you try to guide them toward independence. Many of the self-care strategies we have detailed in the second section of this workbook are similar to the nurturing care you provide for you children.

It's important for you to make your own nurturing a high priority. Be certain that you eat enough of the right foods and that you get the exercise you need. It is easy to neglect these two basics when you're busy attending to other people's needs. Rest and relaxation are also important parts of your self-nurturing. Taking a nap or reading a book may seem self-indulgent when you have many other pressing duties, but taking a little time out of your busy day to relax will repay you with more energy later.

If you are able to nurture yourself, you will find you lead a more balanced life. Balance is created by incorporating many different facets into your life. For example, if you spend too much time on one type of activity, such as work, you will eventually begin to long for a balancing activity, such as play. Nurturing yourself, demonstrating your love for yourself, means listening to your physical and mental needs for variation and balance. Honor your needs. Don't force yourself into a pattern that has been cut from the material of your perfectionism and self-criticism.

Living with Others and Loving Yourself

You have read many suggestions in this chapter for showing love to yourself. If you have incorporated the hope-enhancing strategies in the previous sections, you will be at ease with the tasks given here. How does self-love actually work in the lives of people who have many other commitments? You saw the small changes made by Bonnie and Ken to ensure that at least one important need was met. Let's look at Donna, whom you have followed throughout this workbook. In her younger years, she was a single parent and had a busy career. Finding time for herself was a daunting task.

✳ **Donna—Making Time for Me**

There is one problem with being a woman in a "man's world." Men who have wives at home don't understand the need to take time away from work to be with your children. When my children were in their early teens and I was a single mother, I was also building my reputation as an attorney. I felt constantly torn between my obligations at work and my responsibilities to my children.

My mother, a successful career woman, had found little time to be involved in my activities when I was young, and I determined that when I had children I would be part of their lives. So, between putting in many hours at work and eking out special time to do the things my children wanted, I felt like my life had become a game of tug-of-war.

How long could I keep up the pace, when the only time I had to rejuvenate myself was my lunch hour and the fifteen minutes before I fell asleep at night? I was stressed. I was cranky and short-tempered. Something was going to have to change. I was taking care of everyone except myself.

I wanted to be the perfect mother, the perfect homemaker, and the perfect lawyer. So what if I had no social life, no romance, no leisure; that was just the price I had to pay to do all the other things. But, I was discovering that I didn't want to buy that bill of goods anymore.

Some major changes in my life were going to have to happen, but what should they be? I made lists (I'm a great list maker, anyway) of what I needed to do to take care of myself and what I simply wanted to do that I never found the time for. From the need list, I selected exercising and reading literature. I consider feeding my mind as important as feeding my body, and my mind was becoming stagnant reading nothing but legal documents. From the list of things I wanted to do, I selected going to movies with friends and having dinner parties.

Now that I had decided which activities would enrich my life and rejuvenate me, I had to figure out how to get the time to do them. Actually, the two activities I wanted to do were the easiest. Although the children were accustomed to having me at home every night, they were old enough to stay by themselves on occasion. I could make time to go to movies. As for dinner parties, the kids would just have to absent themselves and keep busy with other activities. I didn't think they would object to those requests.

Finding the time to meet the two needs I had selected was harder. I needed to exercise often and probably during the day. I didn't want to miss the important events and interests of my children, and the mornings were too busy to schedule in another activity

Since I had some amount of control over my time, I decided to take an hour four days a week to play racquetball. Several other attorneys I knew liked to play, and I made arrangements to play with them. To do this meant that my billable hours would decrease by approximately six each week, so I thought it would be wise to talk with one of the senior partners first. As I had feared, he was not pleased and suggested that I make up the hours on the weekend. I stood my ground, however, and told him that my own health depended on getting some physical activity. He finally agreed, a little grudgingly. I had some guilt about not being the perfect lawyer, but I (and he) was just going to have to get used to it.

Finding the time to read literature was even more difficult, and the guilt was constant for a while. I had a cozy chair in my bedroom where I planned to read. I told the children that for an hour each evening I would be off-limits. If they had things to tell me, unless it was an emergency, they would have to wait until I was finished reading. Either they had a hard time understanding the importance of what I was doing, or they simply forgot. For the first several weeks one after the other would barge in to talk to me. Each time

I shooed them off I felt guilty. Isn't mothering supposed to be constantly on tap?

Eventually they learned not to disturb me, but even then I felt guilty for a while. Was I being a good enough mother? Maybe I was, actually, because children need limits. They need to recognize other people's boundaries, and my kids were learning a good lesson. Because I was taking time out every evening for myself, it meant that the house was not as neat and orderly as it had been. Another lesson for my children was to work as a family at keeping the house clean. My ideas of perfection were changing, but I found I was still an excellent mother.

Most importantly, I was finally being a friend to myself. I began to feel better both physically and emotionally. I started liking the person I saw in the mirror. Everyone benefited, and I really began to love who I was.   ✳

We know from following Donna through many parts of her life, that she is a person high in hope. Her story illustrates the guilt she felt for not living up to her idea of perfection. It took courage for her to defy the senior partner, and it took strength to set boundaries with her children. Loving yourself can be difficult, even for high-hope people such as Donna; however, hope makes the process easier. If your hope is increasing, as it will as you do the work in this book, your love for yourself will increase right along with your willpower and waypower.

Guidelines and Goals for Loving Yourself

The theme of this chapter, having a good relationship with yourself, is learning to take the good care of *yourself* that you give to others. In order to do that, you must be willing to make yourself a high priority, and in doing so, you may come up against the wishes and expectations of others. Making yourself a priority takes courage and strength. You must be willing to chance the annoyance or even anger expressed by other people. You must be willing to disappoint those you care about on occasion, because you also care about yourself.

Learn to distinguish between needs and wants, and be able to understand the importance of each in your life. Learn also to express your thoughts to others. Remember that they can't read your mind. Once you have explained the reasons behind your actions, it's up to them to accept what you need to do for yourself. You are a lovable and a valuable person. It is unlikely that you will be rejected simply because you are acting for your own good.

Learning to love yourself will enhance your hope, just as increasing your hope will make it easier to care for yourself. Loving yourself and hopeful thinking nourish each other and, in turn, your life will increase in satisfaction dramatically. Here are some goals you can use along with your hope strategies to increase both your hope and your love for yourself.

1. Understand your needs and your wants.

2. Listen to your needs and wants.

3. Spend time with/by yourself. Learn to enjoy your own company.

4. Do some of the things *you* want to do rather than always acquiescing to others' wishes.

5. Don't ask permission. You are an adult, make your own decisions.

6. Make and use your self-love mantra.

7. Change your notion of what is perfect.

8. Learn to ask for help when you need it.

9. Take care of your body.

10. Nourish your mind.

11. Work on eliminating guilt, apologies, and feeling selfish.

Now that you are improving your relationship with yourself, the next chapter takes you into the realm of your relationships with others. Bear in mind, however, that you are of primary importance because without your own well-being, no other relationship will be truly satisfying.

16

Hope in Your
Relationships with Others

In chapter 15, you learned the importance of your relationship with yourself. You learned that loving yourself is a prerequisite to loving others. Loving yourself, in addition, is necessary to accepting the love that others have for you. Your relationship with yourself provides the foundation upon which all the other relationships you have are built.

We suggested strategies and provided examples illustrating the ways you could improve your relationship with yourself. If you have spent many years without the benefits of self-love, you may be reluctant to try the assignments given. We have pointed out that, when you attempt to change an existing life pattern, you may encounter resistance from other people in your life. Your friends and family have been accustomed to your behaving in a certain way, especially in regard to the way that you have met their needs. When you change your behavior, even to a small extent, they also must make an adaptation.

It's important for you to have the willpower to risk encountering your loved ones' displeasures. If they truly love you, they do so for who you are, and not only for what you do for them. Thus, their annoyance will be short-lived—only a bump on the journey that is your life. The benefits to you and to your relationships with others are enormous.

Once you have learned to love yourself and to take good care of your own needs and wants, you will be able to have equality with your lover, your partner, and your friends. You will be a better parent to your children, because you will be able to maintain appropriate boundaries. You will model self-sufficiency and independence in your relationship with yourself, while demonstrating interdependence in your relationship with others.

This chapter is about your relationships with others. Using the life domains given in chapter 7, we will discuss your relationships in the areas of romance, family, and friends. Because your work in chapter 16 may have some temporarily unsettling effects on these relationships, here are a few caveats to remember.

In the stories that you read, changes were made one step at a time, and they were small. We suggested that you discuss what you wanted and needed with the people whose lives might be affected. Communication, of course, is one vital component of good relationships, and it's important for you to be able to talk about what you require for yourself. Once you have explained what you require and why it is important you have laid all the groundwork possible for other people's acceptance. You must then allow them, on their own, to come to terms with changes that you are undergoing. This is the difficult part for people who are accustomed to meeting the needs of others rather their own.

To minimize the stress on your relationships with others, it is important to start with small steps and not to make your changes too rapidly. You have lived with your needs for a long time and may not have spoken of them to anyone. Remember, however, that other people cannot read your mind, and so your requests may come as a complete surprise to them. Just as we have reminded you to be patient with yourself, you also must be patient with the other people in your life who are not accustomed to your new behaviors. It will take them time to become used to your taking care of yourself, just as it will take time for you to learn this new way of being.

This chapter on relationships begins with the romantic domain, then moves to the family, and finally, the social arena—friendships. The assumption underlying all of the suggestions and strategies for having hope in your relationships is that you love yourself, or that you are in the process of developing your self-love. Hopeful thinking, as well, is a must in positive relationships with others. You have learned many ways to enhance your willpower and waypower, and you will use these to achieve the goals suggested in this chapter.

Romantic Relationships

The importance of romance in your life can vary. When you are young, romance may have filled your thoughts and desires, but as you get older, other domains may become more important. Not everyone needs romance, although being loved and loving others is essential to happiness. Romance is not the same thing as lust or sex. Men often consider the culmination of a successful romantic liaison to be sexual contact, whereas women frequently consider emotional attachment as the primary goal.

Romance involves feelings of being valued and cherished. During a romantic relationship, the partners show a fascination with each other that can border on obsession. Thoughts of each other are constantly present, either consciously or just under the surface. During this initial phase, you see yourself as your loved one sees you. Love may bloom on your face, giving you a glow that hides your imperfections from yourself. If you don't love yourself, it is less obvious to you during this stage of romance because you are loved by someone else.

If you don't love yourself, you may jump from one romance to another. Being adored by someone else can act as a salve for self-doubts. If you lack self-love, you will look to others to save you from being with yourself. Popular love songs are odes to this type of behavior, and they reinforce the frequency and normalcy of self-doubts. Although such thoughts may be frequent, they are not healthy. Needing to be with another to save you from being alone is a sign that you don't like your own company and don't care for yourself. If this sounds familiar, you are looking to someone else to meet your needs. It is important to be able to turn to *yourself* to fill such needs.

Assuming that your romance is not based on a need to avoid yourself, you are in a position to establish a genuine relationship with the object of your affections. In the phase that follows the initial attraction, you return to reality and begin the process of really getting to know the other person. In the beginning, you saw yourself through the infatuated eyes of the other person, and now you realize that you are still you. How will you tell the other person about the real you? How will you discover what he or she is all about?

Getting to Know Each Other

How candid are you when you tell another person about yourself? If you like who you are, you will find pleasure in this activity. If you have not learned to love yourself, however, you will be selective about what you disclose. If you are just starting a new romance, or are in the early stages of one, now is a good time to begin to be honest about yourself. Realize that if you're not honest, you will never believe that you are loved for who you are.

In the early stages of a relationship, you have the opportunity to show that you expect to have your needs met, just as you expect to meet those of the other person. In the previous chapter, you learned how to begin identifying your own needs and setting up conditions for meeting those needs. In a new relationship, you can do this without having to deal with a long-established pattern. You can ask for what you want and need and begin the important work of boundary setting.

When you begin a new relationship, do you try so hard to please the other person that you neglect yourself? If you don't love yourself, this is probably the case. While concentrating on the needs of the other person can be attractive and pleasing, it portrays an unrealistic picture of who you are. Pleasing your partner to the exclusion of yourself puts you in a one-down position in the relationship, and with that game established in the beginning, it's difficult to change the rules later.

Use your hope-enhancing skills to get your relationships off on the right foot. Consider the goals and guidelines you learned in the previous chapter as targets to aim for in your new relationship. Decide which need or want will be your first goal. Because this is a two-way relationship, ask yourself how you would like your partner to help you achieve your goal. Think of ways to communicate what you want, and consider the responses that you would find acceptable. Use your willpower thinking by putting your plan into action, even if this task produces anxiety.

To illustrate this process, here is the story of Corey and David. They are just beginning their relationship. They each have been married before and are in their early thirties. Corey has a son and daughter, and David has no children. Corey tells this story about using hope lessons to learn to have an equal relationship.

❋ Corey—I Don't Want to Repeat the Past

My husband left me for another woman five years ago, and I was devastated and confused. I thought I had been the perfect wife. Our house was immaculate, I was a superb cook, and we never argued because I always gave him what he wanted—I thought. The woman he left me for was my age, and wasn't any better looking than I, but, as he told me, she was a lot more independent. I thought I was being a good wife, but he thought I was being too passive.

During the past five years, I have done a lot of work on myself. When I look back on it, I realize that I didn't speak up for what I wanted. I was afraid he would leave me if I were demanding—ironically, he left me anyway. I am able now to admit to myself the things I need, and even the things I want. One thing is certain: my next relationship is going to be different than my last.

I met David at a meeting of the Sierra Club, and we were instantly attracted to each other. I had joined that group because I wanted to meet people with similar interests to mine, not expecting to find a new relationship. I really wasn't hunting for a partner, like some of my friends. In fact, I was rather enjoying my own freedom. So, it was with caution that I began this new relationship.

I had spent so much of my time coming to terms with being alone that I had not given much thought to what I would want in another relationship. Now that it was upon me, I knew I had to give it some thought.

As I do with many things, I made a list. What characteristics in a partner did I need? What did I want? I labeled some qualities as "required" and some as "preferred." Under the required category,

I put "sensitive and willing to listen to me," while under preferred I put "handsome and tall." Of course, there were other qualities, both required and preferred, but I decided to be certain he met my first few required qualifications before proceeding further.

David was tall and he was handsome. He was also sensitive to environmental concerns, but would he be sensitive to me? Nothing that involves people is clear cut, of course, and I found that sometimes he was an empathic listener, and sometimes he wasn't. In the past, when my husband tuned me out, I assumed that it was because I didn't have anything worthwhile to say. I wasn't willing to accept that view now, but former habits of thought die hard.

When David interrupted me or changed the subject, as he did more often than I would have liked, my old self-doubts would come back. My first reaction was to criticize myself for talking trivia, but then I was able to stop that thought and focus on what was going on between us. I had to find a good way to tell him that I needed him to really listen to me when I talked.

When I was alone, I rehearsed a number of scenarios where I told him what I needed. When we were together, however, it was more difficult to talk about. I knew it was because I wasn't accustomed to speaking up for my needs, but I also knew that if I didn't do it, I wouldn't want to continue the relationship. So, the next time he interrupted me, I told him that if our relationship was going to work for me, I needed him to listen to the things I had to say. I went on to explain a bit about my past relationship, and how it was new for me to speak for what I needed. He seemed to be surprised, but he also said he would pay closer attention. I was pleased that he hadn't gotten angry with me, and that gave me courage to speak my mind when it happened again.   ✳

Given Corey's history, speaking up for what she needed took courage. She had learned some painful lessons in her marriage, and she was determined not to repeat the past. She used hopeful thinking by finding appropriate pathways to achieve her goal of being heard, and she used willpower thinking by reminding herself that, if she wanted the relationship to be a good one, she was going to have to be more confrontational with David.

David was somewhat surprised when Corey said she needed him to listen to her better. His former wife had never suggested that he was insensitive or a poor listener, but then she always let him guide the conversations. In addition, David never really had discussed personal or emotional aspects of his relationships, and so Corey's request was uncomfortable for him. Here is David's story of the way the relationship developed.

✳ David—This Is All New Territory

When I first met Corey, I was attracted by her good figure and her pretty face. I had been divorced for three years, and the dating scene still wasn't comfortable. I'd been out with a few women but hadn't really wanted more than a few dates with any of them. Corey was not only sexy, but she was smart and interested in some of the same things I was. There was immediate electricity between us that I had not felt for some time.

Our friendship started with coffee after the Sierra Club meeting. Soon we progressed to dinners and a few movies. One of the things I noticed about Corey was that she really liked to talk. We took a long drive one afternoon down the Pacific Coast Highway, and I would have been very content to enjoy the scenery quietly. Corey, however, had all sorts of things she wanted to talk about ranging from ecology to religion. I know I lost interest in the conversation. Talking just wasn't what I wanted right then.

A few days later, as we were having a drink in our favorite pub, Corey told me that she got the feeling I didn't listen to her much or care about the things she had to say. I was really caught off guard. In part she was right, but I also thought I acted like I was interested. Although I was confused, I said I would try to listen better.

Later that evening, I gave some serious thought to what she had said. I knew from what she told me that her husband had discounted her in subtle ways, and that she still felt somewhat insecure. I really liked and respected Corey, and I didn't want to treat her the same way. However, I also didn't want to be blamed for something I wasn't doing. We were going to have to talk about it some more, and I was really on unfamiliar ground talking about my feelings.

Corey's confrontation caused me to think back on my marriage. I realized that I might have done to my wife what Corey's husband had done—dominated the conversations. I had to ask myself if I really did care about what she had to say, or did I just want to have a sexual relationship with her. When I considered it, I knew I wanted a relationship with her that would go beyond sex.

If I wanted to make this relationship work, I was going to have to find ways to communicate equally. I decided that one thing I could do would be to focus my attention on Corey when she spoke and really try to listen to what she said. This would be a new behavior for me in friendships, even though I was accustomed to listening at work.

I decided to go one step further and tell Corey about the thoughts and feelings I had after our confrontation. Discussing personal subjects felt as if I would be exposed and vulnerable. If I wanted to have a deeper relationship with this woman, however, I had better learn to be more open. Our conversation went very well, and she seemed aware of how hard it was for me. She became more warm and loving, and thanked me for the effort.

David's experience was similar to Corey's in that they both had to overcome their discomfort in order to learn to talk to each other. They both set goals that would help them communicate better, and they both had the same bigger and shared goal of developing a good relationship. They each had to find ways to communicate their thoughts and feelings, and they were able to exercise willpower thinking because they knew the relationship depended upon it.

David's and Corey's stories illustrate how hopeful thinking can be used to help form a romantic relationship. Even if you have no baggage to overcome from past relationships, you will want to be able to set boundaries and expect to have many of your needs and wants satisfied. As you start a new relationship, consider how you want it to be. Establishing those conditions will become your goals within the relationship. You know the strategies to use for achieving your goals now, so it's up to you.

Perfectionism in Relationships

Perfectionism, as we discussed in chapter 15, can be a sign of a lack of self-love. The desire for perfection stems from criticisms that you internalized when you were a child. Perfectionism is not only personally destructive, but also destroys relationships. You have seen that this quality feeds your self-doubts, causing you to feel unworthy of having your needs met. When you expect perfection of another person, you will either drive that person away or create self-doubts in them that are similar to your own. Neither condition is healthy for a relationship.

If you are a faultfinder and rarely completely satisfied with others, you are demonstrating perfectionist characteristics. The people around you eventually may stop trying to please you, they may withdraw their affections, and finally may leave. Letting go of perfectionism is difficult. If you find yourself criticizing other people frequently, you can use the hope-enhancement process to change this behavior.

Your first step is to consider what and who you criticize most often. Being aware of when you are most likely to do it will allow you to establish goals for those situations. Your next step is to determine ways to cope with your desire to criticize. You may tell yourself to keep quiet, or you may find an uncritical way of saying what you wish to say. Ask yourself how important the situation really is. Is it important enough for someone else to feel bad? *If you are a critical person, it is likely that you have been criticized.* You know how it feels, and that can be a strong deterrent.

The beginning of a new relationship is a good time to examine your perfectionist tendencies. A word of warning is warranted on this point, however. It can be difficult to determine when your expectations are reasonable and when they are not. If you're a person who does not expect to have your needs met, you may be critical, but you also may keep your thoughts to yourself until they build into resentment. Or, if the opposite is the case and you ask someone else to satisfy all of your needs, you may become unduly critical if your partner does not comply.

The solution to this dilemma is to communicate. It is vital to the success of all relationships that the people involved learn to talk to each other. You must learn to express your thoughts, and you must listen attentively to your partner. The strategies you have learned for enhancing hope can help you achieve this goal.

Matching Your Hope

Now that you are in the process of enhancing your own hope, and you can see the positive changes that can happen in your life, you will want your partner to have high hope as well. When the partners in a relationship differ greatly in their waypower and willpower thinking, difficulties are likely to arise. The person who is low in hope may think that the one who is high in hope is being unrealistic—a Pollyanna. The high-hope partner may have different goals, will see these goals as possible because he or she can perceive ways to reach them, and will have the mental energy to pursue these objectives.

The partner who is high in hope may think that the low-hope person is depressed, negative, and not willing to try hard enough to reach his or her goals. In this circumstance, it is the high-hope person who is in the better position to understand, and possibly even assist, the low-hope partner in using hopeful thought. Hope is infectious, and your high-hope thoughts and actions may provide sufficient incentive to encourage the other person to try your approach.

If your *prospective* partner in a relationship does not have high hope, it's unwise to believe you can make him or her change once you are well into an intimate commitment. In the early stages of the relationship, you will need to discuss the differences that you see. Living with a low-hope person who can not or will not change creates an atmosphere in which you are constantly bombarded by the other individual's negative thinking. Undoubtedly, with your high-hope thinking, you can cope with such low-hope thoughts, but why choose that situation if you are in a position to prevent it now?

If you already are in a relationship in which your partner has low hope, and you think he or she may be receptive to what you're learning in this book, talk about what you have discovered and your progress. If, however, you meet with skepticism, continue with your personal work and let your achievements speaks for themselves. Remember that one of the rules for maintaining high waypower is to avoid friendships or relationships where you are praised for *not* coming up with ways to solve problems. Similarly, avoid relationships where you are encouraged to lower your sights and settle for less than you want.

Hope Is Good Communication

Of the many couples we have seen in counseling, the vast majority experience a failure to communicate with each other as the root of their relationship's problems. Communication means the willingness to disclose thoughts and feelings that you consider private and personal—those that may cause you to feel vulnerable. This means telling the other person what you expect, need, and want in the relationship. But communication also is a two-way street. It means that you're willing to listen and really *hear* what the other person has to tell you. Genuine communication is risky, because your feelings can be hurt and you might feel angry. The outcome of developing good communication, however, is well worth the struggle that it may take to get there.

You can use hope strategies to learn more effective communication, while good communication also nourishes hope. If you and your partner share the common goal of learning to share your thoughts and feelings, even if this is new to either of you, you can follow the hope-enhancing guidelines you learned in section II to facilitate that goal. The methods you learned in section I, exploring your hope and its origins, will prove helpful as you communicate your thoughts and feelings. The introspection you practiced in understanding yourself through your stories will give you valuable personal information to disclose to your partner as you learn to communicate better.

Be patient with yourself and your partner as you learn to communicate. Start with small goals. For example, you might examine how it is that you have different likes and dislikes in music or art. This type of subject will be less threatening than, for example, discussing behaviors that you don't care for in the other person. Agree to avoid areas that are central to each of your identities in the beginning. Learn to talk and listen, to share ideas about easy subjects. With each success, it will become easier to move closer to the more central issues in your identities and your relationship.

Sharing Goals in Your Relationship

As you have learned, identifying your goals is the beginning point in your hope-enhancement work. Discussing your goals with your partner is an excellent way to begin learning how to communicate, as well as determining how compatible you are in hope. You may find that you have different short-term goals, which is understandable when two people lead different lives. For a relationship to work over time, however, it is important to agree on at least some of the major, long-range goals. For example, how do you each view marriage? Do you want children? How do you envision your lives in five or ten years? Communicate about these issues—they are important.

As you discover each other's goals, you also will discover how you each use waypower and willpower thinking. Can your partner think of many ways to achieve his or her goals? How motivated is your partner to go after those goals? How does he or she assess the chances for success? If you are beginning a long-term relationship, and feel that having high hope is vital to you, this can be a litmus test for your future compatibility. Pay attention to the information you get. Do you share a hopeful approach to your future? These answers are critical to your future happiness.

Romancing with Hope

High-hope people have more successful relationships, whether those are romantic or with friends and family. When two high-hope people come together, the relationship has even greater potential.

Thus far, we have instructed you in ways to bring hope to your existing romantic relationship and to determine the level of hope in potential relationships. Through your work in this book you are developing your love for yourself, and you will find that you want to live in relationships where hope enhancement is valued. Hope is infectious, but it helps to have good communication to inform your partner of the changes you are making. Work with your partner to enhance hope. Share the exciting things you're learning and doing. Allow your enhanced hope to influence your romantic relationship.

Hope and Family Relationships

In sections I and II, you learned how influential the messages you received about hope were to you as a child. They could determine the difference between the high-hope and the low-hope adult. Now that you are enhancing your hope, you have the potential to influence others in your life who are important to you.

Families come in all types of configurations from the large extended group, to a single parent with one child. If you have an adult partner as part of your family, you will find the previous part of this chapter concerning romantic relationships to be applicable to that part of your family. This section of the chapter focuses primarily on your role as a parent. As a parent, you are in an ideal position to nourish hope in your children. Your young children look to you for the necessary guidelines and structure of their lives. You can work with them to set goals, brainstorm ways to reach their goals, and then give them the positive encouragement that will fuel their energy to achieve success. All of the lessons you have learned in this book can be taught to your children, and in teaching them you will reinforce your own high hope.

Nourishing hope in your children is one of the most rewarding gifts that a parent can give. Even teenage children, who would prefer you to think they are no longer under your influence, will see changes in you as you learn the hope-enhancing strategies in this book. You will be providing a model for your adolescents, showing that change is possible. They will see you set new goals and find ways to go after them, and they will notice the renewed energy that you have to work for your objectives.

Another important gift that you can give your children is to teach them to love themselves. As they see you learning to meet your needs and establish your boundaries, they will learn that it's not only doable, but that it is also a preferred behavior. Children usually have very little trouble asking for what they want, and these requests offer you good opportunities to teach them the difference between wants and needs. You also can teach them the most effective ways to meet their needs and get what they want. Use the hope strategies to teach your children to meet their needs, just as you used them to learn to care for yourself.

Perfectionism and Family Relationships

Having a high-hope family also involves a relaxation of your perfectionist standards. You have seen the association between criticism and perfectionism, and you have learned that critical comments are destructive both to positive feelings about oneself, and to one's feelings of hope. If you want to give your family the gift of high-hope, you must learn to be less critical of both yourself and of them.

Criticism is a poor way to teach your children the things you want them to learn, but teaching lessons may be the last reason you choose to criticize. You may be critical of your family in an attempt to bolster your own self-esteem. You may reason that your family is a reflection of you, and therefore they must be perfect so that you will appear in a good light. Or, you may convert your self-criticism into finding fault with others. Whatever may underlie this behavior, it can be destructive to those you love.

You have seen how perfectionism, faultfinding, and criticism can be reduced through the strategies you used to enhance your hope. Use those same techniques now to enhance the hope in your family by reducing your expectations of perfection. Teach your children the important lessons in life through appropriate explanations and praise for their efforts. Both children and adults flourish when their efforts are approved and commended.

Behavioral psychology has provided valuable lessons on how people learn, and the best conditions under which you can teach them new things. Hope theory, and the strategies we have detailed in this book, are consistent with these principles of learning.

A person learns best when given positive feedback for each effort made toward a goal. Even if the effort is not immediately successful, using a rethinking strategy and trying another route will be a positive experience. Punishing yourself through negative critical comments, or making critical remarks to your family, will not help either of you to improve. On the contrary, it only will reinforce the low-hope thoughts and behaviors of your loved ones.

Establishing Family Goals

You have learned that goal setting is part of daily living. You have examined goals in your life arenas, and you have learned to establish goals in your romantic relationships. Having shared goals will enhance the hope experienced by you and your family. Try using family meetings to discuss what goals each member has established for him or herself, and talk about the ways family members can be supportive of one another.

Children should be encouraged to have personal long-range as well as short-term goals. The family, as a unit, can have goals in which each member can participate. For example, one goal can be keeping the house clean. Each person can have a list of chores that constitutes his or her contribution to the overall achievement of a well-kept house. The benefits of such a strategy are obvious. Not only is one person no longer responsible for all the work, but other members of the family learn to be responsible participants in a group effort. Using these strategies to achieve family goals enhances not only hope, but the relationships within the family as well.

In chapter 15 you read the story of Bonnie, who found that establishing her boundaries helped her children to become more independent. The following vignette is told by Maggie, who, at age thirteen, found her own sense of personal responsibility growing, as her mother established personal boundaries, began to meet her own needs, and developed higher hope.

✳ Maggie—Learning Responsibility

My mother and I have lived alone since my father left and married someone else. He moved to another city with his new wife and her children, so I rarely see him. My mother is still sad about the divorce, but she says I make her life worth living. I know she is trying to be both a mother and a father to me, and she tries to give me everything I want.

I guess I want a lot. I want to have all the clothes the other girls have, and I want to have the CDs and all the other stuff. My mother worked very hard, and when she came home she did all the housework, cooking, and laundry. She wanted our house to be perfect—but it didn't have to be. She was busy constantly and I never got to spend time with her. If I sound spoiled, maybe I am a little.

My mother reached a point where she was nervous and cranky all the time. She would yell at me and I would yell back, and our relationship was getting pretty bad. She decided that she needed to spend more quality time with me, and she also had to have time for herself. So, she told me I would have to start helping out around the house—and I wasn't too happy about that.

Together we worked out a pretty fair division of the things that needed to get done, and she was willing to give a little on having the house look great all the time. I won't say it all went smoothly from the beginning. I kept forgetting to do things like take out the trash, unload the dishwasher, or feed the cat. I really resented having to keep my room clean all the time, and she finally gave in on that and just made me keep the door shut.

It's been a little over six months now and we have things worked out better. Even though I didn't like having those responsibilities at first, I'm learning to do the things I will have to do as an adult. My mom is feeling better, too. She doesn't have to spend the whole weekend cleaning the house, so we have time to do something together—like buying me new clothes.

＊

When teenagers are expected to assume new and not always fun responsibilities, they often balk. It's important to persist, however, because it is only through participating in such communal family activities that children can learn cooperative relationships. Maggie was learning to have a two-way relationship with her mother, and that lesson will serve her well as she becomes an adult.

Hope in Friendships

People who are low in hope in the social arena have fewer and less satisfactory friendships than those who are high in hope. If your low-hope is augmented by your lack of self-love, you may not see yourself as being worthy of friendships. You may think that you have little to offer another person. If you don't enjoy your own company, you probably believe that others will not want to be with you either. How can you use hope to develop better friendships?

The first step, of course, is to decide whether you really want to have friendships. If you are lonely and have scored low on the social area of the Domain-Specific Life-Hope Scale, you will want to consider which, and what type, of friends you would like to have. If you don't think you have especially good social skills, one of your first goals might be to take a class to learn how to meet people and to make conversation.

If you think that a lack of self-love is part of the reason you have low hope in the social domain, then along with the hope strategies detailed in chapter 15, you may wish to seek the professional help of a counselor or therapist. Remember that high-hope people don't hesitate to ask for help from others. The ability to meet people and develop friendships involves a set of skills that can be learned. By establishing each skill as a goal and taking small steps toward it, you can achieve high hope in your social life, and you will be well rewarded for your efforts.

Perfectionism in Friendships

Do you make friends, only to be disappointed later when you find that they are not who you expected them to be? This happens occasionally to everyone, but if it occurs frequently to you, you may have unrealistic expectations for your friends.

Perfectionism can have the same negative effects on friendships that it has on romantic and family relationships, and for many of the same reasons. You may be substituting your self-criticism for criticism of others. If you're trying to live up to your perfectionistic standards, you probably expect others to do the same and are irritated with them when they don't. If this description fits you, it's important for you to examine the standards that you have for yourself and your friends. Use the same strategies to rid yourself of destructive perfectionism with your friends that you learned to use with your romantic and family relationships.

To illustrate hope in friendships, here is the story of Esme, who has had a difficult time making and keeping friendships.

❋ Esme—Learning to Like People

I looked up my name once in one of those books that tells the meaning of different names. Esme is supposed to mean "one who is held in great esteem." If that is the case, I was certainly misnamed, because I never used to feel valued by the people whom I considered my friends. My life is different now and I have some close friends, but I had to change some things to get there.

All through elementary and secondary school I had very few girlfriends. I was way too tall, too skinny, and not at all pretty. I couldn't play sports because I had asthma, and I had such bad allergies that my nose was constantly running. The kids called me "Snuffalufagus," like the character on television. I hated being me, and I hated all the other kids my age.

I tried to do well in school and received good grades, and I got along well with my teachers. I always thought that when I became an adult, I would find people who would want to be my friends. That hasn't been entirely true. To begin with, I didn't know how to initiate friendships very well. I was never sure what to say to people or how to take the first step toward getting to know them better. As time went on, however, and I developed more interests, it got somewhat easier to get to know other people.

The real problem with my friendships was that, after a while, my new friends acted in ways that I didn't like or respect. For example, I found out that one friend was talking about me behind my back. Another friend told me, to my face, that she didn't think I wore my hair in a flattering way. When these situations occurred, I just wanted to go away and hide. I certainly didn't want those people to be my friends anymore.

Finally, I became so disappointed in my social life that I began to examine what part I was playing in those failures. I realized that as a young person I had not learned the give-and-take necessary to have good friendships, and that I would have to learn it now—better late than never. I also realized that I had very high expectations of myself, and that I thought my friends should live by those same standards. Again, this was a reflection of my lack of flexibility with others.

At first, I felt as if I were starting from zero in learning to develop friendships. Actually, I had quite a few skills on which to build. I knew how to make conversation and I had interesting things to talk about. As my first goal, I asked a few friends to dinner—something I had never done before. That event turned out successfully and started a stream of reciprocal invitations.

My next goal, approached little by little, was to stop criticizing my friends. Each time I found myself looking for faults, I examined what I was doing and how it would affect the friendship. Eliminating fault finding has been difficult, and I have not succeeded completely. I have been able to maintain my friendships for well over a year, however, and now I find that I really enjoy this part of my life. ✳

Esme used strategies for enhancing hope to develop and maintain her friendships. Her low social hope was due, in part, to the negative experiences that she had as a child, as well as to her own critical and perfectionist attitudes. Whether your social hope is similar to Esme's, or unsatisfactory in some other manner, you'll find that the strategies in this book will help you to have better and happier friendships.

Goals and Guidelines for Hope in Relationships

Throughout this section, you have seen that love, both of self and of others, is a critical variable in having good relationships. You have seen how perfectionism and critical behavior toward others can diminish your relationships. You also have seen how the strategies you learned earlier in this book can be used to develop and maintain relationships with lovers, family, and friends. Here is a list of goals that will enhance both hope and your relationships.

1. Identify what you value most in each of your relationships. Concentrate on those aspects rather than the qualities you don't like.

2. Learn to set personal boundaries.

3. Once you have learned to meet your own needs, teach others how to meet theirs.

4. Work to eliminate your perfectionism and faultfinding.

5. Learn to instruct your children with praise, and reward them for their efforts.

6. Learn to be patient with yourself and others. Relationships take time to grow.

7. Learn to be flexible—allow others to do things their way and live up to their own standards.

8. Set small goals for your relationships—in the long run you will benefit from making your changes slowly.

9. Continue to use all your hope strategies for every aspect of your relationships.

A Relationship for You

Now that you have reached the end of this book, you have developed a working knowledge of the hope process. You have examined hope in a number of contexts and have seen how you can use hope to solve specific problems. But, if you have learned the strategies in this book, you have done much more than solve problems. You have acquired a skill, a new frame of mind, that you will use for the rest of your life. Treat yourself to a lifelong relationship with a high-hope person—*you!*

A Hopeful Afterword

As a writer of this workbook I wanted to share a story about my own hope journey and the creation of this book. Approximately six years ago, I was privileged to read the manuscript for C. R. Snyder's *The Psychology of Hope* (1994). I immediately was filled with enthusiasm for bringing the theoretical ideas of the book into the applied world of counseling and education. At this same time, I was moved by a speech given by the Reverend Jesse Jackson, who said that what minorities and the poor need is hope. I began an odyssey into both researching and writing about nurturing hope, especially in underprivileged young people. This workbook, self-help that is geared for adults, represents a new direction and the beginning of a lifetime dream.

I grew up in a family of professional men and creative women. My grandmother wrote poetry, my mother was a writer, and I, too, always thought that I would be a writer as well. After a twenty-six-year-long career as an educator, therapist, and researcher, I'm beginning to move in the direction of expository writing. The stories in this workbook are based on the lives of real people, many of whom were my clients, and I also have drawn from my own life. The stories are about high-hope people and people in the process of developing greater hope.

Everything in this book is possible and achievable. I am proof of that. I have raised five children, spending much of that time as a single parent, and have had a full-time and rewarding career. I have coped with many of the concerns discussed in this book and have found that my high-hope always has held me in good stead.

Throughout the writing of this book I have worked closely with Rick Snyder, my colleague, friend, and erstwhile mentor. Like so many women of my generation, it has taken a long time to believe that I could accomplish my major life dreams. Rick, who has gently prodded me to believe in myself, has helped me along the way.

Use the lessons learned in this book. They have worked for me, and they will work for you. Although I began this venture as a high-hope person, through the continued use of these hope-enhancing strategies, my hope has continued to grow. And as my own hope has grown, so too have I come to believe that we all need to see that hope spreads to more and more people—hope for the many rather than the few. I am convinced that many of us have little or no idea how far we can go and how much we can achieve. Dare to dream, and dare to pursue the goals that anchor those dreams. Go ahead and hope for the impossible—and watch when it turns into the probable.

Recommended Reading

Hope, hope-building strategies, and related information.

C. R. Snyder. 1994. *The Psychology of Hope: You Can Get There from Here*. New York: The Free Press.

Burns, David D. 1980. *Feeling Good: The New Mood Therapy*. New York: Avon.

Bourne, Edmund J. 1994. *The Anxiety and Phobia Workbook*, 2nd ed. Oakland, Calif.: New Harbinger Publications, Inc.

Locke, E. A., and G. P. Latham. 1984. *Goal Setting: A Motivational Technique That Works*. Englewood Cliffs, N.J.: Prentice Hall.

Taking care of yourself

Cash, Thomas F. 1997. *The Body Image Workbook*. Oakland, Calif.: New Harbinger Publications.

Gender, ethnicity, and aging

For women

Christian Smith, Linda K. 1990. *Becoming a Woman Through Romance*. New York: Routledge.

For men and women

Clance, P. R. 1985. *The Imposter Phenomenon: Overcoming the Fear That Haunts Your Success*. Atlanta: Peachtree.

Ethnicity

Vacc, Nicholas A., and Joseph P. Wittmer. 1980. *Let Me Be Me: Special Populations and the Helping Professional.* Munice, Ind.: Accelerated Development.

Aging

Bortz II, Walter M. 1996. *Dare to Be One-hundred.* New York: Fireside.

Hess, Beth B., and Elizabeth W. Markson. 1995. *Growing Old in America.* New Brunswick, N.J.: Transaction Publishers.

Relationships

Relationship with self

Forrest, Jan. 1998. *Coming Home to Ourselves: Journaling to Wholeness.* Westline, Mich.: Heart to Heart Press.

Relationship with a partner

Kirshenbaum, Mira. 1999. *The Ten Prescriptions to Heal Your Relationships.* New York: Avon Books.

Family relationships—helping your children

Snyder, C. R., Diane McDermott, William Cook, and Michael A. Rapoff. 1997. *Hope for the Journey: Helping Your Children Through Good Times and Bad.* Boulder, Colo.: Westview.

Satir, Virginia. 1972. *Peoplemaking.* Palo Alto, Calif.: Science and Behavior Books.

Social relationships

Pilisuk, Marc, and Susan Hiller Parks. 1986. *The Healing Web: Social Networks and Human Survival.* Hanover, N.H.: The University Press of New England.

More New Harbinger Titles

THE POWER OF FOCUSING

Takes you step by step through a process of listening to your body, finding words or images to express the feelings that emerge, and letting those messages lead to insights, decisions, and positive change.   *Item POF $12.95*

CLAIMING YOUR CREATIVE SELF

The inspiring stories of thirteen women who were able to keep in touch with their own creative spirit open the door to new definitions of creativity and to the kind of transforming ideas that can change your life.
        Item CYCS $15.95

GOODBYE GOOD GIRL

The dozens of women whose stories are told in this book confirm that it may be scary to challenge the "good girl" rules, but the results can be astonishing, inspiring, and well worth the struggle.   *Item GGG $12.95*

SIX KEYS TO CREATING THE LIFE YOU DESIRE

Why is the road to satisfaction so difficult to find? This book helps you recognize your core issues and take the steps you need to take to create the life you really desire.   *Item KEY6 $19.95*

WANTING WHAT YOU HAVE

Shows how proven cognitive therapy principles can hyelp make it possible to achieve contentment and meet the challenges of modern life with balance and serenity.   *Item WANT $18.95*

Call toll-free 1-800-748-6273 to order. Have your Visa or Mastercard number ready. Or send a check for the titles you want to New Harbinger Publications, 5674 Shattuck Avenue, Oakland, CA 94609. Include $3.80 for the first book and 75¢ for each additional book to cover shipping and handling. (California residents please include appropriate sales tax.) Allow four to six weeks for delivery.

Prices subject to change without notice.

Some Other New Harbinger Self-Help Titles